C000195E84

MARKS & MONOGRAMS

MARKS &
MONOGRAMS

The Decorative Arts
1880-1960

MALCOLM HASLAM

COLLINS & BROWN

Published by Collins & Brown,
London House, Great Eastern Wharf,
Parkgate Road, London SW11 4NQ

Produced by Cameron Books,
PO Box 1, Moffat, Dumfriesshire DG10 9SU, Scotland

Designed by Ian Cameron
Edited by Jill Hollis

First edition published 1977 by Lutterworth Press
as *Marks and Monograms of the Modern Movement*

This revised and enlarged edition first published 1995

1 3 5 7 9 8 6 4 2

British Library Cataloguing-in-Publication Data:
A catalogue record for this book is available from the
British Library

ISBN 1 85585 024 9

Printed and bound in Great Britain

CONTENTS

CONTENTS

INTRODUCTION

Eighteen years ago, when compiling the precursor of this book, I used as a criterion of a person's or firm's inclusion the extent to which they had contributed to the evolution of the Modern Movement in architecture and design. Indeed, the title of the book was *Marks and Monograms of the Modern Movement 1875-1930*, and its viewpoint was derived from the precepts of Sir Nikolaus Pevsner's *Pioneers of the Modern Movement from William Morris to Walter Gropius*. Knowledge and understanding of modernism in the decorative arts was at that time still largely based on Pevsner's book which had first been published as long ago as 1936. Today, however, new ideas have emerged and different attitudes prevail.

During the last two decades, collecting decorative arts of the late nineteenth and twentieth centuries has expanded enormously. Academic research, ever wider and deeper, has provided the collector with the necessary tools; attics and cellars have been ransacked, flea-markets have been combed to supply each new craving. We have been engulfed by the flood of objects that has appeared and have been overwhelmed by the number and variety of the styles, materials and techniques used by the decorative artists of the period.

The bare bones provided by Pevsner have taken on flesh and there has now emerged a much more complex organism than we had ever been led to expect. For instance, Art Nouveau is now considered to have been as much an expression of Freudian angst as the harbinger of steel and glass architecture, and Art Deco has been recognised as a phenomenon that rivals modernism in its artistic and historical significance. In the light of such hugely expanded knowledge, and to take account of the radical shifts in collectors' interests, it quickly became apparent that any new guide to marks and monograms of the period would have to be very considerably more extensive than the slim volume that appeared in 1977, and that any title invoking the Modern Movement would now be unduly limiting.

One of the prejudices overthrown by all the attention paid to modern decorative arts was the hidebound concept of an 'antique'. Even as late as the 1960s, most authorities held that an object had to be over a hundred years old to qualify as an antique, and it was exclusively antiques that were sold in antique shops, exhibited in museums or auctioned at Sotheby's and Christie's.

INTRODUCTION

Histories of the decorative arts never extended beyond 1850, and *The Connoisseur's Complete Period Guides*, published in 1968, ended with 'Early Victorian'. Even in 1977, when *Marks and Monograms of the Modern Movement* was published, one felt quite bold in taking its coverage up to a date as recent as 1930.

But the hundred-year rampart quickly crumbled, and collectors swarmed into ever more recent decades. By the late 1970s, people were collecting objects from the 1950s that were barely a quarter of a century old. When the time-span of this book was considered, it was decided that the cut-off year should be 1960, and even this is already beginning to appear rather old-fashioned in terms of the latest trends in collecting. However, adding thirty years to the span covered by the previous book, as well as including a greatly increased number of marks from the earlier period, was going to make the book so much bigger that there was a risk of it turning into a ponderous and unwieldy tome, which would be difficult to use and awkward to carry. It was considered preferable to produce something that could reasonably be described as a 'handbook'.

Although the concept of modernism has been more or less banished from the thinking behind this book, it should not be assumed that the principles of post-modernism have been applied in its creation. The post-modernist attitude to the decorative arts of the past may be summarised as a belief that they provide an assortment of ready-made, mix-and-match styles to be plundered at will for the benefit of the present-day consumer. But historical styles, like all other aspects of the environment, should be carefully preserved, and to be preserved they have to be understood. I hope that, by providing collectors with a little more knowledge, this book will contribute to a greater understanding and a more fulfilling enjoyment of the late nineteenth and twentieth-century decorative arts.

Malcolm Haslam
London, 1995

HOW TO USE THIS BOOK

The marks are arranged in five main sections according to medium –
Ceramics, Glass, Metalwork & Jewellery, Graphics, Furniture & Textiles. Glass
includes stained glass; graphics includes applied graphic art such as posters,
book design and illustration, but not print-making where the artist's intention
has been simply to replicate an image.

The main sections are arranged by country. The order of countries is
always the same, but all countries do not necessarily appear in every section.
Included under Austria are all the territories that formed the Austro-Hungarian
Empire from 1866 to 1919, even if they subsequently became independent
states (e.g. Czechoslovakia, Hungary). Scandinavia embraces Denmark, Finland,
Norway and Sweden.

Under each country firms and individuals are listed in alphabetical order.
The words 'manufacturer' or 'manufacturing' imply that a firm was essentially
a commercial enterprise; guilds, workshops and other associations of artists
and craftsmen/women are designated as such. Designers and decorators listed
as working for a firm were not necessarily employees; in many instances, their
services were bought by the firm on an *ad hoc* basis, and they may well have
worked for other firms as well. In the case of a designer/decorator whose
mark is illustrated, the entry lists all the different firms for which he/she
worked; otherwise, a designer's or decorator's other activities can be ascertained
by consulting the index.

If an individual was primarily a painter, sculptor or architect, this is indicated
at the beginning of the entry. The descriptions 'designer', 'decorator', etc.
refer only to work in the particular medium under which the entry appears.
At the end of the entry, the individual's activities in other media are mentioned.
If his/her marks in other media are shown elsewhere in the book, they can
be found by referring to the index.

Individuals are listed under the countries where the work bearing the
mark(s) shown was executed. If he/she was not a national of that country, a
nationality is given.

As well as being an encyclopedia of marks and monograms, this book
serves as a directory of prominent European and American decorative artists

working during the period. The references given in the index to a particular name provide a comprehensive account both of activities in the various media and of the different firms for which he/she worked.

To identify a mark which includes a name and/or initials, refer first to the index. If the mark is a monogram, look first in the index under the most prominent letter in the monogram, and then under the other letters of which it is composed. If the mark is a device without any name, initials or monogram, try to identify its country of origin and then search the appropriate section.

A mark shown in this book is not necessarily reproduced at its actual size, which may vary according to the dimensions of the object bearing the mark. No significance should be attached to the size of illustration of any mark, nor to the relative sizes of marks in a particular section or entry.

The selection of marks shown in this book has necessarily been somewhat arbitrary. The broad aim has been to reproduce the marks which appear on the most collectable items, at the same time as including as many as possible of the rarer marks which even experienced collectors would be unlikely to recognise.

In order to include as many marks as possible, slight variations have been omitted: an object bearing a mark which is only a little different to one illustrated is not necessarily a fake. It should be remembered that the correctness of the mark on an object is no guarantee of authenticity.

MARKS
&
MONOGRAMS

BRITISH CERAMICS

ADAMS, John (1882-1953)

Potter, designer, decorator. Worked for B.*Moore; co-founder of *Carter, Stabler & Adams. Painted monogram.

ALLAN, Hugh (1862-1909)

Painter, potter, designer. Set up *Allander Pottery. Incised initials.

ALLANDER POTTERY (1904-08)

Pottery established by H.*Allan. Incised mark.

ALLER VALE ART POTTERIES (c.1881-1901)

ALLER VALE

Manufacturers. In 1901 merged with *Watcombe Pottery. Impressed mark.

ARBEID, Dan (b.1928)

Potter, designer. Impressed initials.

ASHBY POTTERS' GUILD (1909-22)

Pottery. In 1922 merged with *Ault. Impressed mark.

ASHTEAD POTTERS (1923-35)

Pottery. Designers include Anne Crawford Acheson (1882-1962), F.*Brangwyn, Donald Gilbert (1900-61), Phoebe Stabler (d.1955), Allan G. Wyon (1882-1962). Printed mark.

AULD, Ian (b.1926)

Potter, designer. Worked at *Odney before setting up his own pottery. Impressed initials.

AULT, William (1887-1922)

Manufacturers. Designers include C.*Dresser. Printed, impressed or moulded mark.

BAILEY, C.J.C. (1864-89)

(†)

Manufacturers. Designers include J.-C.*Cazin (*see* French ceramics), E.*Kettle, R.W.*Martin, John Pollard Seddon (1827-1906). Impressed (†) and incised marks.

BARE, Ruth (1880-1962)

Sculptor, designer, decorator.
Worked for *Della Robbia.
Painted/incised initials.

BARLOW, Arthur Bolton (1845-79)

Designer, decorator. Worked for
*Doulton (Lambeth).
Incised initials.

BARLOW, Florence Elizabeth (d.1909)

Designer, decorator. Worked for
*Doulton (Lambeth).
Incised monogram.

BARLOW, Hannah Bolton (1851-1916)

Designer, decorator. Worked for
*Doulton (Lambeth).
Incised monogram.

BARNARD, Harry (1862-1933)

Designer, decorator, modeller.
Worked for *Doulton (Lambeth),
*Macintyre, *Wedgwood.
Incised initials.

BARNES, William (fl.1945-60)

Potter, designer, decorator. Worked
independently before joining
*Pilkington in 1948.
Incised monogram.

BARNSLEY, Grace *see* DAVIES, Grace.

BARON, William Leonard (1863-1937)

Potter, designer, decorator. Worked for *Brannam, *Doulton (Lambeth) before setting up in 1895 his own pottery which was taken over by Brannam in 1939.
Incised signature.

BARRON, Paul (1917-83)

Potter, designer, decorator.
Impressed initial.

BAYES, Gilbert (1872-1953)

GILBERT BAYES

Sculptor, modeller, designer.
Worked for *Doulton (Lambeth).
Moulded signature.

BEARDMORE, Evelyn Hope (c.1886-1972)

Designer, decorator. Worked for B.*Moore, *Wedgwood.
Painted monogram.

BELLS, A.E. (fl.1895-1905)

ÆB

Decorator, designer. Worked for *Della Robbia.
Painted/incised initials.

BENTHALL POTTERY CO. (est.c.1862)

SALOPIAN

Manufacturers of 'Salopian Art Pottery' and other wares. Designers include Gertrude Hermes (fl.c.1935).
Impressed mark.

BESWICK, John (est.1897)

BESWICK
ENGLAND

Manufacturers. Designers include Albert Hallam (fl.c.1950), Jim Hayward (fl.c.1950), Colin Melbourne (fl. c.1950).
Printed marks.

BEW, John (1897-1954)

Potter, designer, decorator. Worked at *Odney for about four years before his death.
Painted monogram.

BIDDER, Joyce (fl.1930-60)

M·JOYCE
BIDDER

Sculptor, modeller. Collaborated with Daisy Borne (fl.1930-60).
Moulded signature.

BILLINGTON, Dora May (1890-1968)

(i)   (ii)

Potter, designer, decorator. Worked for B.*Moore before setting up her own pottery.
Painted (i), incised (ii) monograms.

BOURNE, Joseph, & Son (est.c.1809)

BOURNE,
DENBY,
ENGLAND.

Manufacturers at Denby Pottery. Products include 'Danesby Ware'.
Impressed or printed marks.

BRADEN, Norah (b.1901)

(i)   (ii)

Potter, designer, decorator. Worked at *Cole, *St Ives and independently.
Impressed (i), painted (ii) monograms.

17

BRAIN, E., & Co. (est.1903)

Manufacturers of 'Foley China'. Designers include John Armstrong (1893-1973), Vanessa Bell (1879-1961), F.*Brangwyn, C.*Cliff, G.M.*Forsyth, Duncan Grant (1885-1978), Barbara Hepworth (1903-75), L.*Knight, P.*Nash, Ben Nicholson (1894-1982), D.*Procter, E.*Procter, Albert Rutherston (1881-1953), G.V.*Sutherland. Printed marks.

BRANGWYN, Frank (1867-1956)

Painter, designer. Designed for *Brain, *Doulton (Burslem), A.J.*Wilkinson. Some ceramics made to his designs by *Ashtead Potters and *St Ives; also designed *graphics, *furniture, textiles. Printed mark.

BRANNAM, C.H. (est.1879)

Pottery run by Charles Hubert Brannam (1855-1937). Designers/decorators include W.L.*Baron, Arthur Braddon (fl.1890-1910), R. Cowie (fl.c.1905), J.*Dewdney. Incised mark.

BRAUNTON POTTERY CO. (1912-71)

Manufacturers. Directed by W.F.*Holland from 1912 to 1921. Impressed mark.

BRETBY ART POTTERY (est.1883)

Manufacturers. Designers include co-founder H.*Tooth.
Impressed mark.

BULLERS STUDIO (1934-52)

Studio opened by manufacturers of electrical and chemical porcelain. Designers/decorators include John L. Cottrell (fl.1935-60), G.M.*Forsyth, Ralph Guy Harris (1891-1963), A.*Hoy, Robert B. Jefferson (b.1929), M.*Leach, A.R.*Potts, W.*Ruscoe.
Printed mark.

BURGESS & LEIGH (est.c.1865)

Manufacturers of 'Burleigh Ware' among other lines. Designers include C.*Rhead.
Printed marks.

BURMANTOFTS FAIENCE (1879-89)

Burmantofts
Faience

BURMANTOFTS
FAIENCE

Art pottery manufactured by Wilcock & Co; the firm was restyled Burmantofts Co. Ltd in 1888 and the following year was incorporated in Leeds Fireclay Co. Designers include Maurice Bingham Adams (1849-1933), William James Neatby (1860-1910).
Impressed marks.

BURSLEM SCHOOL OF ART

Pottery class taught by W.*Ruscoe.
Impressed mark.

BUSHEY HEATH POTTERY (1921-33)

Pottery. Decorators include
F.*Passenger.
Printed mark.

BUTLER, Frank A. (fl.1872-1911)

Designer decorator. Worked for
*Doulton (Lambeth).
Incised monogram.

BUTTERTON, Mary (fl.1874-94)

Designer, decorator. Worked for
*Doulton (Lambeth).
Painted monogram.

CAIGER-SMITH, Alan (b.1930)

Potter, designer, decorator.
Painted monogram.

CALUWÉ, Marianne de (fl.1890-1910)

Decorator, modeller. Worked for
*Della Robbia.
Painted/incised initials.

CAPES, Mary (fl.1870-90)

Designer, decorator. Worked for
*Doulton (Lambeth).
Painted monogram.

CARDEW, Michael (1901-81)

Potter, designer, decorator. Worked
at Abuja Pottery Training Centre
(est.1951) in Nigeria, *St Ives, Volta
Pottery (est.1946) in Ghana,
*Wenford Bridge Pottery,
*Winchcombe Pottery.
Impressed initials, monogram.

CARTER & CO. (est.1873)

Manufacturers. Designers include
Dora M. Batty (fl.1920-30), Edward
Bawden (1903-89), John Farleigh
(1900-65), Joseph Roelants
(fl.c.1920), Reginald Till
(1895-1978), James Radley Young
(1867-1933).
Incised mark.

CARTER, STABLER & ADAMS (est.1921)

(i)

(ii)

(iii)

(iv)

(v)

Manufacturers. Designers include
J.*Adams, Dora M. Batty (fl.1920-
30), Edward Bawden (1903-89),
Truda Carter (1890-1958), Robert B.
Jefferson (b.1929), E.*Manners,
H.*Stabler (see British metalwork),
Phoebe Stabler (d.1955).
Impressed (i), impressed or printed
(ii, iii), printed (iv, v) marks.

CASSON, Michael (b.1925)

Potter, designer, decorator.
Impressed monogram.

CLIFF, Clarice (1899-1972)

Designer, decorator. Worked for
*Brain, *Wilkinson, *Newport.
Printed signature.

COLE POTTERY (1924-46)

Pottery set up by K.*Pleydell-
Bouverie. Other potters who worked
there include N.*Braden.
Impressed mark.

COLLARD, Charles (1874-1969)

Potter, designer, decorator. Worked
for *Aller Vale, *Hart & Moist,
*Longpark before managing
*Crown Dorset and *Honiton.
Impressed, incised signatures.

COLLIS, Charles (1880-c.1967)

Designer, decorator. Worked for
*Della Robbia, *Doulton (Burslem),
Wardle & Co.
Painted/incised initials.

COMPTON POTTERY (c.1898-1956)

Pottery founded by Mary S. Watts
(1849-1938).
Impressed mark.

22

COOPER, Susie (b.1902)

Designer, decorator. Designed for *Gray before setting up her own firm, Susie *Cooper Pottery. Incised signatures and painted monograms.

COOPER, Susie, Pottery (est.1932)

Manufacturers directed by S.*Cooper. Printed marks.

COOPER, Waistel (b.1921)

Potter, designer, decorator. Painted signature.

COPER, Hans (1920-81)

German potter, designer working in England. Impressed initials.

COX, George J. (fl.1910-30)

Potter, designer, decorator. From 1914 worked in USA. Incised mark and monogram.

CRANE, Walter (1845-1915)

Painter, designer. Designed for
*Maw, *Minton, *Pilkington,
*Wedgwood; also designed stained
glass, furniture, textiles, carpets,
wallpapers, posters, books (*see*
British graphics).
Painted monogram and rebus.

CRAVEN DUNNILL & CO. (1872-1951)

CRAVEN DUNNILL & Co

Manufacturers. Designers include
L.F.*Day, George Goldie (1828-
1927), T.R. Spence (fl.c.1890),
Alfred Waterhouse (1830-1905).
Printed, impressed marks.

CROWAN POTTERY (1946-62)

Pottery. Designers include founder
Harry Davis (1910-86).
Impressed mark.

CROWN DORSET ART POTTERY (est.1905)

Pottery set up and run by C.*Collard.
Impressed mark.

CUNDALL, Charles E. (b.1890)

Painter, designer, decorator.
Worked for *Pilkington.
Painted monogram.

DALTON, William Bower (1868-1965)

Potter, designer, decorator. From
1941 to c.1960 worked in USA; also
designed furniture.
Incised monogram.

DAVIES (*née* BARNSLEY), Grace (b.1896)

Potter, designer, decorator. Decorated pottery made by *Wedgwood. In 1934 she and her husband Oscar Davies opened Roeginga Pottery. Painted monograms.

DAVIS, Derek (b.1926)

Potter, designer, decorator. Painted signature.

DAY, Lewis Foreman (1845-1910)

Designer. Worked for *Craven Dunnill, J.C. Edwards, *Maw, *Pilkington, *Torquay; also designed stained glass, silver, jewellery, books, furniture, textiles, wallpapers. Painted monogram.

DAYSH, Barbara (fl.c.1925)

Designer, decorator. Worked at *Farnham. Incised monogram.

DELLA ROBBIA POTTERY (1894-1906)

Pottery. Designers and decorators include R.*Bare, A.E.*Bells, C.*Collis, Thomas Collcutt (1840-1924), C.*Dressler (co-founder), J.*Fogo, C.*Manzoni, H.S.*Rathbone (co-founder), E.M.*Rope, Gertrude *Russell, C.A.*Walker. Painted/incised mark.

DE MORGAN, William Frend (1839-1917)

Manufacturer, potter, designer. Designs by himself and H.*Ricardo were executed at his pottery. Decorators include Joe Juster (fl.1880-1900), C.*Passenger, F.*Passenger; also designed stained glass.
Impressed marks.

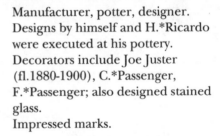

DE TREY, Marianne (b.1913)

Potter, designer, decorator.
Impressed monogram, mark.

DEWDNEY, James (fl.1880-1910)

Designer, decorator. Worked for C.H.*Brannam.
Incised monogram.

DOULTON & CO., Burslem (est.1882)

(†)

Manufacturers. Designers/decorators include F.*Brangwyn, Arthur Charles Eaton (fl.c.1900), Harry Nixon (b.1886), C.J.*Noke, Harry Tittensor (1886-1942), C.*Vyse.

ROYAL
DOULTON
FLAMBE

Printed/impressed (†), printed
marks.

DOULTON & CO., Lambeth (1858-1956)

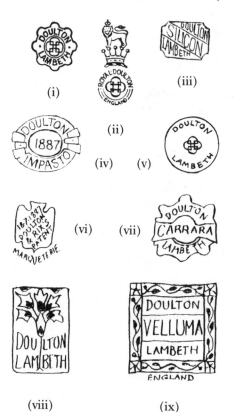

(i)

(ii)

(iii)

(iv)   (v)

(vi)   (vii)

(viii)   (ix)

Manufacturers.
Designers/decorators include
A.B.*Barlow, F.E.*Barlow,
H.B.*Barlow, H.*Barnard,
W.L.*Baron, G.*Bayes, John Broad
(fl.1875-1920), F.A.*Butler,
M.*Butterton, M.*Capes, Reco
Capey (1898-1991), Richard Garbe
(1876-1957), A.L.*Harradine,
A.*Hoy, V.*Huggins, Frances Lee
(fl.1875-90), E.*Lewis, F.*Lewis,
E.D.*Lupton, M.V.*Marshall,
F.C.*Pope, H.*Simeon,
E.*Simmance, Margaret E.
Thompson (fl.1890-1920),
G.*Tinworth, Helen Walters
(fl.c.1950), L.*Watt.
Impressed (i-iv), printed (v-x)
marks.

(x)

DRESSER, Christopher (1834-1904)

Designer. Designed for *Ault,
*Linthorpe, *Minton, *Minton's
Art-Pottery, *Old Hall, *Torquay,
*Watcombe, *Wedgwood; also
designed *glass, *metalwork,
furniture, textiles, carpets,
wallpapers.
Impressed signature.

DRESSLER, Conrad (1856-1940)

Sculptor, potter, designer, modeller, decorator. With H.S.*Rathbone founded *Della Robbia Pottery. In 1897 set up his own pottery and founded Art Pavements and Decorations Ltd.
Incised monogram.

DUCKWORTH, Ruth (b.1919)

Potter, designer, decorator.
Impressed initials.

DUNN (née WADE), Constance E. (fl.1925-50)

Potter, designer, decorator.
Impressed initial.

ELTON, Sir Edmund (1846-1920)

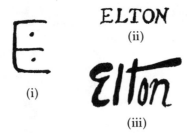

Potter, designer, decorator.
Incised (i), impressed (ii), painted (iii) signatures.

EPTON, Charlotte (1902-70)

Potter, designer, decorator.
Impressed signature.

FARNHAM POTTERY (est.1873)

Pottery run by successive generations of Harris family.
Designers/decorators include W.H.

Allen (fl.1890-1940), B.*Daysh, Agnes Hall (fl.c.1920), Ada Hazell (fl.c.1900), M.*Leach. Impressed marks.

FINCH, Ray (b.1914)

Potter, designer, decorator. Worked at and ran *Winchcombe Pottery. Impressed monogram.

FISHLEY, Edwin Beer (1832-1912)

Potter, designer, decorator. Incised signature.

FOGO, John (d.1980)

Designer, decorator. Worked for *Della Robbia. Painted/incised monogram, initials.

FORSYTH, Gordon Mitchell (1879-1952)

Potter, designer, decorator. Designed for *Brain, *Bullers, *Gray, Minton Hollins, *Pilkington, *Wilkinson. Painted rebus.

GORDON, William (fl.1939-55)

Sculptor, potter, designer, decorator; also designed metalwork. Painted mark.

GRAY, A.E., & Co. (1912-61)

Manufacturers. Designers include
S.*Cooper, G.M.*Forsyth, S.C.
Talbot (fl.1940-60).
Printed marks.

HAILE, Thomas Sam (1909-48)

Potter, designer, decorator.
Impressed monogram.

HAMADA, Shoji (1894-1978)

Japanese potter, designer, decorator
who worked at *St Ives.
Impressed signature.

HAMMOND, Henry Fauchon (1914-89)

Potter, designer, decorator.
Impressed monogram.

HARDING, Deborah N. (fl.c.1930)

Potter, designer, decorator.
Incised initials

HARRADINE, Arthur Leslie (d.1965)

Designer, modeller. Worked for
*Doulton (Lambeth), *Doulton
(Burslem) and other factories.
Painted/incised initials.

HART & MOIST (1896-1935)

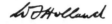

Partnership running the Devon Art
Pottery (previously the Exeter Art
Pottery). Designers include
C.*Collard.
Impressed mark.

HOLLAND, William Fishley (1888-1971)

Potter, designer, decorator. Worked
for grandfather E.B.*Fishley and
*Braunton before establishing his
own pottery.
Incised signature.

HOLYROOD POTTERY (1918-27)

Pottery established by Henry Wyse
(1870-1951).
Impressed mark.

HONITON POTTERY (1918-47)

COLLARD
HONITON
ENGLAND

Pottery run by C.*Collard.
Impressed mark.

HOPKINS, Alfred G. (fl.1910-35)

Potter, designer, modeller, decorator.
Worked for *Doulton (Lambeth)
before setting up his own pottery.
Incised signature.

HOWELL & JAMES (est.c.1820)

HOWELL & JAMES
SPECIAL MAKE

Retailers of pottery (*inter alia*) who organised classes in china painting from 1876 to c.1890.
Printed mark.

HOY, Anita [Agnete] (b.1914)

Danish potter, designer, decorator working in England from 1940. Worked for *Bullers, *Doulton (Lambeth) and independently. Painted/incised monogram, signature.

HUGGINS, Vera (fl.1923-50)

Designer, decorator. Worked for *Doulton (Lambeth). Incised monogram.

JOYCE, Richard (1873-1931)

.R.

Designer, decorator. Worked for *Bretby, Moore Bros, *Pilkington. Painted monogram.

KEMP, Dorothy (b.1905)

Potter, designer, decorator. Worked at *St Ives and elsewhere. Impressed monogram.

KETTLE, Edgar (1842-77)

Potter, designer, decorator. Worked for *Bailey and independently. Incised signature, monogram and rebus.

KING, Jesse Marion (1876-1949)

Designer, decorator; also designed jewellery, books (*see* British graphics), textiles, wallpapers. Painted initials and marks.

KNIGHT, Laura (1877-1970)

Painter, designer. Designed for *Brain, *Wilkinson; also designed posters. Painted signature.

LAUDER, Alexander (1836-1921)

Architect, designer, decorator. Worked for *Lauder & Smith and independently. Incised signature.

LAUDER & SMITH (1876-c.1890)

Manufacturers of 'Devon Art Pottery'. Designers include partner A.*Lauder. Incised mark.

LEACH, Bernard (1887-1979)

Potter, designer, decorator. Set up pottery at *St Ives. Impressed (i), impressed or painted (ii) and painted (iii) initials.

(i)

(ii)

(iii)

LEACH, David (b.1911)

Potter, designer, decorator. Worked at *St Ives and elsewhere before establishing *Lowerdown Pottery. Impressed initials.

LEACH, Michael (1913-85)

Potter, designer, decorator. Worked at *Bullers, *St Ives, *Farnham before establishing *Yelland Manor Pottery. Impressed initials.

LESSORE, Elaine Thérèse (1883-1944)

Painter, decorator, modeller. Decorated ceramics made by *Wedgwood. Painted monogram.

LEWENSTEIN, Eileen (b.1925)

Potter, designer, decorator. Impressed mark.

LEWIS, Esther (fl.1877-97)

Designer, decorator. Worked for *Doulton (Lambeth). Painted monogram.

LEWIS, Florence (fl.1875-97)

Designer, decorator. Worked for *Doulton (Lambeth). Painted monogram.

LIBERTY & CO. (est.1875)

MADE FOR
LIBERTY&C°

Retailers. Sold work by *Aller Vale, *Brannam, *Bretby, *Burgau (see German ceramics), *Burmantofts, *Cantagalli (see Italian ceramics), *Compton, *Della Robbia, *Doulton (Lambeth), *Farnham, M.*Läuger (see German ceramics), *Macintyre, *Moorcroft, Wardle & Co., *Wileman, *Zsolnay (see Austrian ceramics), *Zuid-Holland (see Dutch ceramics); also retailed *glass, *metalwork, *jewellery, *furniture, textiles, carpets. Printed mark.

LINTHORPE ART POTTERY (1879-89)

LINTHORPE

Pottery directed by H.*Tooth. Designers include C.*Dresser. Impressed mark.

LONGPARK POTTERY CO. (1903-40)

LONGPARK
TORQUAY

Manufacturers. Designers/decorators include C.*Collard. Impressed mark.

LOWERDOWN POTTERY (est.1956)

Pottery established by D.*Leach. Impressed mark.

LUNN, Dora (1881-c.1955)

Potter, designer, decorator. Established Ravenscourt Pottery in 1916. Incised monogram, signature.

LUPTON, Edith D. (d.1896)

Designer, decorator. Worked for
*Doulton (Lambeth).
Incised initials.

MACBETH, Ann (1875-1948)

Designer, decorator; also designed
embroideries, textiles, metalwork.
Painted initials.

MACINTYRE, James, Co. (est.c.1850)

Manufacturers. Designers include
H.*Barnard, William *Moorcroft.
Printed mark.

MACKENZIE, Warren (b.1924)

American potter, designer, decorator
working at *St Ives from 1950 to
1952.
Impressed initials.

MANNERS, Erna (fl.1910-30)

Potter, designer, modeller,
decorator. Designed for *Carter,
Stabler & Adams.
Painted monogram.

MANZONI, Carlo (d.1910)

Potter, designer, decorator. Ran the Granville Pottery before joining *Della Robbia.
Incised monogram.

MARLOW, Reginald (fl.1925-40)

Potter, designer, decorator. Impressed mark, painted monogram.

MARSHALL, Mark Villars (d.1912)

M.V.M.

Designer, modeller, decorator. Worked for Brown-Westhead, Moore & Co., *Doulton (Lambeth), *Martin Brothers and independently.
Incised initials.

MARTIN BROTHERS (1873-1915)

Pottery run by brothers Charles Douglas Martin (1846-1910), E.B.*Martin, R.W.*Martin, W.F.*Martin. Designers/decorators include M.V.*Marshall, W.E.*Willy.
Incised and impressed marks.

MARTIN, Edwin Bruce (1860-1915)

Potter, designer, decorator working with *Martin Brothers.
Incised initials.

MARTIN, Robert Wallace (1843-1924)

Sculptor, designer, modeller, decorator. Designed for *Bailey before setting up *Martin Brothers. Incised signature.

MARTIN, Walter Fraser (1857-1912)

Potter, designer, decorator working with *Martin Brothers. Incised signature.

MATHEWS, Heber (c.1907-59)

Potter, designer, decorator. Incised initials.

MAW & CO. (est.1850)

Manufacturers. Designers include W.*Crane, L.F.*Day, George Goldie (1828-87), John Pollard Seddon (1827-1906), George Edmund Street (1824-81), Matthew Digby Wyatt (1820-77), Charles Henry Temple (fl.1887-1906). Impressed mark.

MELLON, Eric James (b.1925)

Potter, designer, decorator. Painted initials and signature.

MIDWINTER, W.R. (est.c.1910)

Midwinter Stylecraft STAFFORDSHIRE ENGLAND CLASSIC SHAPE 5-61

Manufacturers. Designers include Hugh Casson (b.1910), Terence Conran (b.1931), Roy Midwinter (1925-90), Jessie Tait (b.1928).

Printed marks.

MINTON (est.1793)

Manufacturers. Designers include Léon Arnoux (1816-1902), C.*Dresser, Augustus Welby Northmore Pugin (1812-52), M.-E.-L.*Solon (*see* French ceramics), Léon Victor Solon (1872-1957), Alfred Stevens (1817-75), Charles Toft (1831-1909), John William Wadsworth (1879-1955).
Printed and impressed marks.

MINTON'S ART-POTTERY STUDIO (1871-75)

Decorating studio. Designers include William S. Coleman (1829-1904), C.*Dresser, Henry Stacy Marks (1829-98).
Printed marks.

MOORCROFT, Walter (b.1917)

Designer, decorator. Worked for father's firm, William *Moorcroft.
Painted initials and signature.

MOORCROFT, William (1872-1945)

Designer, decorator. Worked for *Macintyre before establishing his own firm, William *Moorcroft.
Painted initials and signature.

MOORCROFT, William (est.1913)

MOORCROFT
BURSLEM

MOORCROFT

Manufacturers. Designers include William *Moorcroft and son Walter *Moorcroft.
Impressed mark.

MOORE, Bernard (1850-1935)

BM.

BERNARD
BMOORE

Potter, designer, decorator. Designers/decorators working in his studio include J.*Adams, E.H.*Beardmore, D.*Billington, R.R.*Tomlinson.
Painted initials and signature.

MURRAY, Keith (1892-1981)

KM

Keith Murray

Architect, designer. Worked for *Wedgwood; also designed *glass.
Printed monogram and signature.

MURRAY, William Staite (1881-1962)

W.S.Murray

Potter, designer, decorator. Worked at *Yeoman Potters before establishing his own pottery.
Incised signature, impressed initial.

MYCOCK, William Salter (1872-1950)

Designer, decorator. Worked for *Pilkington.
Painted monogram.

NASH, Paul (1889-1946)

Paul Nash

Painter, designer. Worked for
*Brain, *Wilkinson; also designed
*glass, textiles, carpets, posters,
books.
Printed signature.

NEWLAND, William (b.1919)

*William
NEWLAND*

Potter, designer, decorator.
Incised signature.

NEWPORT POTTERY CO. (est.1920)

*Clarice Cliff
NEWPORT POTTERY
ENGLAND*

Manufacturers run from c.1920 by
*Wilkinson. Designers include
C.*Cliff.
Printed mark.

NIXON, Harry (b.1886)

·ℍ·

Designer, modeller, decorator.
Worked for *Doulton (Burslem).
Painted monogram.

NOKE, Charles John (1858-1941)

Noke

Potter, designer, modeller,
decorator. Worked for *Doulton
(Burslem).
Painted signature.

NORTON, Wilfred and Lily (fl.1925-50)

Sculptors, potters, modellers.
Husband and wife working
independently and in collaboration
making ceramic figures.
Incised joint monogram.

ODNEY POTTERY (1937-56)

 ODNEY

Pottery. Among potters who worked there were I.*Auld and J.*Bew. Impressed mark.

OLD HALL EARTHENWARE CO. (est.1861)

Manufacturers. Designers include C.*Dresser.
Printed mark.

OMEGA WORKSHOPS (1913-19)

Workshops started by Roger Fry (1866-1934) where pottery was manufactured and decorated. Designers/decorators include Fry, Vanessa Bell (1879-1961), Henri Gaudier-Brzeska (1891-1915), Duncan Grant (1885-1978), Percy Wyndham-Lewis (1882-1956); workshops also produced *furniture, textiles, carpets. Incised or painted mark.

PASSENGER, Charles (fl.1880-1920)

Decorator. Worked for W.F.*De Morgan.
Painted initials.

PASSENGER, Fred (fl.1880-1933)

Decorator. Worked for W.F.*De Morgan, *Bushey Heath.
Painted initials.

PEARSON, John (fl.1895-1925)

Designer, decorator; also made
*metalwork.
Painted monogram.

PILKINGTON TILE & POTTERY CO. (est.1892)

Manufacturers.
Designers/decorators include
W.*Barnes, W.*Crane,
C.E.*Cundall, L.F.*Day,
G.M.*Forsyth, R.*Joyce,
W.S.*Mycock, E.T.*Radford,
J.L.*Spencer, Charles Francis
Annesley Voysey (1857-1941).
Printed (†) and impressed marks.

PINCOMBE, Helen Edith (b.1908)

Potter, designer, decorator.
Impressed monograms.

PLEYDELL-BOUVERIE, Katharine (1895-1985)

Potter, designer, decorator. Worked
at *St Ives before establishing *Cole
Pottery.
Impressed monograms.

POPE, Francis C. (fl.1880-1920)

F.C.P.

Designer, decorator, modeller.
Worked for *Doulton (Lambeth).
Incised initials.

POTTS, Anne R. (fl.1933-65)

Anne B. Potts.

Designer, modeller, decorator.
Worked for *Bullers and
independently.
Incised signature.

POWELL, Alfred Hoare (1865-1960)

Designer, decorator. Worked for
*Wedgwood and independently;
also decorated furniture and
designed textiles.
Painted monogram.

POWELL, Louise (1882-1956)

Designer, decorator. Worked for
*Wedgwood and independently;
also made illuminated manuscripts.
Painted monogram.

PROCTER, Dod (1891-1972)

Dod Procter.

Painter, designer. Worked for *Brain,
*Wilkinson; also designed posters.
Printed signature.

PROCTER, Ernest (fl.1925-50)

Ernest Procter

Painter, designer. Worked for *Brain,
*Wilkinson; also designed posters.
Printed signature.

QUICK, Kenneth (1931-63)

Potter, designer, decorator. Worked
at *St Ives before establishing
*Tregenna Hill.
Impressed monogram.

RADFORD, Edward Thomas (c.1860-1937)

E.T.R.

Potter, designer. Worked for
*Burmantofts, *Doulton (Lambeth),
*Linthorpe, *Pilkington,
*Wedgwood.
Incised initials.

RATHBONE, Harold Stewart (1858-1929)

Potter, designer, decorator. With
C.*Dressler established *Della
Robbia.
Painted/incised monograms.

RAVILIOUS, Eric William (1903-42)

Painter, designer. Worked for
*Brain, *Wedgwood, *Wilkinson;
also designed glass, furniture,
posters, books.
Printed marks.

RHEAD, Charlotte (1889-1947)

(i)

Designer, decorator. Worked for
*Burgess & Leigh, Ellgreave Pottery
Co., *Richardson, H.J. Wood.
Painted (i, ii) and printed (iii, iv)
signatures.

(ii)

Lottie Rhead Ware

(iv)

(iii)

45

RICARDO, Halsey (1854-1928)

Architect, designer. In partnership with W.F.*De Morgan, 1888-98. Painted monogram.

RICHARDS, Frances E. (c.1869-1931)

Potter, designer, decorator. Painted monogram.

RICHARDSON, A.G., & CO. (est.1915)

Manufacturers of 'Crown Ducal' ware. Designers include C.*Rhead. Printed marks.

RIE, Lucie (b.1902)

Austrian potter, designer, decorator working in England from 1938. Impressed monogram.

RODGERS, Gwladys M. (b.1887)

Decorator, designer. Worked for *Pilkington. Painted initial.

ROPE, Ellen Mary (1855-1934)

Sculptor, designer, modeller, decorator. Worked for *Della Robbia. Painted/incised signature.

RUSCOE, William (fl.1925-60)

Sculptor, potter, modeller. Taught modelling class at *Burslem School of Art; worked for *Bullers. Incised or painted monograms.

RUSKIN POTTERY (1898-1935)

Pottery established by W.H.*Taylor. Impressed marks.

RUSSELL, Gertrude (fl.1900-10)

Designer, decorator. Worked for *Della Robbia. Painted/incised monogram.

SADLER, E. (1912-c.1920)

Manufacturers of 'Devonia Art Pottery'. Taken over by *Brannam. Incised mark.

ST IVES POTTERY (est.1920)

Pottery established by B.*Leach. Potters who worked there include N.*Braden, M.*Cardew, C.*Epton, S.*Hamada, D.*Kemp, D.*Leach, W.*Mackenzie, K.*Pleydell-Bouverie, K.*Quick. Some stoneware made to designs by F.*Brangwyn. Impressed marks.

SHELLEY POTTERIES (1925-66)

Manufacturers. Previously *Wileman & Co. Designers include Mabel Lucie Attwell (1879-1964), Hilda Cowham (1873-1964). Printed mark.

SIMEON, Harry (fl.1894-1936)

Designer, modeller, decorator.
Worked for *Doulton (Lambeth).
Incised initials.

SIMMANCE, Eliza (fl.1873-1928)

Designer, decorator. Worked for
*Doulton (Lambeth).
Incised monogram.

SIMPSON, W.B., & Sons (est.1870)

Manufacturers, decorators.
Designers include James Moyr Smith
(fl.1865-95); also produced stained
glass, metalwork, wallpapers.
Impressed mark.

SPENCER, John L. (b.1904)

Painter, designer, decorator,
modeller. Worked for *Pilkington.
Painted/incised monogram.

SUTHERLAND, Graham Vivian (1903-80)

Painter, designer. Worked for
*Brain, *Wilkinson; also designed
glass, textiles, tapestries, posters.
Printed signature.

TAPLIN, Millicent Jane (1902-80)

Designer, decorator. Worked for
*Wedgwood.
Painted monogram.

TAYLOR, William Howson (1876-1935)

Potter, designer. Established
*Ruskin Pottery.
Painted rebus, monogram.

TINWORTH, George (1843-1913)

Sculptor, designer, modeller,
decorator. Worked for *Doulton
(Lambeth).
Incised monogram.

TOMLINSON, Reginald Robert (1885-1978)

Designer, decorator. Worked for
Minton Hollins, B.*Moore, Crown
Staffordshire Porcelain Co.
Painted monogram.

TOOTH, Henry (fl.1879-1900)

Designer. Manager at *Linthorpe,
co-founded *Bretby.
Impressed monogram.

TORQUAY TERRA-COTTA CO. (1875-1909)

Manufacturers.
Designers/decorators include
L.F.*Day, C.*Dresser, A.*Fisher (*see*
British metalwork).
Impressed or printed marks.

TOWER, James (1919-88)

James Tower

Potter, designer, decorator.
Incised signature.

TREGENNA HILL POTTERY (1955-60)

Pottery established by K.*Quick. Impressed mark.

TUCKFIELD, Denise K. *see* WREN, Denise K.

TUSTIN, Sidney (b.1914)

Potter, designer, decorator. Worked at *Wenford Bridge, *Winchcombe. Impressed mark.

UPCHURCH POTTERY (1913-61)

Pottery. Designers include E.*Spencer (*see* British metalwork). Impressed and incised marks.

VERGETTE, Nicholas (1923-74)

Potter, designer, modeller, decorator. Moved to USA, 1958. Painted initial and monogram.

VYSE, Charles (1882-1971)

Potter, designer, modeller, decorator. Worked for *Doulton (Burslem) and independently. Incised monogram and signature, and painted initials.

WADE, Constance E. *see* DUNN, Constance E.

WALFORD, James (b.1913)

Potter, designer, decorator.
Impressed monogram.

WALKER, Cassandia Ann (fl.1895-1910)

Designer, decorator. Worked for
*Della Robbia.
Painted/incised initials.

WASHINGTON, Robert J. (b.1913)

Potter, designer, decorator.
Impressed initials.

WATCOMBE POTTERY (est.1869)

Manufacturers. Designers include
C.*Dresser.
Printed mark.

WATT, Linnie (fl.1870-95)

Painter, designer, decorator.
Worked for *Doulton (Lambeth).
Painted signature.

WEDGWOOD, Josiah, & Sons (est.1759)

Manufacturers.
Designers/decorators include
H.*Barnard, Edward Bawden
(1903-89), W.*Crane, G.*Davies,
L.F.*Day, C.*Dresser, P.*Follot (*see*
French metalwork), Richard Garbe
(1876-1957), M.*Goupy (*see* French

51

WEDGWOOD, Josiah, & Sons (continued)

glass), Emile Lessore (1805-76), William Lethaby (1857-1931), Arnold Machin (b.1911), K.*Murray, A.H.*Powell, L.*Powell, E.W.*Ravilious, John Skeaping (1901-80), Victor Skellern (b.1909), M.J.*Taplin, L.*Whistler, R.J.*Whistler, N.*Wilson.
Impressed and/or printed marks.

WELLS, Reginald Fairfax (1877-1951)

COLDRVM

Sculptor, potter, designer, modeller, decorator; also designed posters.
Impressed marks.

WENFORD BRIDGE POTTERY (est.1939)

Pottery established by M.*Cardew. Other potters working there include S.*Tustin.
Impressed mark.

WHISTLER, Laurence (b.1912)

Designer. Worked for *Wedgwood; also engraved glass.
Printed mark.

WHISTLER, Rex John (1905-44)

Painter, designer. Worked for
*Wedgwood; also illustrated books
and designed posters.
Printed mark.

WILEMAN & CO. (1892-1925)

Manufacturers of 'Foley' ware.
Subsequently *Shelley Potteries.
Designers include Rowland James
Morris (1847-1909), Frederick
Alfred Rhead (1856-1933), F.H. and
H.G.*Rhead (*see* American
ceramics), Walter Slater
(c.1865-1938).
Printed mark.

WILKINSON, A.J. (est.1885)

Manufacturers. Designers include
John Armstrong (1893-1973),
Vanessa Bell (1879-1961),
F.*Brangwyn, J. Butler (fl.c.1900),
C.*Cliff, G.M.*Forsyth, Duncan
Grant (1885-1978), Barbara
Hepworth (1903-75), L.*Knight,
P.*Nash, Ben Nicholson
(1894-1982), D.*Procter, E.*Procter,
Albert Rutherston (1881-1953),
G.V.*Sutherland.
Printed marks.

WILLY, Walter Edward (fl.1875-95)

Designer, decorator. Worked for
*Martin Brothers.
Incised signature.

WILSON, Norman (b.1902)

Potter, designer. Worked for
*Wedgwood.
Impressed initials.

WILTSHAW & ROBINSON (est.1890)

Manufacturers of 'Carlton Ware'.
Printed marks.

WINCHCOMBE POTTERY (est.1926)

Pottery set up by M.*Cardew. Other
potters working there include Elijah
Comfort (c.1860-1945), R.*Finch,
S.*Tustin.
Impressed mark.

WORCESTER ROYAL PORCELAIN CO.

Manufacturers.
Designers/modellers include James
Hadley (1847-1903), Phoebe Stabler
(d.1955), John William Wadsworth
(1879-1955; art director 1915-30).
Printed mark.

WREN (*née* Tuckfield), Denise K. (1891-1979)

Potter, designer, modeller,
decorator.
Incised initials and signature.

YELLAND MANOR POTTERY (est.1956)

Pottery established by M.*Leach.
Impressed mark.

YEOMAN POTTERS (c.1915-20)

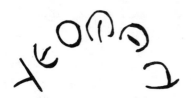

Collaboration between painter
Cuthbert Fraser Hamilton (1884-
1959) and W.S.*Murray.
Incised marks.

AMERICAN CERAMICS

ALBERHILL POTTERY (1912-14)

ALBERHILL

Pottery run by A.W.*Robertson for the Alberhill Coal and Clay Company.
Impressed mark.

AMERICAN ENCAUSTIC TILING COMPANY (1875-1935)

Manufacturers. Designers include H.T.*Mueller, F.H*Rhead, L.*Rhead, Leon Victor Solon (1872-1957).
Moulded marks.

AMERICAN ENCAUSTIC
TILING Co Limited
NEW YORK

ARC-EN-CIEL POTTERY COMPANY (1903-05)

Manufacturers.
Designers/decorators include J.*Lessell.
Impressed mark.

AREQUIPA POTTERY (1911-18)

Pottery attached to tuberculosis sanatorium. Artistic directors were successively F.H.*Rhead, Albert L. Solon (fl.1910-30), Fred H. Wilde (fl.1885-1920).
Incised (†) and impressed marks.

56

ASBURY, Lenore (fl.1894-1931)

L A

Designer, decorator. Worked for
*Rookwood.
Painted initials.

ATLAN CERAMIC ART CLUB (1893-1921)

Association of amateur decorators
in Chicago. Among instructors was
F.D.*Koehler.
Painted mark.

AVON FAIENCE CO. *see* VANCE/AVON FAIENCE COMPANY

AVON POTTERY (1886-88)

AVON

Pottery established by Karl
Langenbeck (1861-1938).
Decorators include James
MacDonald (fl.1880s).
Impressed mark.

BAGGS, Arthur Eugene (1886-1947)

aEB

Potter, designer, decorator.
Worked for *Marblehead, *Cowan
and independently.
Incised initials.

BAKER, Contance Amelia (fl.c.1900)

C A B

Designer, decorator. Worked for
*Rookwood.
Painted initials

BATCHELDER TILE COMPANY (1909-32)

**BATCHELDER
LOS ANGELES**

Pottery established by
E.A.*Batchelder (*see* American
graphics).
Moulded mark.

BENNETT, John (1840-1907)

Bennett,
101 Lex Ave N.Y.

Potter, designer, decorator.
Worked for *Doulton (Lambeth)
(*see* British ceramics) before
emigrating in 1877 to the USA
where he established his own
pottery.
Painted signature.

BINNS, Charles Fergus (1857-1934)

English potter, designer. Worked
for *Worcester Royal Porcelain (*see*
British ceramics) before settling in
the USA. Director of New York
School of Clayworking.
Incised initials.

BISHOP, Irene (fl.1880-1925)

J. B   **I.B.**

Designer, decorator. Worked for
*Rookwood.
Painted initials.

BOOKPRINTER, Anna Marie *see* VALENTIEN, Anna Marie

BRAUCKMAN, Cornelius W. (1864-1952)

BRAUCKMAN
ART
POTTERY

Potter, designer. Established
*Grand Feu.
Impressed mark.

BROUWER, Theophilus Anthony, Jr (1864-1932)

Brouwer

Painter, potter, designer,
decorator. Established *Middle
Lane Pottery and subsequently

Brouwer Pottery; also designed and made metalwork and carved wood. Incised signature.

BUFFALO POTTERY (est.1901)

Manufacturers. Products include 'Deldare Ware'. Designers/decorators include Ralph Stuart (c.1877-1945). Factory also made tableware for the *Roycroft community (*see* American furniture) designed by D.*Hunter (*see* American graphics). Printed marks.

BURGESS, Levi J. (fl.c.1905)

Designer, decorator. Worked for *Weller. Painted initials.

BYRDCLIFFE POTTERY (est.c.1903)

Pottery established by Edith Penman (fl.1900-30) and Elizabeth R. Hardenbergh (fl.1900-30) and associated with Byrdcliffe arts and crafts community. Other designers/decorators include Zulma Steele (fl.1910-30). Community also produced metalwork, furniture, textiles. Impressed mark.

59

CALIFORNIA FAIENCE (1915-30)

Pottery. Made 'California Porcelain' in collaboration with West Coast Porcelain. Incised marks.

CAMBRIDGE ART POTTERY COMPANY (1901-08)

CAMBRIDGE

Manufacturers. Designers include C.B.*Upjohn. Impressed mark.

CHELSEA KERAMIC ART WORKS (1872-89)

CHELSEA KERAMIC ART WORKS ROBERTSON & SONS.

Manufacturers. Designers/decorators include J.*Day, F.X.*Dengler, G.W.*Fenety, John Gardner Low (1835-1907), A.*Osborne, A.W.*Robertson, H.C.*Robertson, Isaac Elwood Scott (1845-1920). Reorganised as *Chelsea Pottery US in 1889. Impressed marks.

CHELSEA KERAMIC ART WORKS ROBERTSON & SONS

CHELSEA POTTERY US (1891-95)

Pottery run by H.C.*Robertson. Subsequently became *Dedham Pottery. Designers/decorators include Joseph L. Smith (fl.c.1890). Impressed mark.

CHICAGO CRUCIBLE COMPANY (c.1920-c.1932)

Manufacturers.
Impressed marks.

CINCINNATI ART POTTERY COMPANY (1880-91)

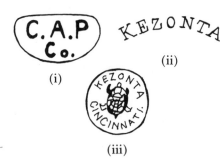

(ii)

(i)

(iii)

Pottery run by T.J.*Wheatley and known as T.J.*Wheatley & Co. until he left in 1882. Among its output was 'Kezonta' ware.
Impressed (i) and printed/impressed (ii, iii) marks.

CLIFTON ART POTTERY (1905-11)

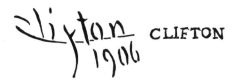

Pottery. Designers include W.A.*Long (co-founder).
Incised and impressed marks.

COWAN POTTERY STUDIO (1912-31)

Cowan Pottery

(†)

COWAN
POTTERY

Pottery established by R.G.*Cowan. Designers/decorators/modellers include Russell Barnett Aitken (b.1910), A.E.*Baggs, Alexander Blazys (fl.1915-40), Paul Bogatay (1905-72), Edris Eckhardt (b.1907), Waylande Gregory (1905-71), Paul Manship (1885-1966), Viktor Schreckengost (b.1906), Thelma Frazier Winter (1903-77).
Incised (†) and impressed marks.

COWAN, R. Guy (1884-1957)

Potter, designer, decorator.
Established *Cowan Pottery Studio.
Incised monogram.

COX, Paul Ernest (1879-1968)

 (i)   (ii)

Potter. Worked for *Newcomb and
independently.
Printed (i) and impressed (ii)
marks.

CROSSWARE POTTERY (est.c.1905)

Pottery established by Nellie Agnes
Cross (fl.c.1900-20)
Relief-moulded mark.

DALLAS POTTERY (1865-82)

DALLAS

Pottery where members of the
Cincinnati Pottery Club decorated
their wares and had them fired.
Impressed mark.

DALY, Matthew Andrew (1860-1937)

Designer, decorator. Worked for
Matt *Morgan, *Rookwood.
Painted initials.

DAY, Josephine (fl.1880-1900)

Designer, decorator. Worked for
*Chelsea Keramic Art Works.
Incised monogram.

DEDHAM POTTERY (1895-1943)

(i)

(ii)

(iii)

(iv)

Manufacturers. Name of *Chelsea Pottery US after it moved to new premises. Designers/decorators include Maud Davenport (fl.c.1905), Joseph L. Smith (fl.c.1895), H.C.*Robertson (art director).
Impressed (i), printed (ii) and incised (iii, iv) marks.

DENGLER, Franz Xavier (fl.c.1880)

Designer, decorator. Worked for *Chelsea Keramic Art Works. Incised monogram.

DENVER CHINA & POTTERY COMPANY (1901-05)

(i)

(ii)

Pottery established by W.A.*Long. Impressed (i) and printed (ii) marks.

DIEDERICH, Wilhelm Hunt (1884-1925)

Sculptor, potter, designer, decorator; also made metalwork. Painted monogram.

DURANT KILNS (1910-30)

Pottery established by Jean Durant Rice (d.1919) and L.*Volkmar. Incised mark.

EPPLY, Lorinda (1874-1951)

Designer, decorator. Worked for
*Rookwood.
Painted monogram.

FAIENCE MANUFACTURING COMPANY (1880-92)

Manufacturers.
Designers/decorators include
E.*Lycett.
Impressed marks.

FENETY, George W. (1854-1933)

Designer, decorator. Worked for
*Chelsea Keramic Art Works; also
designed embroideries, textiles.
Incised initials.

FERRELL, Frank L. (fl.1900-30)

Designer, decorator. Worked for
*Owens, *Peters & Reed,
*Roseville, *Weller.
Painted signature and initials.

FRACKELTON, Susan Stuart Goodrich (1848-1932)

Potter, designer, decorator.
Incised monogram.

FRY, Laura Anne (1857-1943)

(†)

Designer, decorator. Worked for
*Lonhuda, *Rookwood and
independently; also made
furniture.
Incised (†) and painted
monograms.

FULPER POTTERY COMPANY (est.1899)

Manufacturers of 'Vasekraft' and other wares.
Impressed marks.

GATES POTTERIES (est.c.1885)

WM. D .GATES

AMERICAN
TERRA-COTTA
CHICAGO

TECO

Teco

Group of firms including American Terra Cotta & Ceramic Company, manufacturers of 'Teco' ware, owned and directed by William Day Gates (1852-1935) who also designed many pieces. Other designers include Fritz Albert (fl.1890-1920), William J. Dodd (1862-1930), Hugh M.G. Garden (1873-1961), William LeBaron Jenney (1832-1907), Fernand Moreau (fl.1890-1920), William Bryce Mundie (1863-1939), Frank Lloyd Wright (1867-1956).
Impressed marks.

GELNER, Sarah (1894-1982)

Designer, decorator. Worked for *Paul Revere.
Painted monogram.

GRAND FEU ART POTTERY (c.1912-c.1918)

GRAND FEU
POTTERY
L. A., CAL.

Pottery established by C.W.*Brauckman.
Impressed mark.

GRUEBY POTTERY (1894-1920)

**GRUEBY POTTERY
BOSTON. U.S.A.**

Manufacturers.
Designers/decoators include Julia H. Bradley (fl.c.1900), Ruth Erickson (fl.c.1900), George Prentiss Kendrick (fl.c.1900), Addison B. Le Boutillier (1872-1951), Annie V. Lingley (fl.c.1900), Norma Pierce (fl.c.1900), Wilhelmina Post (fl.c.1900), Kiichi Yamada (fl.c.1900).
Impressed marks.

HALCYON POTTERY (1910-13)

Pottery directed by A.W.*Robertson.
Impressed marks.

**HALCYON
CALIF.**

HAMPSHIRE POTTERY COMPANY (1871-1923)

(i)   (ii)

Manufacturers.
Designers/decorators include C.*Robertson.
Printed (i, ii) and impressed (iii) marks.

(iii)

HARPER, Helen M. (fl.c.1895)

HMH

Designer, decorator. Worked for *Lonhuda.
Incised monogram.

HAUBRICH, Albert (1875-1931)

Designer, decorator. Worked for
*Owens, *Weller.
Painted/incised signature, initials.

HEROLD, John J. (1871-1923)

J.H.

Potter, designer, decorator.
Worked for *Owens and *Roseville
before establishing Herold China
Co. in 1908.
Painted/incised initials.

HOMER LAUGHLIN CHINA COMPANY (est.1873)

Manufacturers of 'Wells Art',
'Fiesta' and other wares.
Designers/decorators include
E.*Lycett, F.H.*Rhead.
Printed marks.

MADE IN U.S.A.

HULL-HOUSE KILNS (1927-c.1940)

Pottery associated with practical
classes at Hull House settlement,
Chicago.
Printed and incised marks.

HUNT, Jonathan Bowne (1876-1943)

Potter, designer. Worked for
*Newcomb College and
*Rookwood.
Incised monogram.

HURLEY, Edward Timothy (1869-1950)

Designer, decorator. Worked for
*Rookwood; also designed
metalwork.
Painted monogram.

IRVINE, Sarah Agnes Estelle (Sadie) (1887-1970)

Designer, decorator. Worked for
*Newcomb College.
Incised initials.

JERVIS, William Percival (1849-1925)

Potter, designer, decorator.
Worked for Craven Art Pottery,
*Rose Valley, *Vance/Avon before
establishing his own pottery at
Oyster Bay, New York, in 1908,
where F.H.*Rhead also worked.
Incised signature and mark.

KENTON HILLS PORCELAINS (1939-42)

Manufacturers.
Designers/decorators include
D.W.*Seyler.
Impressed mark.

KOEHLER, Florence D. (1861-1944)

Painter, designer, decorator. Worked for *Atlan Ceramic Art Club, *Rookwood and independently; also made jewellery, enamels.
Painted initials.

LESSELL ART WARE COMPANY (1911-12)

Pottery established by J.*Lessell.
Impressed mark.

LESSELL, John (c.1871-1925)

Potter, designer, decorator. Worked at *Arc-en-Ciel, Art China Co., *Owen China Co. *Owens, *Weller and established *Lessell Art Ware Company.
Painted/incised initials, signature.

LITTLEJOHN, Cynthia Pugh (1890-1959)

Designer, decorator. Worked for *Newcomb College.
Incised monogram.

LONG, William A. (1844-1918)

Potter, designer, decorator. Worked for *Clifton, *Lonhuda (co-founder), *Owens, *Weller and established *Denver China & Pottery Co.
Incised monogram.

LONHUDA POTTERY (1892-94)

Pottery. Designers/decorators include L.A.*Fry, H.M.*Harper, W.A.*Long (co-founder), S.R.*McLaughlin, J.R.*Spaulding. Impressed marks.

LOW, J. & J.G., Art Tile Works (1879-83)
LOW, J.G. & J.F., Art Tile Works (1883-1907)

J&J.G.LOW
PATENT
ARTTILE WORKS
CHELSEA
MASS U.SA.

J.G.&J.F.LOW.
ART TILE WORKS.
CHELSEA.
MASS. U.S.A.
COPYRIGHT
BY J.G.&J.F. LOW
1885

Manufacturers. Designers include co-founder John Gardner Low (1835-1907), A.*Osborne. Moulded marks.

LYCETT, Edward (1833-1909)

E Lycett

Painter, potter, designer, decorator. Worked for Battam and Copeland & Garrett in Britain before emigrating to the USA where he worked for *Faience Manufacturing Company, *Homer Laughlin, Jersey City Pottery, Union Porcelain Works and independently. Painted signature.

McCANDLESS, Cora (fl.c.1900)

Designer, decorator. Worked for *Owens. Incised/painted initials.

McDONALD, William Purcell (1865-1931)

W.P.McD.   **WᶜD**

WPMᶜD   **WPMcᶜ**

Designer, decorator. Worked for
*Rookwood.
Painted initials, monogram.

McLAUGHLIN, Mary Louise (1847-1939)

LMᶜL

Lo'santi

Potter, designer, decorator. Made
'Losanti Ware'; also made stained
glass, metalwork, furniture,
needlework.
Painted initials, monogram and
marks.

McLAUGHLIN, Sarah R. (fl.c.1900)

SL

Designer, decorator. Worked for
*Lonhuda.
Incised monogram.

MARBLEHEAD POTTERY (1904-36)

Pottery. Designers/decorators
include A.E.*Baggs, Arthur Irwin
Hennessey (fl.c.1910), E.D.
(Hannah) Tutt (fl.c.1910).
Impressed mark.

MARKHAM POTTERY (1905-21)

Markham

Pottery established by Herman C.
Markham (1849-1922).
Incised mark.

MERRIMAC POTTERY COMPANY (1902-08)

Manufacturers.
Impressed/incised mark.

MEYER, Joseph Fortune (1848-1931)

Potter, designer. Worked at
*Newcomb College, *New Orleans.
Incised monogram.

MIDDLE LANE POTTERY (1894-1902)

Pottery established by
T.A.*Brouwer Jr.
Impressed or incised mark.

MORAVIAN POTTERY & TILE WORKS (est.1898)

Pottery established by Henry
Chapman Mercer (1856-1930).
Impressed (i, ii) and moulded (iii)
marks.

(i)   **MORAVIAN**

(ii)   (iii)

MORGAN, Matt, Pottery Company (1883-85)

Pottery established by painter and
designer Matthew Somerville
Morgan (c.1839-90).
Designers/decorators include
M.A.*Daly, H.T.*Mueller.
Impressed mark.

MOSAIC TILE COMPANY

Manufacturers.
Designers/decorators include
H.T.*Mueller, H.G.*Rhead.
Moulded mark.

MUELLER, Herman T. (1854-1941)

Designer, modeller. Worked for
*American Encaustic Tiling, Matt
*Morgan, *Mosaic Tile Co.,
*Mueller Mosaic Tile Co.
Moulded monogram.

MUELLER MOSAIC TILE COMPANY (1909-38)

Manufacturers established by
H.T.*Mueller.
Moulded mark.

NEWCOMB COLLEGE POTTERY (est.1895)

Pottery established at Tulane
University, New Orleans.
Designers/decorators include
P.*Cox, J.B.*Hunt, S.A.E.*Irvine,
C.P.*Littlejohn, J.F.*Meyer,
L.*Nicholson, M.T.*Ryan,
M.G.*Sheerer, A.F.C.*Simpson,
K.E.*Smith, F.E.*Walrath,
S.E.*Wells.
Impressed/painted marks.

NEW ORLEANS ART POTTERY (1888-89)

Pottery run by J.F.*Meyer and
G.E.*Ohr.
Incised mark.

NEWTON, Clara Chipman (1848-1936)

C¹.CN   C.H   🕷

Designer, decorator. Worked for
*Rookwood and independently.
Painted initials and monogram.

NICHOLS, Maria Longworth (1849-1932)

M.L.N.

MLS

Designer, decorator. Worked at
*Dallas Pottery before establishing
*Rookwood and worked
independently. (In 1886 married
B. Storer.)
Painted initials.

NICHOLSON, Leona (1875-1966)

⎣N

Potter, designer, decorator.
Worked for *Newcomb College.
Incised initials.

NORTHWESTERN TERRA COTTA COMPANY (1907-20)

NORWETA
(i)

NORWETA
(ii)

Manufacturers. Designers include
Fritz Albert (fl.1890-1920),
Fernand Moreau (fl.1890-1920).
Impressed (i) and printed (ii)
marks.

NOURSE, Mary Madeline (1870-1959)

M.N.

Designer, decorator. Worked for
*Rookwood and independently.
Painted initials.

ODELL & BOOTH BROTHERS (1880-85)

O&BB

Manufacturers.
Impressed marks.

OHR, George E. (1857-1918)

Potter, designer, decorator.
Founded Biloxi Art Pottery,
worked for *New Orleans Art
Pottery.
Impressed and incised marks.

OSBORNE, Arthur (fl.1870-1900)

English designer, modeller,
decorator working in the USA.
Worked for *Chelsea Keramic Art
Works, J.& J.G.*Low Art Tile
Works.
Moulded monogram.

OVERBECK, Elizabeth G. (1875-1936)

E

Potter. Worked at *Overbeck
Pottery (co-founder).
Incised initial.

OVERBECK, Hannah B. (1870-1931)

Designer, decorator. Worked at
*Overbeck Pottery (co-founder).
Incised initial and monogram,
painted signature.

OVERBECK, Mary Frances (1878-1955)

Designer, decorator. Worked at
*Overbeck Pottery (co-founder).
Incised initials.

OVERBECK POTTERY (est.1911)

Pottery run by sisters
E.G.*Overbeck, H.B.*Overbeck,
Margaret Overbeck (1863-1911),
M.F.*Overbeck.
Incised mark.

OWEN CHINA COMPANY (1903-32)

Manufacturers of 'Swastika
Keramos' and other wares.
Designers/decorators include
J.*Lessell.
Moulded mark.

OWENS, J.B., Pottery Company (est.1891)

Manufacturers.
Designers/decorators include
F.L.*Ferrell, A.*Haubrich,
J.J.*Herold, J.*Lessell, W.A.*Long,
C.*McCandless, H.M.*Ross,
R.L.*Shoemaker, H.*Smith,
W.H.*Stemm, M.*Timberlake,
S.*Timberlake.
Impressed marks.

OWENSART

OZARK POTTERY COMPANY (c.1906-c.1910)

Pottery established by sculptor
Robert Porter Bringhurst
(1855-1925); ware called 'Zark'.
Incised/impressed mark.

PAULINE POTTERY (1882-1909)

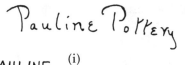

(i)

PAULINE (i)
POTTERY

CHICAGO

(ii)

(iii)

Pottery established by Pauline
Jacobus (1840-1930).
Incised (i) and impressed (ii, iii)
marks.

PAUL REVERE POTTERY (1906-42)

P.R.P   S.E.G.
(i)   (ii)

(iii)   (iv)

Pottery established at 'Saturday
Evening Girls', a Boston club for
young female immigrants.
Designers/decorators include
S.*Gelner.
Painted (i, ii) and printed (iii, iv)
marks.

PERRY, Mary Chase (1868-1961)

M C P   Perry

Potter, designer, decorator.
Worked as an independent
decorator before establishing
*Pewabic Pottery.
Painted initials and signature.

PETERS & REED (1898-1921)

ZANE WARE
MADE IN USA

Manufacturers.
Designers/decorators include
F.L.*Ferrell, Adam Reed (d.1922).
Impressed mark.

PEWABIC POTTERY (est.1903)

(i)

(ii)

Pottery established by Horace
James Caulkins (1850-1923) and
M.*Perry (founder).
Impressed (i, ii) and incised (iii)
marks.

Pewabic
Detroit

(iii)

PILLSBURY, Hester W. (fl.c.1900)

Ħ   J-Ꝑ

Designer, decorator. Worked for
*Roseville, *Weller.
Painted/incised monograms.

POILLON POTTERY (c.1901-28)

POILLON
Woodbridge
N.J.

Pottery established by Clara Louise
Poillon (d.1936).
Incised mark.

POOR, Henry Varnum (1888-1971)

HP   +Ṽᑭ

Painter, potter, designer,
decorator.
Painted monograms.

PULLMAN, John Wesley (1886-1931)

WP

Designer, decorator. Worked for
*Rookwood.
Painted initials.

REDLANDS POTTERY (c.1904–c.1909)

Pottery established by Wesley H.
Trippett (1862-1913).
Relief-moulded marks.

RETTIG, Martin (1869-1956)

Designer, decorator. Worked for
*Rookwood.
Painted initials.

RHEAD, Frederick Hurten (1880-1942)

Rhead

ʁ

Potter, designer, decorator.
Worked for Wardle & Co. and
*Wileman (*see* British ceramics)
before settling in the USA in 1902.
Worked for *American Encaustic
Tiling Co., *Arequipa, *Homer
Laughlin, *Jervis, *Rhead Pottery,
*Roseville, *University City,
*Vance/Avon, *Weller.
Incised signature and monogram.

RHEAD, Harry G. (1881-1950)

H Rhead

Potter, designer, decorator.
Worked for Wardle & Co. and
*Wileman in Britain before settling
in the USA c.1908. Worked for
*Roseville, *Mosaic Tile Co.,
Standard Tile Co.
Painted signature.

RHEAD (née WHITCOMB), Lois (fl.1910-30)

Designer, decorator. Worked for
*American Encaustic Tiling Co.,
*Rhead Pottery.
Painted monogram.

RHEAD POTTERY (1913-17)

Pottery. Designers/decorators include founder F.H.*Rhead, L.*Rhead.
Impressed mark.

ROBERTSON, Alexander W. (1840-1925)

Potter, designer, decorator. Worked for *Alberhill, *Chelsea Keramic Art Works, *Halcyon, *Roblin.
Incised and impressed initials.

ROBERTSON, Cadmon (fl.1900-25)

Potter, designer, decorator. Worked for *Hampshire.
Impressed mark (a tribute to his wife, Emoretta).

ROBERTSON, Fred H. (1880-1952)

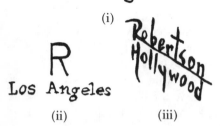

(i)

(ii)   (iii)

Made 'Robertson Pottery' (1906-52), latterly with son George B. Robertson (1907-66).
Impressed (i, ii) and incised (iii) marks.

ROBERTSON, Hugh Cornwall (1844-1908)

Potter, designer. Worked for *Chelsea Keramic Art Works, *Chelsea Pottery US, *Dedham.
Incised monogram.

ROBINEAU, Adelaide Alsop (1865-1929)

(i)   (ii)

Potter, designer, decorator. Worked independently and for The Onondaga Pottery Company and *University City. Raised (i) and impressed (ii) monograms.

ROBLIN ART POTTERY (1898-1906)

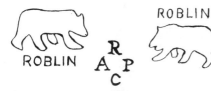

Pottery established by Linna Irelan (fl.c.1900) and A.W.*Robertson. Impressed marks.

ROOKWOOD POTTERY (1880-1967)

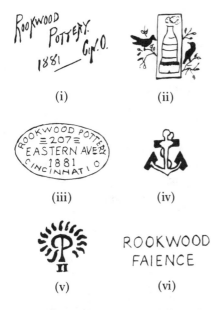

(i)   (ii)

(iii)   (iv)

(v)   (vi)

Manufacturers. Designers/decorators include L.*Asbury, C.A.*Baker, I.*Bishop, A.M. Bookprinter (*see* A.M. Valentien), M.A.*Daly, L.*Epply, L.A.*Fry, J.B.*Hunt, E.T.*Hurley, F.D.*Koehler, W.P.*McDonald, C.C.*Newton, M.L.*Nichols (founder), M.M.*Nourse, J.W.*Pullman, M.*Rettig, S.*Sax, K.*Shirayamadani, S.A.*Toohey, A.*Van Briggle, J.D.*Wareham, G.*Young. Painted/incised (i), printed (ii, iii), printed/impressed (iv), impressed (v) marks, and moulded (vi) mark on tiles.

ROSE VALLEY POTTERY

(†)

Pottery. Designers/decorators include W.P.*Jervis. Printed (†) and moulded marks.

ROSEVILLE POTTERY COMPANY (1890-1954)

Manufacturers of 'Rozane Ware', etc. Designers/decorators include F.L.*Ferrell, J.J.*Herold, H.W.*Pillsbury, F.H.*Rhead, H.G.*Rhead, R.L.*Shoemaker, H.*Smith, M.*Timberlake, S.*Timberlake, G.*Young. Impressed marks.

ROSS, Hattie M. (fl.c.1900)

Designer, decorator. Worked for J.B.*Owens, *Weller. Incised/painted monogram.

RYAN, Mazie Teresa (1880-1946)

Designer, decorator. Worked for *Newcomb College. Painted signature.

SAX, Sara (fl.1896-1931)

Designer, decorator. Worked for *Rookwood. Painted initials and monogram.

SEYLER, David W. (fl.1935-70)

(i)   (ii)

Sculptor, modeller, designer, decorator. Worked for *Kenton Hills and independently. Incised (i) and moulded (ii) initials.

SHEERER, Mary Given (1865-1954)

Designer, decorator. Worked for
*Newcomb College.
Incised initials.

SHIRAYAMADANI, Kataro (1865-1948)

Japanese designer, decorator
working in the USA. Worked for
*Rookwood.
Incised signature.

SHOEMAKER, R. Lillian (fl.c.1900)

Designer, decorator. Worked for
J.B.*Owens, *Roseville.
Printed/incised initials,
monogram.

SICARD, Jacques (1865-1923)

French potter designer, decorator.
Worked for C.*Massier(see French
ceramics) in France before settling
in the USA where he worked for
*Weller.
Painted signature.

SIMPSON, Anna Frances Connor (1880-1930)

Designer, decorator. Worked for
*Newcomb College.
Incised monogram.

SMITH, Helen (fl.c.1905)

Designer, decorator. Worked for
J.B.*Owens, *Roseville, *Weller.
Incised signature.

SMITH, Kenneth E. (b.1907)

Potter, designer. Worked for
American Art Clay Co., *Newcomb
College.
Incised initials.

SPAULDING, Jessie R. (fl.c.1895)

Designer, decorator. Worked for
*Lonhuda.
Incised monogram.

STEMM, William H. (fl.c.1900)

Designer, decorator. Worked for
J.B.*Owens, *Weller.
Painted/incised initials,
monogram.

STOCKTON ART POTTERY COMPANY (1896-1900)

Manufacturers of 'Rekston' and
other wares.
Impressed mark.

STORER, Maria Longworth *see* NICHOLS, Maria Longworth

TIFFANY, Louis Comfort (1848-1933)

Designer. Worked for his own
pottery; also designed *glass,
stained glass, mosaics, metalwork,
jewellery, textiles, wallpapers.
Incised monogram.

TIMBERLAKE, Mae (fl.c.1900)

Designer, decorator. Worked for
J.B.*Owens, *Roseville, *Weller.
Painted/incised signature, initials.

TIMBERLAKE, Sarah (fl.c.1900)

Designer, decorator. Worked for
J.B.*Owens, *Roseville, *Weller.
Painted/incised initials.

TOOHEY, Sara Alice (fl.1887-1931)

Designer, decorator. Worked for
*Rookwood.
Painted monograms.

UNIVERSITY CITY POTTERY (1907-15)

School of ceramic art directed by
T.*Doat (*see* French ceramics) as
part of the American Woman's
League. Members of staff include
Edward Dahlquist
(1877-1927), Emile Diffloth
(1856-1933), F.H.*Rhead,
A.A.*Robineau.
Impressed and incised marks.

UPJOHN, Charles Babcock (1866-1953)

Potter, designer, modeller.
Worked for *Cambridge Art
Pottery, Trent Tile Co., *Weller,
and established C.B. Upjohn
Pottery Co.
Incised monogram.

VALENTIEN, Albert Robert (1862-1925)

Potter, designer, decorator.
Worked for *Rookwood before
establishing *Valentien Pottery.
Painted initials.

VALENTIEN (née BOOKPRINTER), Anna Marie (1862-1947)

Potter, designer, decorator.
Worked for *Rookwood (as
Bookprinter) before establishing
*Valentien Pottery.
Painted initials.

VALENTIEN POTTERY (1911-13)

Pottery established by
A.R.*Valentien and wife
A.M.*Valentien.
Impressed mark.

VAN BRIGGLE, Artus (1869-1904)

Potter, designer, modeller,
decorator. Worked for *Rookwood
before establishing *Van Briggle
Pottery.
Painted initials.

VAN BRIGGLE POTTERY (est.1901)

Pottery established by A.*Van
Briggle and continued by his wife
Anne after his death.
Incised/impressed marks.

VANCE/AVON FAIENCE COMPANY (1901-08)

(i)

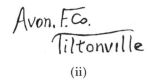

(ii)

(iii)

Manufacturers. Name changed from Vance to Avon in 1902. Designers/decorators include W.P.*Jervis, F.H.*Rhead. Impressed (i), incised (ii) and impressed/printed (iii) marks.

VAN DER MEULEN & WYKSTRA ART POTTERY (1906-09)

Pottery established by Theake F. Van Der Meulen (fl.1900-10) and Gerrit Wykstra (fl.1900-20). Impressed mark.

VOLKMAR, Charles (1841-1914)

CHAS . VOLKMAR

Painter, potter, designer, decorator. Ran his own pottery at various locations before establishing *Volkmar Kilns. Incised monogram, impressed signature.

VOLKMAR, Leon (1879-1959)

Potter, designer. Worked at *Durant Kilns, *Volkmar Kilns. Incised initial.

VOLKMAR KILNS (1903-14)

VOLKMAR KILNS,
METUCHEN, N.J.

Pottery established by father and son C.*Volkmar and L.*Volkmar. Impressed mark.

WALLEY, William Joseph (1852-1919)

W J W

Potter, designer, decorator.
Impressed initials.

WALRATH, Frederick E. (1871-1921)

Walrath
Pottery

Potter, designer, decorator.
Taught at Mechanics Institute,
Rochester, New York, and worked
for *Newcomb College.
Incised mark.

WALRICH POTTERY (1922-30)

(i)

WALRICH
Berkeley, Cal.

(ii)

Pottery established by James A.
Wall (1877-1952) and wife
Gertrude Rupel Wall (1881-1971).
Impressed (i, ii) and incised (iii)
marks.

WALRICH

(iii)

WANNOPEE POTTERY (1892-1903)

(i)

(ii)

Manufacturers of 'Scarabronze'
and other wares. Designers include
A.H. Noble (fl.c.1900), Charles
Reynolds (fl.c.1900).
Impressed (i) and
impressed/moulded (ii) marks.

WAREHAM, John Dee (1871-1954)

Designer, decorator. Worked for
*Rookwood.
Incised initials.

WELLER, S.A., Pottery Company (1894-1948)

Manufacturers.
Designers/decorators include
L.J.*Burgess, F.L.*Ferrell,
A.*Haubrich, J.*Lessell,
W.A.*Long, H.W.*Pillsbury,
F.H.*Rhead, H.M.*Ross, J.*Sicard,
H.*Smith, W.H.*Stemm,
M.*Timberlake, S.*Timberlake,
C.B.*Upjohn, T.J.*Wheatley.
Incised (†) and impressed marks.

WELLS, Sabina Elliott (fl.1900-10)

S.E.W.

Designer, decorator. Worked for
*Newcomb College.
Incised initials and signatures.

WHEATLEY, Thomas Jerome (1853-1917)

Painter, potter, designer,
decorator. Worked for *Coultry,
*Weller, T.J.*Wheatley & Co., and
independently. Established
*Wheatley Pottery Co.
Incised signature.

WHEATLEY, T.J., & Company (1880-82)

Name given to *Cincinnati Art
Pottery Co. whilst it was run by
T.J.*Wheatley.
Incised mark.

WHEATLEY POTTERY COMPANY (1903-27)

Pottery established by
T.J.*Wheatley.
Monogram on paper label.

WHITCOMB, Lois *see* RHEAD, Lois

YOUNG, Grace (1869-1947)

Designer, decorator. Worked at
*Rookwood, *Roseville.
Painted monogram.

ZANESVILLE ART POTTERY (1900-20)

LA MORO

Manufacturers of 'La Moro' and
other wares.
Impressed mark.

FRENCH CERAMICS

AIRE-BELLE (1895-1905)

Aire - Belle

Pottery established by
A.C.H.*Rossollin.
Painted mark.

ALAPHILIPPE, Ferdinand (1880-1910)

F. alaphilipps

Potter, designer, decorator.
Incised signature.

ANKER, Albert (1831-1910)

ÅNKER

Painter, designer, decorator.
Worked for T.*Deck.
Painted signature.

ARNOUX, Guy (1890-1951)

GUY ARNOUX

Painter, designer, decorator.
Worked for *Montières; also
designed posters.
Painted signature.

ARTIGAS, Josep Llorens (b.1892)

LLORENS-ARTIGAS   ARTIGAS

(i)   (ii)

LA

(iii)

Spanish potter, designer,
decorator, who worked for many
years in France. Made ceramics
decorated by G.*Braque, R.*Dufy,
A.*Marquet, J.*Miró.
Painted (i) and incised (ii)
signatures, painted/incised
monogram (iii).

AVISSEAU, Charles-Jean (1796-1861)

Potter, designer, decorator.
Incised signature and monogram.

BACQUET, Auguste (1873-1930)

Potter, designer, decorator.
Incised rebus.

BACS (1916-c.1926)

BACS
Golfe Juan
CANNES-EDEN

Pottery established by J.-B.*Barol,
Marius Alexandre (1880-1959),
Jean Carle (fl.1900-40), François
Sicard (fl.1900-40), who had all
worked previously for C.*Massier.
Printed mark.

BARK, Nils Ivan Joakim de (1863-1930)

Swedish painter and potter
working in France.
Incised signatures.

BARLUET & CIE (1876-1920)

CRE IL
B. & Cⁱᵉ
MONTEREAU

Manufacturers. Took over
*Lebeuf, Milliet & Cie.
Designers/decorators include
F.*Bracquemond (see French
metalwork), E.F.*Rousseau.
Printed mark.

BAROL, Jean-Baptiste (1873-1966)

Barol

Potter, designer, decorator.
Worked for *Bacs (co-founder),
C.*Massier, *Picarde.
Painted signature.

BAUDIN, Eugène (1853-1918)

Baudin

Potter, designer, decorator.
Established Poterie de *Monaco
where he worked with his son
P.A.*Baudin.
Impressed signature.

BAUDIN, Paul Adolph (1879-1931)

Baudin   Paul Baudin

Potter, designer, decorator.
Worked at Poterie de *Monaco
and subsequently at St Briac.
Painted signatures.

BENNER, Emmanuel (1836-96)

E. Benner

Painter, designer, decorator.
Worked for T.*Deck.
Painted signature.

BESNARD, Jean (1889-1958)

Jean Besnard

Potter, designer, decorator.
Worked for *Primavera and
independently.
Incised signature.

BEYER, Paul (1873-1945)

B
E
Y
E
R

Potter, designer, decorator.
Incised signature.

BIGOT, Alexandre (1862-1927)

Potter, designer, decorator. Made ceramics designed by, among others, A.*Charpentier (*see* French metalwork), P.-F.*Fix-Masseau, Jacques Froment-Meurice (1864-1948), H.*Guimard, A.-J.*Halou, Paul Jouve (1880-1973), L.*Majorelle (*see* French metalwork), A. de *Manneville, P.*Roche (*see* French metalwork), R. de *Saint Marceaux, Henri Sauvage (1873-1923), Carl Wilhelm Vallgren (1855-1940), H.C. van de *Velde (*see* German ceramics). Incised signature, impressed mark.

BOISSONNET, Alexis (1879-1956)

A ß

Potter, designer, decorator. Painted initials.

BRAQUE, Georges (1882-1963)

G.B.

G Braque

Painter, designer, decorator. Decorated ceramics made by J.L.*Artigas; also designed textiles, tapestries. Painted initials and signature.

BRÉCY, Henri (fl.1880-1930)

Sculptor, designer, decorator. Worked for *Sèvres. Painted monogram.

BUSSIÈRE, Ernest (1863-1937)

Sculptor, modeller. Worked for *Keller & Guérin; also designed glass. Painted signature.

BUTHAUD, René (b.1886)

Painter, potter, designer, decorator. Designed ceramics for *Primavera before setting up his own pottery.
Painted monogram.

CARANZA, Amédée de (fl.1870-1906)

Designer, decorator. Worked for *Longwy, J.Vieillard & Cie, C.*Massier; also decorated *glass.
Painted signature.

CARRIÈRE, Ernest (1858-1908)

Designer, modeller, decorator. Worked for T.*Deck, *Sèvres.
Moulded signature.

CARRIÈS, Jean (1855-94)

Sculptor, potter, designer, decorator.
Incised signature.

CAZAUX, Edouard (1889-1974)

Sculptor, potter, designer, decorator; also made glass.
Painted monogram and mark, painted/incised signature.

CAZIN, Jean-Charles (1841-1901)

Painter, potter, designer, decorator. Worked in England for C.J.C.*Bailey (*see* British ceramics) before setting up his own pottery in France.
Incised signature.

CAZIN, J.-M. Michel (1869-1917)

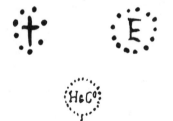

Sculptor, potter, designer, decorator; also designed *metalwork.
Incised signature and relief-carved monogram.

CHAPLET, Ernest (1835-1909)

Potter, designer. Worked for *Haviland & Co., *Laurin, and independently. Made ceramics that were designed and decorated by P.*Gauguin, and cast sculptures by A.*Rodin in ceramic.
Impressed rebus (*chaplet* is French for rosary).

CHAUVIGNÉ, Auguste (1829-1904)

Potter, designer, decorator.
Painted monogram.

CHÉRET, Joseph (1838-94)

Sculptor, designer, modeller. Worked for *Sèvres; also designed glass, metalwork, furniture.
Incised signature.

COCTEAU, Jean (1889-1963)

Painter, designer, decorator. Decorated ceramics made by Atelier Madeline-Jolly. Designed for *Rosenthal (*see* German ceramics); also designed posters, textiles, and for the stage. Painted signature.

DALPAYRAT, Pierre-Adrien (1844-1910)

Potter, designer. Made ceramics designed by, among others, M.*Dufrène (for La *Maison Moderne) and sculptors Constantin Meunier (1831-1905) and A.*Voisin-Delacroix. Painted signature and impressed marks.

DAMMOUSE, Albert-Louis (1848-1926)

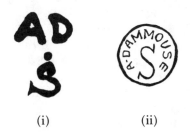

(i)   (ii)

Potter, designer, decorator. Worked for *Gérard-Dufraisseix-Abbot, *Haviland & Co., Théodore *Haviland, J.Pouyat, and ran workshop in Sèvres with brother E.A.*Dammouse; also made glass. Painted initials and impressed mark.

DAMMOUSE, Edouard Alexandre (1850-1903)

E·Ɖ

Designer, decorator. Worked for A.-L.*Dammouse, *Haviland & Co., *Laurin. Painted initials.

DANGAR, Anne (1887-1951)

MSDG.

Australian painter, potter, designer, decorator working in France. Worked at the artists' colony Moly-Sabata (Isère). Painted initials.

DANTON, Frédéric (1874-1932)

F·DANTON

Potter, designer, decorator; also manufactured carpets. Painted signature.

DAX (fl.c.1930)

DAX

Manufacturers. Impressed mark.

DECK, Théodore (1823-91)

TD **TH·DECK·**

(i) (ii)

(iii)

(iv)

Potter, designer, decorator. Worked for *Sèvres and ran his own studio where he employed E.*Lachenal. Made ceramics designed/decorated by A.*Anker, E.*Benner, Jean Benner (1836-1906), E.*Carrière, E.C.*Escallier-Légerot, Eugène Gluck (1820-98), P.*Helleu, A.A.*Hirsch, E.E.A.*Lachenal. C.*Moreau-Nélaton, A.L.*Regnier, Sophie Schaeppi (1852-1921) and others. Impressed monogram (i) and signature(ii), painted initials (iii), relief-moulded mark (iv).

DECOEUR, Emile (1876-1953)

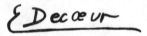

Potter, designer. Worked with E.E.A.*Lachenal and

F.P.O.*Rumèbe before setting up his own pottery. Designed for *Sèvres. Made ceramics modelled by sculptors L.-E.*Lambert, Théodore Rivière (1857-1912) and others.
Incised signatures, monogram and mark.

DÉCORCHEMONT, François-Émile (1880-1971)

Painter, potter, designer, decorator; also made *glass.
Impressed signature.

DELACHENAL, Louis (1897-1966)

Potter, designer, decorator. Worked for *Sèvres and independently.
Impressed marks and painted monogram.

DELAHERCHE, Auguste (1857-1940)

(i)   (ii)

Potter, designer, decorator. Incised (i) and impressed (ii, iii) signatures, impressed monogram (iv), painted initials (v).

(iii)   (iv)   (v)

DELPIERRE, Francine (1913-68)

5

Potter, designer, decorator.
Painted monogram.

DENBAC (1909-52)

Denbcic

Pottery established by René Denert
(fl.c.1905-40).
Impressed mark.

DESMANT, Louis-Etienne (1844-1902)

Desmant

Potter, designer, decorator.
Painted signature.

DESMANT, Lucien-Adolphe (1875-1929)

Lucien Desmant

Potter, designer, decorator.
Painted signature.

DOAT, Taxile Maximin (1851-1938)

Potter, designer, decorator.
Worked for *Sèvres, *University
City Pottery (*see* American
ceramics) and independently.
Incised monogram.

DUFRÈNE, Maurice (1876-1955)

M. DUFRENE

(i)

N. DuFReNE

(ii)

Designer, decorator. Designed
ceramics made by P.-A *Dalpayrat
for La *Maison Moderne and by
*Boch (*see* Belgian ceramics) for
La Maîtrise (Galeries Lafayette);
also designed glass, metalwork,
furniture, textiles, carpets.
Printed signature (i), incised
signature (ii).

DUFY, Raoul (1877-1953)

Painter, designer, decorator.
Decorated ceramics made by
J.L.*Artigas; also designed textiles,
tapestries.
Painted signature.

DUMESNIL, Guy (fl.1920-40)

G. Dumesnil

Designer, decorator. Worked for
*Montières.
Incised/painted signatures.

Guy Dumpsnil

ESCALIER DE CRISTAL, L' (est.1802)

Escalier de Cristal
Paris.

Retail shop and decorating studio
run by Pannier Frères from c.1885;
also sold and decorated glass, and
sold and made metal mounts.
Printed mark.

ESCALLIER-LÉGEROT, Eléonore Caroline (1827-88)

ꓜ.

Painter, designer, decorator.
Worked for T.*Deck, *Sèvres.
Painted monogram.

ETLING (fl.c.1925)

Retailers who commissioned
ceramic items from potters
including M.*Guillard; also
commissioned *glass, *metalwork.
Impressed mark.

FAVRE, Gisèle (fl.1935-60)

gisèle Favre

Potter, designer, decorator.
Worked as one of Les *Quatre
Potiers and independently.
Painted signature.

FEURE, Georges de (1868-1943)

de Feure

Dutch painter, designer, living in
France. Designed porcelain made
by *Gérard-Dufraisseix-Abbot for
*Maison de l'Art Nouveau; also
designed *glass, posters (*see* French
graphics), furniture, textiles,
carpets.
Printed signature, impressed
monogram.

FIX-MASSEAU, Pierre-Félix (1869-1937)

F Masseau Fix. Masseau

Fix. Masseau

Sculptor, modeller. Worked for
A.*Bigot, E.E.A.*Lachenal.
Incised signatures.

FOUQUET, Pierre (b.1909)

fouquet

Potter, designer, decorator.
Incised signature.

FOURMONT, Marius Frédéric (1878-1953)

M Fourmont

Potter, designer, decorator.
Painted signature.

FOURNIER, Anatole (fl.1878-1926)

AF

Decorator. Worked for *Sèvres.
Painted monogram.

FRUMERIE-KJELLBERG, Agnes de (1869-1937)

Swedish sculptor, designer, decorator working in France until 1930. Modelled ceramics made by E.E.A.*Lachenal; also designed glass, metalwork, furniture. Incised signatures.

GALLÉ, Émile (1846-1904)

(†)

Manufacturer, designer. Made ceramics designed by V.*Prouvé and others, as well as by himself; also made *glass, *furniture. Impressed (†) and painted marks.

GAUGUIN, Paul (1848-1903)

Painter, sculptor, designer, modeller, decorator. Work fired by E.*Chaplet. Painted signature.

GAZIELLO, Jean Baptiste (1871-1957)

Potter, designer, decorator. Worked for D.*Massier and J.*Massier before establishing his own pottery. Painted signature.

G.D.V. (est.1877)

Bruère
G. D. V.

Manufacturers.
Designers/decorators include
Claude Demay (1850-1918)
Painted mark.

GÉBLEUX, Léonard (fl.1882-1930)

Decorator. Worked for *Sèvres.
Painted monogram.

GENSOLI, Maurice (b.1892)

maurice Gensoli

Potter, designer, decorator.
Worked for *Sèvres and
independently.
Incised signature, impressed mark
incorporating monogram.

GENTIL BOURDET (est.1901)

Manufacturers.
Impressed marks.

GENTIL
BOURDET
ARCHITECTES
CERAMISTES

GÉRARD-DUFRAISSEIX-ABBOT (est.c.1885)

FRANCE

Manufacturers. Designers include
Edward Colonna (1862-1948), A.-
L.*Dammouse, G. de *Feure,
Frédéric Hexamer (fl.1869-1906).
Manufactured porcelain for
*Maison de l'Art Nouveau.
Printed mark.

GILLET, Numa François (1868-1940)

Painter, sculptor, potter, designer.
Collaborated with Georges
Auguste Jules Delvaux (1834-1909).
Incised monogram and signature.

GLATIGNY, Atelier de (fl.c.1900)

Group of deliberately anonymous
potters, designers, decorators at
Versailles.
Impressed mark.

GRITTEL, Emile (1870-1953)

E.S   E.Grittel

Painter, sculptor, potter.
Incised initials and signature.

GRUBER, Jacques (1870-1936)

J.Gruber

Designer. Worked for *Mougin
and *Rambervillers; also designed
*glass, stained glass, bookbindings,
furniture.
Incised signature.

GUÉDEN, Colette (fl.c.1925)

CJ   Colette Gueden

Designer, decorator. Worked for
*Primavera.
Painted initials and signature.

GUILLARD, Marcel (fl.c.1925)

Marcel Guillard

Potter. Made ceramics for *Etling.
Impressed signature.

GUIMARD, Hector (1867-1942)

Architect, designer. Designed ceramics for A.*Bigot, *Muller, *Sèvres; also designed stained glass, metalwork, furniture, carpets.
Impressed monogram.

HALOU, Alfred-Jean (1875-1939)

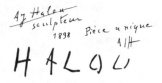

Sculptor, designer. Worked for A.*Bigot.
Incised signatures.

HAVILAND & CO. (1843-1925)

H&Cᴼ

HAVILAND ε Cᴼ

Manufacturers.
Designers/decorators include Jean-Paul Aubé (1837-1916), F.*Bracquemond (see French metalwork), E.*Chaplet, Léon Philibert Couturier (1823-1901), A.-L.*Dammouse, E.A.*Dammouse, Frédéric Hexamer (fl.1869-1906), F.*Lafond, H.-L.*Lambert, L.*Parizot, Jean-Désiré Ringel d'Illzach (1847-1916).
Impressed marks.

HAVILAND, Théodore (est.1893)

Théodore Haviland
Limoges
FRANCE

Manufacturers.
Designers/decorators include Antoine Bourdelle (1861-1929), A.-L.*Dammouse, Jean Dufy (b.1888), M.*Goupy (see French glass), Suzanne Lalique (b.1899), E.-M.*Sandoz.
Printed marks.

HB (VERLINGUE & CIE) (est.1917)

Manufacturers.
Designers/decorators include
François Bazin (fl.c.1925), Jacques
Nam (fl.1920-40), René Quilivic
(fl.c.1925).
Painted mark.

HELLEU, Paul (1859-1927)

P H.

Painter, designer, decorator.
Worked for T.*Deck.
Painted initials.

HENRIOT, Jules (est.c.1860)

HENRIOT
QUIMPER
——

Manufacturers.
Designers/decorators include
Emile Bachelet (fl.c.1925),
Mathurin Meheut (1882-1958), J.E.
Sevellec (fl.c.1925).
Painted mark.

HIRSCH, Auguste Alexandre (1833-1912)

AAH

Painter, designer, decorator.
Worked for T.*Deck.
Painted monogram.

HOENTSCHEL, Georges (1855-1915)

Potter, designer, decorator; also
designed furniture.
Impressed monogram.

IVANOFF, Vassil (1897-1973)

Russian painter, potter, designer,
decorator working in France.
Incised signature.

JEANNENEY, Paul (1861-1920)

Potter, designer, decorator. Cast sculptures by A.*Rodin in ceramic. Incised signature.

KELLER & GUÉRIN (est.1830)

(†)

Manufacturers with works at Lunéville and the *Saint-Clement factory. Designers/decorators include E.*Bussière, E.E.A.*Lachenal, L.*Majorelle (*see* French metalwork).
Painted (†) and impressed marks.

KIEFER, Frédéric (1894-1977)

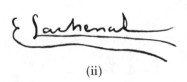

Potter, designer, decorator. Impressed signature.

LACHENAL, Edmond Edouard Achille (1855-1948)

LACHENAL

(i)

Potter, designer, decorator. Worked for T.*Deck before establishing his own studio. Cast in ceramic sculptures by P.-F.*Fix-Masseau, A. de *Frumerie-Kjellberg and others. Worked for *Keller & Guérin; also decorated glass.
Painted (i, ii), impressed (iii) and printed (iv) signatures.

(ii)

(iii)

(iv)

LACHENAL, Raoul Pierre (1885-1956)

Potter, designer, decorator.
Incised/painted signature.

LAFOND, Félix (fl.c.1870-85)

Painter, designer, decorator.
Worked for *Laurin, *Haviland &
Co. and independently.
Incised signature.

LALLEMANT, Robert T. (fl.c.1920-40)

Potter, designer, decorator.
Painted signature.

LAMARRE, Alphonse Adolphe (1837-1922) and Georges François (1867-1944)

Father and son designers,
decorators. Worked for *Pillivuyt.
Painted joint signature.

LAMBERT, Henri-Lucien (1836-1909)

Painter, designer, decorator.
Worked for *Haviland & Co.
Painted monogram.

LAMBERT, Léon-Eugène (b.1865)

Sculptor. Designed pieces made by
E.*Decoeur.
Incised signature.

LASSERRE, Henri (fl.1886-1930)

Decorator. Worked for *Sèvres.
Painted monogram.

LAURENT-DESROUSSEAUX, Henri Alphonse Louis (1862-1906)

Painter, designer, decorator. Collaborated with H.-L.-C.*Robalbhen; also designed and decorated glass. Painted signatures.

LAURIN (fl.1860-1910)

LAURIN

Manufacturers. Designers/decorators include E.*Chaplet, E.A.*Dammouse, F.*Lafond. Printed mark.

LEBEUF, MILLIET & CIE (1841-76)

Manufacturers, subsequently *Barluet & Cie. Designers/decorators include F.*Bracquemond (*see* French metalwork), E.*Rousseau. Printed mark.

LEE, William (fl.c.1900)

Potter, designer. Incised initials.

LE FAGUAYS, Pierre (b.1892)

LE FAGUAYS

Sculptor. Modelled ceramic figures for *Sèvres and Arthur Goldscheider; figures also cast in glass, bronze. Moulded signature.

LENOBLE, Emile (1875-1940)

Potter, designer, decorator.
Impressed monogram.

LENOBLE, Jacques (1902-67)

Potter, designer, decorator.
Incised initial, painted monogram.

LÉVY-DHURMER, Lucien (1865-1953)

Painter, designer, decorator.
Worked for C.*Massier.
Impressed (i) and painted (ii)
signatures.

LION, Amand Eugène Albert (1867-1945)

Potter, designer.
Incised signature and impressed
rebus.

LOEBNITZ, Jules (1836-95)

J.LŒBNITZ
PARIS

Manufacturers. Made architectural
ceramics designed by Eugène
Viollet-le-Duc (1814-79) and other
leading architects.
Impressed mark.

LONGWY (est.18th century)

Manufacturers.
Designers/decorators include A.
de *Caranza. Made ceramics sold
by *Pomone and *Primavera.
Impressed marks.

LUCE, Jean (1895-1964)

Potter, designer, decorator; also designed *glass.
Painted monogram.

LURÇAT, Jean (1892-1966)

Painter, designer, decorator. Worked at *Sant-Vicens; also designed tapestries (*see* French furniture).
Painted signature.

MAISON DE L'ART NOUVEAU (1895-c.1905)

Firm of retailers founded by Siegfried Bing (1838-1905). Commissioned ceramics designed by Edward Colonna (1862-1948), G. de *Feure, and manufactured by *Gérard-Dufraisseix-Abbot; also retailed and supervised design and production of glass, furniture, textiles, carpets, embroideries, *metalwork and jewellery.
Printed mark.

MAISON MODERNE, La (1899-1902)

Retailers. Sold ceramics designed by M.*Dufrène (made by P.-A.*Dalpayrat), A.W.*Finch (*see* Belgian ceramics) and Abel Landry (fl.1890-1910); also sold glass, metalwork, jewellery, furniture, textiles.
Printed mark.

MANNEVILLE, André de (fl.c.1900)

Sculptor, designer, Worked for A.*Bigot.
Incised signature.

MARQUET, Albert (1875-1947)

marquet

Sculptor, designer, decorator.
Decorated ceramics designed by
J.L.*Artigas.
Painted signature.

MASSIER, Clément (1844-1917)

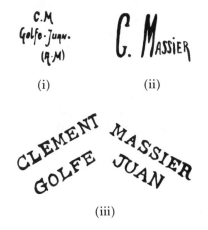

C.M
Golfe-Juan.
(A.M)

(i)

C. MASSIER

(ii)

CLEMENT MASSIER
GOLFE JUAN

(iii)

Potter. Worked with O.*Milet
before establishing his own
pottery. Designers/decorators
working there include Marius
Alexandre (1880-1959),
J.-B.*Barol, A. de *Caranza, Jean
Carle (fl.1900-40), L.*Lévy-
Dhurmer, François Sicard
(fl.1900-40), J.*Sicard (*see*
American ceramics).
Painted (i, ii) and impressed
marks.

MASSIER, Delphin (1836-1907)

D M
V.

Potter, designer, decorator. At his
own pottery in Vallauris
designers/decorators include
J.B.*Gaziello.
Painted initials.

MASSIER, Jérôme, fils (1850-1916)

JEROME
MASSIER
Fils

J.Ma.

Potter, designer, decorator.
Among those who worked at his
pottery was J.B.*Gaziello.
Painted signatures.

MASSIER-MILET (fl.c.1878)

Collaboration between C.*Massier and O.F.*Milet. Some work decorated by Eugène Froment (1820-1900).
Painted mark.

MASSOUL, Félix (1869-1942)

Potter, designer, decorator. Incised initial, painted signature.

MATISSE, Henri (1869-1954)

Painter, sculptor, designer, decorator. Decorated ceramics made by A.F.*Metthey.
Painted signature.

MAYODON, Jean-Léon (1893-1967)

Potter, designer, decorator. Worked for *Sèvres and independently.
Painted initials.

METTHEY, André Fernand (1871-1920)

Potter, designer, decorator. Made ceramics decorated by Pierre Bonnard (1867-1942), André Derain (1880-1954), Othon Friesz (1879-1949), Maximilien Luce (1858-1941), H.*Matisse, Odilon Redon (1840-1916) Georges Rouault (1871-1958), L.*Valtat (*see* French graphics), Kees van Dongen (1877-1958), M.*Vlaminck, Edouard Vuillard (1868-1940).
Incised signature and impressed monogram.

MILET, Optat Félix (1838-1911)

O.MILET
Sèvres

Designer, decorator. Worked for
*Sèvres, collaborated with
C.*Massier (*see* Massier-Milet), and
established his own studio.
Painted signature and monogram.

MILET, Paul Jean (1870-1950)

Designer, decorator. Worked for
father O.F.*Milet and ran studio
after his retirement
Impressed/printed mark.

MINIL, André (fl.c.1900)

andre minil

Potter, designer, decorator.
Worked in collaboration with
P.*Pacton.
Incised signature.

MIRÓ, Joán (1893-1983)

Miro

Painter, designer, decorator.
Decorated ceramics made by
J.L.*Artigas and *Sant-Vicens.
Painted signature.

MONACO, Poterie de (1906-25)

Poterie
de
Monaco

Pottery established by E.*Baudin
and after his death run by his son
P.A.*Baudin.
Printed mark.

MONT-CHEVALIER, Faïencerie du (1882-c.1920)

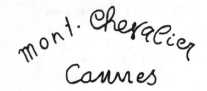

Pottery established by Léon Castel (fl.1880-1910).
Painted/incised mark.

MONTIÈRES (1920-38)

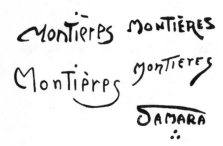

Manufacturers, previously Faïencerie *Picarde.
Designers/decorators include G.*Arnoux, G.*Dumesnil, P.*Motton, G.*Tribout. Made 'Samara' ware for *Pomone.
Impressed/printed marks.

MOREAU-NÉLATON, Camille (1840-97)

Painter, designer, decorator.
Worked for T.*Deck and independently.
Painted signature.

MOREAU-NÉLATON, Etienne (1859-1927)

Painter, potter, designer, decorator.
Painted/incised monogram.

MOTTON, Pierre (fl.1920-40)

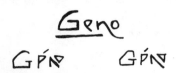

Designer, decorator. Worked for *Montières.
Painted marks (in honour of his granddaughter Geneviève).

MOUGIN FRÈRES (1903-60)

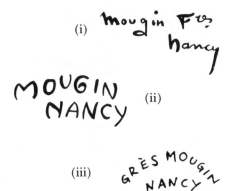

(i)

(ii)

(iii)

Pottery run by brothers Joseph (1876-1961) and Pierre (1880-1955) Mougin. Designers include Emile Bachelet (fl.c.1925), E.*Bussière, J.*Cayette (*see* French glass), J.*Descomps (*see* French glass), A.*Finot (*see* French glass), L.*Majorelle (*see* French metalwork), V.*Prouvé, Ernest Wittman (b.1846).
Incised (i, ii) and impressed (iii) marks.

MULLER, Emile, & Cie (est.1854)

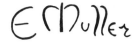

Manufacturers. Designers include A.*Charpentier (*see* French metalwork), G.*Combaz (*see* Belgian graphics), E.S.*Grasset (*see* French graphics), H.*Guimard, Henri Levasseur (b.1853), Constantin Meunier (1831-1905), Jean-Désiré Ringel d'Illzach (1847-1916), I. de *Rudder (*see* Belgian ceramics), H.*Stoltenberg-Lerche, H. de *Toulouse-Lautrec (*see* French graphics), James Vibert (1872-1942), P.*Wolfers (*see* Belgian ceramics, metalwork).
Incised mark.

NAUDOT, Camille-Victor (1862-1938)

Potter, designer, decorator.
Painted monogram and signature.

PACTON, Abbé Pierre (1856-1938)

Potter, designer, decorator.
Worked in collaboration with A.*Minil.
Incised monogram.

PARIZOT, Léon (fl.c.1880)

Painter, decorator. Worked for
*Haviland & Co.
Painted monogram.

PARVILLÉ, Louis Léon (1830-85)

Architect, potter, designer,
decorator.
Painted monogram and signature.

PERROT, Théodule (b.1856)

Potter, designer.
Incised signature.

PICARDE, Faïencerie (1915-20)

(i)   (ii)

Manufacturers, subsequently
*Montières. Designers/decorators
include J.-B.*Barol, François Sicard
(fl.1900-40).
Impressed (i) and painted/incised
(ii) marks.

PIERREFONDS, La Société faïencerie héraldique (est.1904)

Manufacturers.
Printed mark.

PILLIVUYT, Charles, Manufacture de porcelaine (est.1853)

Manufacturers. Designers/
decorators include Jules-Auguste
Habert-Dys (1850-1924) and father
and son A.A. and G.F.*Lamarre.
Printed mark.

POINTU, Jean Marie (1843-1925)

Potter. Worked for *Laurin before setting up a pottery with his son L.*Pointu.
Painted rebus, impressed initial.

POINTU, Léon (1879-1942)

Potter. Worked with his father J.M.*Pointu.
Incised signature ('Pointu fils').

POMONE (est.1923)

Decorative art department of Paris store Bon Marché. Sold ceramics made by *Longwy and 'Samara' ware made by *Montières; also sold glass, metalwork, furniture, textiles, carpets.
Printed mark.

PORTANIER, Gilbert (b.1926)

Potter, designer, decorator.
Painted signature.

PRIMAVERA, Atelier (est.1912)

(i)

(ii)   (iii)

Decorative art department of Paris store Les Grands Magasins du Printemps. Sold ceramics by J.*Besnard, R.*Buthaud, C.*Guéden, Claude Lévy (fl.c.1925), *Longwy, Marcel Renard (fl.c.1925), Madeleine Sougez (fl.c.1925); also sold glass, metalwork, furniture, textiles, carpets.
Incised (i) and printed (ii, iii) marks.

PROUVÉ, Victor (1858-1943)

V. Prouvé

Painter, sculptor, designer.
Worked for E.*Gallé, *Mougin
Frères; also designed glass,
metalwork, jewellery, furniture,
embroidery, textiles.
Incised signature.

PULL, Georges (1810-89)

PULL

Potter, designer, decorator.
Incised signature.

QUATRE POTIERS, Les (est.1936)

Pottery operated by Pierre-André
Favre (fl.1910-40), his wife Marie
Thérèse Favre-Lanoa (fl.1910-40)
and their daughters Anne Favre
(fl.1935-55) and G.*Favre.
Painted mark.

QUENNOY, Charles (fl.c.1900)

Decorator. Worked for *Sèvres.
Painted monogram.

RAMBERVILLERS, S.A. des Produits Céramiques de (est.1885)

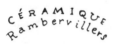

Manufacturers. Designers include
J.*Cayette (*see* French glass),
H.*Bergé (*see* French glass), Jean-
Baptiste Alphonse Cytère
(1861-1941) J.*Grüber, R.
Jeandelle (fl.c.1900), L.*Majorelle
(*see* French metalwork), Charles
Louis Eugène Virion (b.1865).
Printed mark.

REDON, Martial (est.1881)

⌐MJ ⌐LR

Manufacturers.
Printed mark.

REGNIER, Antony Ludovic (1835-1909)

A L REGNiER

Painter, designer, decorator.
Worked for T.*Deck.
Painted signature.

RENOLEAU, Alfred (1854-1930)

R.enoleau

Potter, designer, decorator.
Painted signature.

ROBALBHEN, Henry-Léon-Charles (fl.c.1900)

Robalbhen   ROBALBHEN

Potter. Collaborated with
H.A.L.*Laurent-Desrousseaux.
Painted signatures.

ROBJ (fl.c.1925)

Robj

Retailers who commissioned
ceramic items from artist potters;
also commissioned glass.
Painted/impressed mark.

RODIN, Auguste (1840-1917)

Rodin

Sculptor, modeller, designer.
Worked for *Sèvres and had
sculptures cast in ceramic by
E.*Chaplet, P.*Jeanneney,
E.E.A.*Lachenal.
Painted signature.

ROSSOLLIN, Alfred Camille Honoré (1863-1947)

Potter, designer, decorator.
Established *Aire-Belle.
Painted monogram.

ROUSSEAU, Eugène François (1827-91)

Retailer, designer, decorator.
Established a studio where
F.*Bracquemond (see French
metalwork), M.-E.-L.*Solon and
others worked. Designed ceramics
manufactured by *Barluet,
*Lebeuf, Milliet and other firms;
also designed decorated and
retailed *glass.
Printed (i) and painted (ii) marks.

RUMÈBE, Fernand Pierre Oscar (1874-1952)

Potter, designer, decorator.
Collaborated with E.*Decoeur
before establishing his own
pottery.
Painted/incised signature and
monogram.

SAINT-CLÉMENT (est.1758)

Manufacturers. In 1892 sold to
*Keller & Guérin.
Painted marks.

SAINT MARCEAUX, René de (1845-1915)

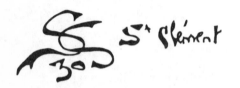

Sculptor, modeller. Worked for
A.*Bigot, *Sèvres.
Moulded signature.

SANDOZ, Edouard-Marcel (1881-1971)

Sculptor, designer. Worked for
Théodore *Haviland; also
designed metalwork.
Printed signature.

SANT-VICENS, Atelier (est.1917)

Pottery. Designers/decorators
include J.*Lurçat, J.*Miró.
Painted mark.

SAVIN, Maurice (1894-1973)

Painter, potter, designer,
decorator.
Painted signature.

SERRÉ, Georges (1889-1956)

Potter, designer, decorator.
Incised initials and signature.

SÈVRES, Manufacture nationale de porcelaine de (est.1756)

Manufacturers.
Designers/decorators include Félix
Aubert (1866-1940), Eric Bagge
(b.1890), Georges Bastard
(1881-1939), Robert Bonfils
(1886-1972), F.*Bracquemond (*see*
French metalwork), H.*Brécy,
Albert-Ernest Carrier-Belleuse
(1824-87), E.*Carrière, J.*Chéret,
T.*Deck, E.*Decoeur,
L.*Delachenal, T.M.*Doat, Jean
Dufy (b.1888), E.C.*Escallier-
Legerot, A.*Fournier, L.*Gébleux,
M.*Gensoli, H.*Guimard,

SÈVRES (continued)

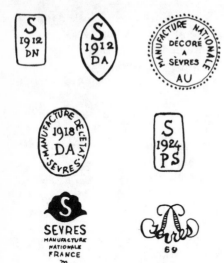

Gustave Jaulmes (1873-1959), L.*Kann (*see* French metalwork), Suzanne Lalique (b.1899), H.*Lasserre, P.*Le Faguays, A.*Léonard (*see* French metalwork), J.-L.*Mayodon, Mathurin Meheut (1882-1958), C.*Quennoy, H.*Rapin (*see* French graphics), A.*Rodin, J.E.*Ruhlmann (*see* French furniture, textiles), R. de *Saint Marceaux, Alexandre Sandier (fl.1890-1916), M.-E.-L.*Solon, L.-J.*Trager.
Printed/impressed marks.

SIMMEN, Henri (1880-1963)

Potter, designer, decorator.
Painted signatures.

SOLON, Marc-Emmanuel-Louis (1835-1913)

Potter, designer, decorator. Worked for *Sèvres and E.F.*Rousseau before moving to England where he worked for *Minton (*see* British ceramics). Painted monograms and signature.

SOUDBININE, Séraphin (1880-1944)

Russian sculptor and potter working in France.
Incised signature and mark.

STOLTENBERG-LERCHE, Hans (1867-1920)

H. ST. Lerche

Norwegian/German painter/sculptor, designer working in France and Italy. Designed for Emile *Muller & Cie; also made glass, metalwork, jewelley. Incised signature.

THARAUD, Camille (1878-1956)

Manufacturer, designer. Made ceramics designed by M.*Goupy (*see* French glass), H.*Rapin (*see* French graphics). Printed signature, printed monogram.

THESMAR, Fernand (1843-1912)

Designer, decorator; also made enamels (*see* French metalwork). Painted monogram.

TRAGER, Louis-Jules (fl.1888-1934)

.I

Decorator. Worked for *Sèvres. Painted monogram.

TRIBOUT, Georges (fl.1920-40)

g.TRiBoub

Painter, architect, designer, decorator. Worked for *Montières. Painted signature.

VALLOMBREUSE, Henri de (1856-1919)

Potter, designer. Incised signature.

VILOTTE, Etienne (fl.1920-40)

Potter, designer, decorator.
Painted signature.

VLAMINCK, Maurice (1876-1958)

Painter, decorator. Decorated ceramics made by A.F.*Metthey.
Painted signature.

VOISIN-DELACROIX, Alphonse (1857-93)

Sculptor, modeller. Collaborated with P.-A.*Dalpayrat.
Incised monogram.

WALTER, Almaric V. (1870-1959)

Potter, designer, decorator; also made *glass.
Painted signature.

ZUMBO, Dominique (1854-1939)

Italian potter, designer, decorator working in France.
Painted signature.

BELGIAN CERAMICS

AUBRY, Edgar (1880-1943)

Potter, designer, decorator.
Incised signature.

BOCH FRÈRES (est.1841)

 BFK

Manufacturers. Among wares
produced were 'Keramis' and 'Grès
Keramis'. Designers/decorators
include P.*Bernard (*see* Belgian
glass), Anna Boch (1848-1936),
C.*Catteau, M.*Dufrène (*see*
French ceramics), A.W.*Finch,
M.*Goupy (*see* French glass),
A.*Hecq, H.*Heemskerk (*see*
French glass), Eugène Paulus
(fl.c.1910), I. de *Rudder, Emile
Diffloth (1856-1933).
Printed/impressed marks.

BOUFFIOULX, Société des Grès d'Art de (fl.20th century)

Pottery run by R.*Guérin.
Designers include Pierre Caille
(fl.c.1930), W.*Harzing (*see* Dutch
ceramics), D.*Ingels, M.*Wolfers.
Incised mark.

CATTEAU, Charles (1880-1966)

French potter, designer, decorator
working in Belgium for *Boch
Frères; also designed *glass.
Printed signature.

CÉRABEL (est.1842)

Manufacturers. Designers include H.C. van de *Velde (*see* German ceramics).
Printed mark.

CLERCK, Oscar de (b.1892)

Sculptor. Modelled figures for *Helman.
Moulded signature.

DUBOIS, Antoine (1905-25)

Pottery, subsequently La Céramique Montoise. Designers/decorators include Antoine Dubois (b.1869), A.*Hecq.
Painted marks.

FINCH, Alfred William (1854-1930)

Painter, potter, designer, decorator. Worked for *Boch Fréres before establishing his own pottery where he made pieces for sale through La *Maison Moderne (*see* French ceramics). Subsequently worked in Finland for *Iris (*see* Scandinavian ceramics).
Incised initials.

GILLIOT & CIE (Manufactures Céramiques d'Hémixem) (1897-1979)

Manufacturers.
Printed mark.

GUÉRIN, Roger (1896-1954)

Potter, designer, decorator. Ran pottery at *Bouffioulx.
Incised signature.

HECQ, Angelo (b.1901)

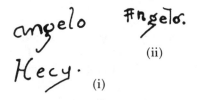

(ii)

(i)

Sculptor. Worked for *Boch Frères, A.*Dubois.
Incised (i) and painted (ii) signatures.

HELMAN, Maison (fl.1920-40)

HELMAN△

Manufacturers. Designers include O. de *Clerck.
Moulded mark.

INGELS, Domien (1881-1946)

Sculptor, designer. Worked for *Bouffioulx, Arthur Goldscheider, *Maes.
Incised monogram.

MAES (est.1880)

CERAMAES

Pottery established by Charles-Louis Maes (fl.c.1890) and carried on by his sons Albert (fl.c.1925) and Jules (fl.c.1925). Designers include D.*Ingels.
Impressed mark.

MOUZIN, Auguste, & Cie (fl.20th century)

Manufacturers.
Impressed marks.

NIMY, Manufacture Royale et Impériale de (1789-1950)

Manufacturers.
Printed mark.

RUDDER, Isidore de (1855-1943)

Sculptor, potter. Modelled figures made by himself, *Boch Frères, E.*Muller (*see* French ceramics), *Vermeren-Coché; also made metalwork and designed bookbindings.
Incised initials and monogram.

SAINT-GHISLAIN, Ateliers d'Art (fl.20th century)

Pottery run by Emile Lombart (b.1859) and Marius Renard (b.1869).
Painted mark.

ST GHISLAIN, Faïencerie de (est.1892)

Manufacturers.
Impressed mark.

VAN DE VELDE, Henry Clemens *see* German ceramics.

VERMEREN-COCHÉ (1852-c.1920)

Manufacturers. Output included figures modelled by I. de *Rudder, M.*Wolfers.
Impressed mark.

WOLFERS, Marcel (fl.c.1920)

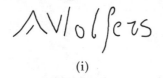

(i)

**MaʀcEL
WolfeʀS**

(ii)

Sculptor, designer. Worked for
*Bouffioulx, R.*Guérin,
*Vermeren-Coché; also made
jewellery and lacquerwork.
Incised (i) and moulded (ii)
signatures.

WOLFERS, Philippe (1858-1929)

Sculptor, designer, decorator.
Worked for *Muller & Cie (*see*
French ceramics); also made
jewellery and designed *glass,
*metalwork, furniture, textiles.
Incised signature.

DUTCH CERAMICS

AGTERBERG, Cris (1883-1948)

Designer, modeller, decorator.
Worked for De *Rijn, Westraven,
*Zenith; also designed *glass,
metalwork.
Printed mark, impressed initials
and signature.

AMPHORA (1908-33)

AMPHORA
HOLLAND

Manufacturers.
Designers/decorators include
P.*Groeneveld, C.J. van der *Hoef,
C.*Lebeau (*see* Dutch glass),
S.*Schellink, R.*Sterken,
Theodorus Verstraaten (1872-1945).
Painted mark.

AMSTELHOEK (1894/5-1910)

AMSTERDAM
·HOLLAND·

Craft workshops including a
pottery. Merged with *Haga (1907)
and De *Distel (1910).
Designers/decorators include C.J.
van der *Hoef; workshops also
produced *metalwork and
furniture.
Impressed/printed marks.

ARNHEMSCHE FAYENCEFABRIEK (est.1907)

Manufacturers. Designers include
W.P.*Hartgring, Cornelis Vet
(b.1908) and co-founders brothers
Jacob Vet (1880-1924) and Klaas
Vet (1876-1943).
Printed marks.

BEGEER, Carel J.A. (1883-1956)

Designer. Worked for *St Lukas; also worked as silversmith. Impressed initials.

BERLAGE, Hendrik Petrus (1856-1934)

Architect, designer. Worked for *Holland; also designed *glass, metalwork, furniture, carpets. Painted monogram.

BOSCH, Jacob Pieter van den (1868-1948)

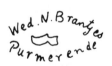

Architect, designer. Worked for *Holland; also designed furniture. Painted monogram.

BRANTJES & CO. (1895-1904)

Pottery. Taken over by *Haga. Designers/decorators include Jan Boeziek (fl.c.1900), J.*Jongert, C.J.*Lanooij, Albert Seinstra (b.1877), Jacob Vet (1880-1924). Painted mark.

BROUWER, Willem Coenraad (1877-1933)

(i)   (ii)

Potter, designer, decorator. Worked for *Goedewaagen before establishing his own pottery. Incised (i, ii) and impressed (iii) marks.

(iii)

COMTE, Adolfe le (1850-1921)

Potter, designer, decorator.
Worked for De *Porceleyne Fles
(artistic director).
Painted signature and initials.

DISTEL, De (1895-1923)

(i)  (ii)

Manufacturers. Took over *Lotus
(1901/02), merged with
*Amstelhoek (1910), taken over by
*Goedewaagen.
Designers/decorators include
Cornelis de Bruin (1870-1941),
J.*Eisenloeffel, W.*Jansen,
C.A.*Lion Cachet, L.*Nienhuis,
T.*Nieuwenhuis, Willem van
Norden (1883-1978).
Printed (i, ii) and painted (iii, iv)
marks.

(iii)

(iv)

DUINVOET (1923-27)

Pottery established by Cor Alons
(1882-1967) and C.J. van *Muijen.
Painted mark.

DUPUIS, Toon (1877-1937)

Sculptor, designer. Modelled
figures for *Haga.
Moulded signature.

EISENLOEFFEL, Jan (1876-1957)

Designer. Worked for De *Distel,
De *Sphinx, De *Woning, *Zuid-
Holland; also made metalwork and
designed glass.
Painted monogram.

E.S.K.A.F. (Eerste Steenwijksche Kunstaardewerkfabriek) (1919-c.1934)

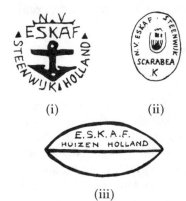

(i)

(ii)

(iii)

ESKAF

(iv)

Manufacturers. Designers include Willem Bogtman (1882-1955), Jan Hessel de Groot (1864-1932), J.*Jongert, Hildo Krop (1884-1970).
Printed (i-iii) and painted (iv) marks.

GELDER, Johanna C. van (b.1891)

Potter, designer. Established her own pottery 'Het Potteke'. In 1919, married A.A. van Rijnbach.
Painted marks.

GIDDING, Jaap (1887-1955)

Painter, designer. Worked for *Goedewaagen, De *Porceleyne Fles, *Regina, *Zuid-Holland; also designed glass.
Painted monogram.

GOEDEWAAGEN (est.1919)

(i)

ROYAL GOEDEWAAGEN
GOUDA
MADE IN Holland

(ii)

Manufacturers. Took over De *Distel (1923). Designers include W.C.*Brouwer, J.*Gidding, W.*Harzing, H.J.*Jansen van Galen, C.A.*Lion Cachet, L.*Nienhuis, Willem van Norden (1883-1978), S.*Schellink, Theo Vos (1887-1948).
Printed (i) and painted (ii) marks.

GROENEVELD, Pieter (b.1889)

Painter, potter. Ran his own pottery and worked for *Amphora. Impressed marks.

HAGA (1904-07)

Manufacturers. Taken over by *Amstelhoek. Designers/decorators include T.*Dupuis, August Falise (1875-1936), C.J. van der *Hoef, C.J.*Lanooij, C.J. van *Muijen, Gerrit J.D. Offermans (1857-1914), Albert Seinstra (b.1877), R.*Sterken, Henri Teixeira de Mattos (1856-1908). Painted marks.

HALPERN, Lee (b.1899)

L. Halpern

LH

Polish-born potter/designer working in Holland until 1940 when she moved to USA. Painted signature, initials.

HAM, Jan van (b.1892)

Potter, designer, decorator. Worked for C.J.*Lanooij, *St Lukas, De *Vier Paddenstoelen (co-founder), *Zenith, *Zuid-Holland. Painted signature.

HAM, Wilhelmus Antonius van (1900-74)

Painter, designer, decorator. Worked for *Zenith and independently. Painted monogram and mark.

HARTGRING, Johannes Hendricus (1876-1951)

Decorator. Worked for
*Rozenburg, *Zuid-Holland.
Painted mark.

HARTGRING, W.P. (b.1874)

Designer, decorator. Worked for
*Arnhemsche Fayencefabriek,
*Rozenburg, *Zuid-Holland.
Painted monogram and marks.

HARZING, Wim (1898-1978)

Sculptor, designer, modeller.
Worked for *Bouffioulx (*see*
Belgian ceramics), *Goedewaagen,
Russel-Tiglia; also designed glass.
Moulded initials.

HEYTZE, Jan Carel (1873-1943)

Designer, decorator. Worked for
*Holland, *Rozenburg, *St Lukas.
Painted mark.

HOEF, Christiaan Johannes van der (1875-1933)

Sculptor, designer, modeller.
Worked for *Amphora,
*Amstelhoek, *Haga, De *Sphinx,
De *Woning, *Zuid-Holland; also
worked as a medallist.
Painted signature,
printed/impressed monograms.

HOLLAND (1893-1920)

Manufacturers.
Designers/decorators include
H.P.*Berlage, J. van der *Bosch,
J.C.*Heytze, J.K.*Leurs,
T.*Molkenboer.
Painted marks.

JANSEN, Willem (1871-1949)

Designer, decorator. Worked for
De *Distel, *Rozenburg, *Zuid-
Holland.
Painted monogram.

JANSEN VAN GALEN, Hendrikus Jan (1871-1949)

Sculptor, designer, modeller.
Worked for *Goedewaagen, *Ram,
De *Sphinx, *Zuid-Holland.
Impressed monogram.

JONGERT, Jacob (1883-1942)

Painter, designer. Worked for
*Brantjes, *E.S.K.A.F.
Painted mark.

KROON, De (1906-10)

Pottery. Designers include Henri
Leonardus August Breetvelt
(1864-1923).
Painted mark.

LANOOIJ, Christiaan Johannes (Chris) (1881-1948)

Painter, potter, designer. Worked for *Brantjes, *Haga, *Zuid-Holland before establishing his own pottery where J. van *Ham and J.F.*Slot worked with him; also designed *glass.
Painted initials and signatures.

LECK, Bart van der (1876-1958)

Painter, potter, designer; also designed posters (see Dutch graphics).
Painted initials.

LEURS, Johannes Karel (1865-1936)

Painter, designer, decorator. Worked for *Holland, *Rozenburg.
Painted initials.

LION CACHET, Carel Adolph (1864-1945)

Designer. Worked for De *Distel, *Goedewaagen, De *Porceleyne Fles, De *Sphinx; also designed posters, bookbindings, furniture, carpets, textiles.
Painted monogram.

LORM, Cornelis de (1875-1942)

Designer. Worked for *Zuid-Holland; also designed *glass.
Printed mark incorporating monogram.

LOTUS (1896-1901/2)

Decorating studio established by
L.*Nienhuis.
Painted mark.

MENDES DA COSTA, Jozeph (1863-1939)

Sculptor, potter, designer.
Incised monogram.

MOLKENBOER, Theo (1861-1960)

Painter, designer. Worked for
*Holland; also designed books.
Printed monogram.

MUIJEN, Cornelus Jacobus van (1886-1971)

Potter, designer, decorator.
Worked for *Haga, *St Lukas and
*Zuid-Holland; subsequently
co-founded De *Vier
Paddenstoelen and *Duinvoet.
Painted initials.

MULLER, Leendert Johan (1879-1969)

Painter, designer. Worked for
*Zuid-Holland.
Painted (i, ii) and printed (iii)
marks.

(i)　　　　(ii)　　　　(iii)

NIENHUIS, Lambertus (Bert) (1873-1960)

Potter, designer. Founded *Lotus
and worked for De *Distel,
*Goedewaagen and independently.
Painted monogram and signature.

NIEUWENHUIS, Theodor Willem (1866-1951)

Architect, designer. Worked for De *Distel; also designed stained glass, metalwork, books (*see* Dutch graphics), furniture, textiles. Impressed monogram.

PORCELEYNE FLES, De (est.1653)

(†)

JT&L
DELFT

Factory operated by Joost Thooft & Labouchère from 1877. Designers/decorators include L.E.F. Bodart (1872-1945), A. le *Comte, J.*Gidding, C.A.*Lion Cachet, H.W. Mauser (1868-1940), Gerrit J.D. Offermans (1857-1914), Wouter Dirk Oosterloo (1879-1955), L.*Senf, J.*Toorop (*see* Dutch graphics). Painted (†) and impressed marks.

RAM (1920-45)

(†)

Pottery established by Henri van Lerven (1875-1945). Designers include Theodoor C.A. Colenbrander (1841-1930), H.J.*Jansen van Galen, Franciscus Johannes Mansveld (1872-1951), R.*Sterken. Painted (†) and printed marks.

REGINA (est.1898)

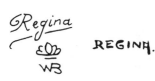

REGINA
WB.
GOUdA
HollANd

Manufacturers. Designers/decorators include G.A. Bonsel (fl.c.1920), J.*Gidding, A. Remiëns (1890-1972), W. de *Vries. Painted marks.

RIJN, De (1918-24)

 de rijn leiderdorp holland

Pottery established by Herman Zaalberg (1880-1958). Designers include C.*Agterberg, Theo van Doesburg (1883-1931), C.*Lebeau (*see* Dutch glass), Jan Schonk (b.1889).
Incised/painted marks.

ROZENBURG (1883-1916)

(i)

(ii)

(iii)

Manufacturers.
Designers/decorators include Theodoor C.A. Colenbrander (1841-1930), Daniel Harkink (1862-1953), C.W.J. t'Hart (fl.1899-1914), J.*Hartgring, W.P.*Hartgring, J.C.*Heytze, W.*Jansen, Jurriaan J. Kok (1861-1919), J.K.*Leurs, Franciscus Johannes Mansveld (1872-1951), D.P.J. de *Ruiter, S.*Schellink, R.*Sterken, J.*Toorop (*see* Dutch graphics), Theodorus Verstraaten (1872-1945), Jan van der Vet (1879-1954).
Painted (i, ii) and printed (iii) marks.

RUITER, Dominicus Petrus Johannes de (1872-1947)

ɗR.

Painter, decorator. Worked for *Rozenburg.
Painted monogram.

ST LUKAS (1909-30)

ST.LᴜKAS UTRECHT

Pottery. Designers/decorators include C.J.A.*Begeer, J. van *Ham, J.C.*Heytze, C.J. van *Muijen, Gerrit J.D. Offermans (1857-1914), Albert Seinstra (b.1877), R.*Sterken, W.*Stuurman (*see* Dutch glass).
Printed mark.

SCHELLINK, Samuel (1876-1958)

S.   ₣.   ₰

Designer, decorator. Worked for
*Amphora, *Goedewaagen,
*Rozenburg.
Painted initials and monogram.

SENF, Leon (1860-1940)

Leon.Senf.   ₤

Designer, decorator. Worked for
De *Porceleyne Fles.
Painted signature and monogram.

SLOT, Johannes Franciscus (1909-74)

JFSLOT   JFS

Potter, designer. Worked for
C.J.*Lanooij before establishing
his own pottery.
Painted signature and initials.

SOCIÉTÉ CÉRAMIQUE (1859-1958)

Manufacturers. Merged with De
*Sphinx.
Printed mark.

SPHINX, De, v/h Petrus Regout & Co. (1899-1958)

(i)

SPHINX

(ii)

(iii)

Manufacturers. Merged with
*Société Céramique to form
Sphinx-Céramique. Designers
include Edmond Bellefroid (1893-
1971), J.*Eisenloeffel, C.J. van der
*Hoef, H.J.*Jansen van Galen,
Johannes Henricus Lint (1889-
1956), C.A.*Lion Cachet, Charles
Vos (1888-1954).
Printed (i), impressed (ii) and
painted (iii) marks.

STERKEN, Roelof (1877-1943)

R.S.

Decorator, designer. Worked for *Amphora, *Haga, De *Kroon, *Ram, *Rozenburg, *St Lukas. Painted initials.

VAILLANT, Henriette (1875-1949)

Sculptor. Modelled figures which were fired at De *Porceleyne Fles. Impressed monogram.

VIER PADDENSTOELEN, De (1920-44)

Pottery started by J. van *Ham, Konrad Mertens (1889-1953), C. van *Muijen, E. Snel (fl.1920-40). Printed mark.

VRIES, Willem de (1908-69)

Potter, designer. Worked for *Regina before establishing his own pottery. Incised signature.

WILDENHAIN, Franz Rudolf (b.1905)

Wildenhain

F. R. W.

German potter, designer, decorator working in Holland between 1933 and 1947 when he moved to the USA. Married M.*Friedlander (*see* German ceramics). Incised mark, signature and initials.

WONING, De (est.1902)

Retailers directed by J.*Eisenloeffel and C.J. van der *Hoef; retailed a wide range of decorative arts. Printed mark.

ZENITH (est. 1915)

Manufacturers. Designers include C.*Agterberg, J. van *Ham, W.A. van *Ham, W.*Stuurman (*see* Dutch glass). Painted mark.

ZUID-HOLLAND (1898-1964)

(i)

(ii)

Manufacturers. Designers/decorators include Henri Leonardus August Breetveld (1864-1923), Theodoor C.A. Colenbrander (1841-1930), J.*Eisenloeffel, J.*Gidding, J. van *Ham, Daniel Harkink (1862-1953), J.*Hartgring, W.*Hartgring, C.J. van der *Hoef, W.*Jansen, H.J.*Jansen van Galen, C.J.*Lanooij, C. de *Lorm, C.J. van *Muijen, L.J.*Muller, Amp Smit (1903-76), Theodorus Verstraaten (1872-1945). Painted (i) and impressed (ii) marks.

GERMAN CERAMICS

ALBOUTS, Wilhelm G. (1897-1971)

Potter, designer, working in
Germany and Norway.
Incised monogram.

ANNABURGER STEINGUTFABRIK (est.1895)

Manufacturers.
Printed mark.

ARZBERG, Porzellanfabrik (est.1886)

Manufacturers. Designers include
Hermann Gretsch (1895-1950),
Heinrich Löffelhardt (fl.c.1955),
F. von *Stockmayer.
Printed mark.

BAMPI, Richard (1899-1965)

Sculptor, potter, designer,
decorator. Worked at *Kandern.
Impressed mark.

BARLACH, Ernst (1870-1938)

E.Barlach

Sculptor. Modelled figures for
*Meissen, H. and R.*Mutz,
*Schwarzburger; also modelled
figures cast in metal.
Moulded signature.

BAUSCHER, Gebrüder (est.1881)

Manufacturers. Designers include P.*Behrens, H.*Christiansen. Printed marks.

BEHRENS, Peter (1868-1940)

Architect, designer. Worked for *Bauscher, A.*Hanke, *Mehlem, *Merkelbach, J.J.*Scharvogel, *Villeroy & Boch. Also designed furniture, textiles, glass, *graphics, *metalwork.
Printed monogram.

BERLIN, Königliche/Staatliche Porzellanmanufaktur (est.1763)

Manufacturers.
Designers/decorators include August Achtenhagen (1865-1938), Adolf Amberg (1874-1913), M.*Friedlander, W.*Gress, H.*Griemert, Karl Himmelstross (1878-1967), Hermann Hugo Hubatsch (1878-1940), E.*Klablena (see Austrian ceramics), G.*Marcks, Rudolf Marcuse (b.1878), A.*Nechansky (see Austrian glass), Adelbert Niemeyer (1867-1932), Edmund Otto (1888-1959), Hermann Pagels (b.1876), Trude Petri-Raben (1906-68), Max Adolf Pfeiffer (1875-1957), Paul Poppke (b.1875), Anton Puchegger (c.1890-1917), Carl Reschke (b.1872), Carl Wilhelm Robra (b.1876), R.*Scheibe, P.*Scheurich (see German graphics), Gerhard Schliepstein (1886-1963), T.*Schmuz-Baudiss, H.*Seger, W.*Stanke, J.*Wackerle, Sigismond Wernekinck

BERLIN (continued)

(1877-1921), Marguerite
Wildenhain (b.1898).
Printed/impressed (i) and printed
(ii) marks.

BONTJES VAN BEEK, Jan (1899-1969)

Potter, designer. Ran his own
pottery and designed for
*Rosenthal and Alfred Ungewiss.
Impressed/incised/painted
monogram.

BUNZLAU, Königliche/Staatliche Keramische Fachschule (est.1897)

Pottery training school.
Incised mark.

BURGAU, Porzellanmanufaktur (est.1902)

Manufacturers founded by
Ferdinand Selle. Designers include
A.*Müller.
Printed mark.

BÜRGELER KUNSTKERAMISCHE WERKSTÄTTEN (est.c.1900)

Pottery. Designers include H.C.
van de *Velde.
Printed mark.

BURRI, Werner (b.1898)

Swiss potter, designer, decorator
working in Germany. Worked for
*Velten-Vordamm and
independently.
Painted/incised monogram.

CADINEN, Königliche Majolika-Werkstätte (fl.c.1900)

Pottery. Designers include
Johannes Götz (b.1865),
L.*Manzel.
Impressed mark.

CARSTENS, Chr., Georgenthal (est.1919)

Manufacturers.
Printed marks.

CARSTENS, Chr., Gräfenroda (est.1919)

Manufacturers. Designers include
Artur Hennig (fl.c.1930).
Printed mark.

CARSTENS, Chr., Neuhandelsleben (est.1900)

Manufacturers.
Designers/decorators include
Mirene Schmidt (fl.c.1930).
Printed mark.

CHRISTIANSEN, Hans (1866-1945)

Painter, designer. Worked for
*Bauscher, *Krautheim &
Adelberg, J. von *Schwarz,
*Villeroy & Boch,
*Wächtersbacher; also designed
glass, metalwork, jewellery, posters,
*furniture, carpets, tapestries,
textiles.
Printed monogram.

DARMSTADT, Grossherzogliche Keramische Manufaktur (est.1906)

Manufacturers. Designers include Karl Georg Huber (b.1872), J.J.*Scharvogel. Impressed marks.

DARMSTADT, Vereinte Kunstgewerbler (fl.c.1905)

Group of Darmstadt designers. Worked for P.*Rosenthal. Printed mark.

DORNHEIM, KOCH & FISCHER (est.1880)

Manufacturers. Printed mark.

DOUGLAS-HILL, Otto Douglas (1897-1972)

Sculptor, potter, designer, decorator. Incised marks.

DRESLER, Paul (1879-1950)

Potter, designer, decorator. Established the Grootenburg Pottery. Impressed mark.

DÜMLER & BREIDEN (est.1912)

Manufacturers. Impressed mark.

DUNTZE, Ursula *see* SCHEID, Ursula

ELSTERWERDA, Steingutfabrik (est.1900)

Manufacturers. Designers include
Siegfried Möller (fl.c.1930).
Printed marks.

ERDMANN SCHLEGELMILCH (est.1861)

Manufacturers.
Printed mark.

FESTERSEN, Friedrich (fl.c.1910)

Festersen

Potter, designer, decorator.
Impressed mark.

FRAUREUTH, Porzellanfabrik (est.c.1860)

Manufacturers.
Printed mark.

FRIEDLANDER, Margarete (b.1898)

Potter, designer. Worked for
*Berlin and independently. Moved
to Holland in 1933 and thence to
the USA in 1947. Married to
F.R.*Wildenhain (*see* Dutch
ceramics).
Painted mark.

FÜRST ADOLF-WERKSTÄTTE FÜR KUNSTKERAMIK
(est.1912)

Manufacturers.
Printed mark.

GAUL, August (1869-1921)

Sculptor, modeller. Modelled figures made by *Meissen, *Nymphenburg, *Rosenthal; work also cast in bronze.
Moulded signature.

GERZ I, Simon Peter (fl.c.1910)

Manufacturers. Designers include A.*Müller.
Impressed mark.

GOEBEL, W. (est.1871)

Manufacturers. Modellers include Sister M.J. Hummel (fl.c.1940).
Printed/impressed marks.

GRESS, W. (fl.c.1925)

w. Gress.

Designer, decorator. Worked for *Berlin, *Rosenthal.
Painted signature.

GRIEMERT, Hubert (b.1905)

Potter, designer, decorator. Established his own pottery. Designed for *Berlin.
Painted/incised monogram.

GRÜNSTADT, Steingutfabrik (est.1801)

Manufacturers.
Printed mark.

GULDBRANDSEN, Julius-Vilhelm (1869-1960)

Danish decorator working in Germany. Worked for *Rosenthal. Painted initials.

HANKE, August (1875-1928)

Potter. Made ceramics designed by P.*Behrens, H.C. van de *Velde, H.*Wewerka, P.*Wynand. Incised signature.

HÄRLIN, Dorkas (1885-1968)

Potter, designer, decorator. Incised monogram.

HEIDER, Max von (b.1839)

Potter, designer, decorator. Worked with his sons Hans (1867-1952), Fritz (b.1868), Rudolf (fl.c.1900). Impressed mark.

HELLMUTH, Leonhard (b.1859)

Designer. Worked for *Merkelbach; also designed carpets, textiles. Impressed monogram.

HEUBACH, Gebrüder (est.1822)

Manufacturers. Designers include Christian Metzger (fl.c.1900), Wilhelm Neuhäuser (fl.c.1900), P.*Zeiller. Printed marks.

HOETGER, Bernhard (1874-1949)

Sculptor. Modelled figures made by *Kandern, *Meissen.
Incised signature.

HOHLT, Otto (1889-1960)

Potter, designer, decorator. Established his own pottery at Katzbach where he was assisted by his sons Albrecht (1928-60) and Görge (b.1930).
Incised mark.

HUTSCHENREUTHER, C.M. (est.1814)

Manufacturers.
Printed marks.

HUTSCHENREUTHER, L. (est.1856)

Manufacturers.
Designers/decorators include Hans Achtziger (fl.c.1950), K.*Severin.
Printed marks.

KAGEL, Wilhelm (1867-1935)

Painter, potter, designer, decorator. Established his own pottery where he was assisted by his son Wilhelm (b.1906).
Impressed/printed mark.

KANDERN, Tonwerke (fl.c.1900-30)

(i)

(ii)

Pottery founded by M.*Läuger. Designers/decorators include B.*Hoetger, E.*Schmidt-Pecht. R.*Bampi also worked there. Impressed (i) and incised (ii) marks.

KARLSRUHE, Grossherzogliche/Staatliche Majolika Manufaktur (est.1901)

Manufacturers. Designers include Franz Blazek (b.1887), Karl-Heinz Feisst (fl.c.1955), Fridegart Glatzle (fl.c.1955), Ludwig König (fl.c.1925), C.*Kornhas, M.*Läuger, G.*Marcks, E.J.*Margold, Adelbert Niemeyer (1867-1932), B.*Paul (*see* German graphics), Emil Pottner (b.1872), R.*Riemerschmid (*see* German metalwork), P.*Scheurich (*see* German graphics), Paul Speck (fl.c.1925), Erwin Spuler (1906-64), Wilhelm Süs (1861-1933), Konrad Taucher (fl.c.1910), H.*Thoma (co-founder), L.*Vierthaler, J.*Wackerle, E.R.*Weiss (*see* German graphics), Karl Maximilian Württemberger (fl.c.1905). Impressed/printed marks.

KEITEL, Otto (1894-1965)

Designer, decorator. Worked for *Rosenthal. Painted monogram.

KORNHAS, Carl (1857-1931)

Sculptor, potter. Work manufactured by *Karlsruhe, *Weingarten. Impressed marks.

KRAUTHEIM & ADELBERG (est.1884)

Manufacturers. Designers include
H.*Christiansen.
Printed mark.

KUHN, Beate (b.1927)

Sculptor, potter, designer. Worked
with K.*Scheid and designed for
*Rosenthal before establishing her
own pottery.
Impressed/incised initial and
mark.

LANDSHUT, Königliche/Staatliche Keramische Fachschule (est.1873)

Technical school.
Impressed mark.

LÄUGER, Max (1864-1952)

PROF. LÄUGER
Made in Germany

Painter, sculptor, potter, designer,
decorator. Founded *Kandern,
worked at *Karlsruhe; also
designed carpets, graphics.
Incised monogram, impressed
signature.

LEHMANN & SOHN, C.A. (est.1895)

Manufacturers.
Printed mark.

LINDIG, Otto (1895-1966)

Sculptor, potter, designer, decorator.
Incised/painted monogram.

MAGNUSSEN, Walter (1869-1946)

Potter, designer. Worked for
J.J.*Scharvogel.
Impressed monograms.

MANZEL, Ludwig (1858-1936)

Sculptor. Worked for *Cadinen.
Incised initials.

MARCKS, Gerhard (b.1889)

Sculptor, potter, designer. Worked
for *Berlin, *Karlsruhe,
*Schwarzburger, *Velten-
Vordamm and independently.
Incised/painted mark.

MARGOLD, Emanuel Josef (1888-1962)

Austrian designer, working largely
in Germany. Worked for *Böck (see
Austrian ceramics), *Karlsruhe,
*Wahliss (see Austrian ceramics),
*Velten-Vordamm, Vereinigte
Wiener und Gmundner Keramik;
also designed glass, jewellery,
posters, furniture, textiles,
wallpaper.
Printed signature.

MEHLEM, Franz Anton (est.1755)

Manufacturers of 'Royal Bonn' and other wares. Designers include P.*Behrens.
Printed marks.

MEIER, Otto (b.1903)

Sculptor, potter, designer, decorator.
Incised/impressed monogram.

MEISSEN, Königliche/Staatliche Porzellanmanufaktur (est.1710)

(i)

(ii)

BÖTTGER
STEINZEUG

(iii)

Manufacturers.
Designers/decorators include August Achtenhagen (1865-1938), E.*Barlach, Arthur Barth (1878-1926), Paul Börner (1888-1976), Theodor Eichler (b.1868), Max Esser (1885-1945), A.*Gaul, K.*Gross (see German metalwork), Konrad Hentschel (1872-1907), Rudolf Hentschel (1869-1951), B.*Hoetger, M.*Høst (see Scandanavian ceramics), Erich Kleinhempel (1874-1947), Hans Meid (1883-1957), Willi Münch-Khe (b.1885) Adelbert Niemeyer (1867-1932), E.*Oehme, J.M.*Olbrich, Max Adolf Pfeiffer (1875-1957), R.*Riemerschmid (see German metalwork), P.*Scheurich (see German graphics), H.C. van de *Velde, H.*Vogeler (see German graphics), Otto Eduard Voigt (1870-1949), Paul Walther (1876-1933), P.*Zeiller.
Painted/incised (i), painted (ii), impressed (iii) marks.

MERKELBACH, Reinhold (est.1845)

Manufacturers. Designers include Friedrich Adler (1878-1942), P.*Behrens, Hans Eduard Berlepsch-Valendas (1849-1921), Leopold Moritz Karl Capeller (1884-1968), Johann Wilhelm Karl Görig (1851-1925), L.*Hellmuth, B.*Mauder (*see* German glass), M.*Prugger, R.*Riemerschmid (*see* German metalwork), H.C. van de *Velde, H.*Wewerka, P.*Wynand. Impressed marks.

METZLER & ORTLOFF, Gebrüder (est.1875)

Manufacturers. Made figures modelled by P.*Zeiller. Printed marks.

MÜLLER, Albin (1871-1941)

Architect, designer. Worked for *Burgau, *Gerz, *Wächtersbacher, *Wahliss (*see* Austrian ceramics); also designed glass, *metalwork. Printed signature.

MUTZ, Hermann (1845-1913)

MUTZ·KERAMIK

(i)

Mutz
Altona

(ii)

Potter, designer. Collaborated with son R.*Mutz. Made ceramics designed by E.*Barlach. Impressed mark (i) and incised signature (ii).

MUTZ, Richard (1872-1931)

Potter, designer. Worked with father H.*Mutz before establishing his own pottery where his work include figures modelled by E.*Barlach, Karl Himmelstross (1878-1967), Richard Küohl (b.1880) and others. Impressed mark.

MUTZE, Walter (1893-1963)

Designer, decorator. Worked for *Rosenthal. Painted initials.

NEUREUTHER, Christian (1869-1921)

Potter, designer, decorator. Worked for *Wächtersbacher. Printed initials.

NYMPHENBURG, Königliche/Staatliche Bayerische Porzellanfabrik (est.1747)

Manufacturers in Bavaria. Designers/decorators include Hans Eduard Berlepsch-Valendas (1849-1921), Franz Blazek (b.1887), A.*Gaul, Hermann Gradl (1869-1934), Theodor Kärner (1884-1966), Adelbert Niemeyer (1867-1932), E.*Oehme, Edmund Otto (1888-1959), Max Rossbach (1871-1947), P.*Scheurich (*see* German graphics), R.*Sieck, J.*Wackerle, Christian Wittmann (fl.c.1910), Willi Zügel (1876-1956). Printed mark.

OBERLAUSITZER KERAMISCHE WERKSTÄTTEN (est.1925)

Pottery run by Paul Jurgel
(fl.c.1930).
Impressed mark.

OEHME, Erich (1889-1970)

Modeller. Worked for *Meissen,
*Nymphenburg.
Moulded signature.

OHME, Hermann (est.1882)

Manufacturers.
Printed mark.

OLBRICH, Josef Maria (1867-1908)

Austrian architect, designer who
settled in Germany in 1899.
Worked for *Meissen, *Villeroy &
Boch, *Wächtersbacher; also
designed *metalwork, jewellery,
furniture, posters.
Printed mark.

OPPEL, Gustav (1891-1978)

Modeller. Worked for *Rosenthal.
Painted monogram.

PAETSCH, Theodor (est.1840)

Manufacturers.
Printed mark.

PAUL, Julius, & Sohn (est.1893)

Manufacturers.
Printed marks.

PRUGGER, Max (1876-1960)

Painter, designer. Worked for
*Merkelbach.
Impressed monogram.

REINHOLD & CO. (est.1739)

Manufacturers.
Impressed/printed mark.

ROESLER, Max (est.1894)

Manufacturers. Designers include
Wolf Kreidl (fl.c.1930), Gustav
Partz (fl.c.1930).
Printed mark.

ROSENTHAL, Philipp (est.1891)

Manufacturers.
Designers/decorators include
J.*Bontjes van Beek, R.*Bryk (see
Scandinavian ceramics),
J.*Cocteau (see French ceramics),
L.*Dasio, A.*Gaul, W.*Gress,
Hermann Gretsch (1895-1950),
K.*Gross (see German metalwork),
J.-V.*Guldbrandsen, Karl
Himmelstross (1878-1967),
Theodor Kärner (1884-1966),
O.*Keitel, B.*Kuhn, Rudolf
Marcuse (b.1878), W.*Mutze,
G.*Oppel, Edmund Otto

(1888-1959), B.*Paul (*see* German graphics), Raymond Peynet (b.1908), Max Adolf Pfeiffer (1875-1957), R.*Scheibe, F. von *Stockmayer, L.*Vierthaler, H.*Vogeler (*see* German graphics), Wilhelm Wagenfeld (b.1900), Bjorn Winnblad (b.1900), T.*Wirkkala (*see* Scandinavian glass), T.*Zoelch. Also manufactured glass. Printed marks.

RUSCHA-KERAMIK (fl.c.1950)

Manufacturers. Incised mark.

SCHALLER, Oscar, & Co. (est.1919)

Manufacturers. Printed mark.

SCHARVOGEL, Jakob Julius (1854-1938)

Potter, designer, decorator. Worked for *Villeroy & Boch before establishing his own pottery, Scharvogel Kunsttöpferei München, where he made ceramics designed by P.*Behrens, L.*Habich (*see* German metalwork), W.*Magnussen, T.*Schmuz-Baudiss. In 1906, established *Darmstadt. Impressed marks.

SCHEIBE, Richard (1879-1964)

Sculptor, painter, designer, modeller. Worked for *Berlin, *Rosenthal, *Schwarzburger, *Velten-Vordamm.
Painted monogram.

SCHEID, Karl (b.1929)

Potter, designer, decorator. Worked with B.*Kuhn before establishing his own pottery where he worked with his wife U.*Scheid.
Impressed mark.

SCHEID (*née* DUNTZE), Ursula (b.1932)

Potter, designer, decorator. Worked with husband K.*Scheid.
Impressed mark.

SCHMIDER, Georg (est.1865)

Manufacturers.
Printed mark.

SCHMIDT-PECHT, Elisabeth (1857-1940)

Potter, designer, decorator. Executed decorative designs by Julius Diez (1870-1957). Worked at *Kandern.
Incised mark and initials.

SCHMUZ-BAUDISS, Theodor (1859-1942)

Potter, designer, decorator.
Designs executed by
J.J.*Scharvogel, *Swaine & Co.
Artistic director of *Berlin
(1908-26).
Printed monograms, painted
signature.

SCHRAMBERGER MAJOLIKAFABRIK (est.1820)

Manufacturers. Designers include
Eva Strikker (fl.c.1930).
Printed mark.

SCHUMANN, Carl (est.1881)

Manufacturers.
Printed mark.

SCHWANDORF, Tonwarenfabrik (est.1863)

Manufacturers.
Printed marks.

SCHWARZ, J. von (est.1859)

Manufacturers. Designers include
H.*Christiansen, Carl Sigmund
Luber (fl.c.1900).
Printed mark.

SCHWARZBURGER WERKSTÄTTEN FÜR PORZELLANKUNST (1908-13)

Schwarzburger Werk-
stätten für Porzellankunst

Pottery founded by Max Adolf
Pfeiffer (1875-1957).
Designers/modellers include
E.*Barlach, Max Esser
(1885-1945), G.*Marcks,
A.*Nechansky (see Austrian glass),
Adelbert Niemeyer (1867-1932),
Otto Pilz (fl.c.1910), Anton
Puchegger (c.1890-1917),
R.*Scheibe, P.*Scheurich (see
German graphics).
Impressed mark.

SEGER, Hermann (1839-93)

Sgr.P

Potter. Worked for *Berlin.
Printed mark.

SEIDLER, Hermann (fl.c.1900)

Seidler

Potter, designer, decorator.
Incised mark and signature.

SEVERIN, Kurt (1896-1970)

Designer, decorator. Worked for
L.*Hutschenreuther, *Rosenthal.
Painted monogram.

SIECK, Rudolf (1877-1957)

RUD. SIECK
BERGKAPELLE.

Painter, designer, decorator.
Worked for *Nymphenburg.
Painted signature.

SÖRNEWITZ-MEISSEN, Steingutfabrik (est.1898)

Manufacturers.
Printed mark.

STANKE, W. (fl.c.1910)

Decorator. Worked for *Berlin.
Painted signature.

STEGER, Milly (1881-1948)

Sculptor, modeller. Worked for
*Rosenthal.
Painted initials.

STEINMANN, K. (est.1868)

Manufacturers.
Printed mark.

STOCKMAYER, Fritz von (1877-1940)

Designer, decorator. Worked for
*Arzberg, *Rosenthal and other
firms.
Painted monogram.

SWAINE & CO. (est.1850)

Manufacturers. Made ceramics
designed by members of
*Vereinigte Werkstätten für Kunst
im Handwerk including
T.*Schmuz-Baudiss.
Printed mark.

TEICHERT, Porzellanfabrik (est.1864)

Manufacturers. Designers include
L*Vierthaler.
Printed mark.

THOMA, Hans (1839-1925)

(i)   (ii)

Painter, designer, decorator. Co-
founder of *Karlsruhe.
Painted (i) and incised (ii)
monograms.

THOMAS & ENS (1903-08)

Manufacturers. Taken over by
*Rosenthal.
Printed mark.

THOMSBERGER & HERMANN (est.1804)

Manufacturers.
Printed mark.

VELDE, Henry Clemens van de (1863-1957)

Belgian architect, painter, designer
working largely in Germany.
Worked for *Bürgeler, *Cérabel
(see Belgian ceramics), A.*Hanke,
*Meissen, *Merkelbach; also
designed glass, *metalwork,
jewellery, posters, bookbindings,
*furniture (see Belgian furniture),
textiles.
Impressed marks and signature.

VELTEN-VORDAMM (fl.20th century)

Manufacturers. Designers include Theodor Bogler (1896-1968), W.*Burri, C.O.*Czeschka (*see* Austrian graphics), G.*Marcks, E.J.*Margold, Antoni Mutter (b.1892), R.*Scheibe. Impressed mark.

VEREINIGTE WERKSTÄTTEN FÜR KUNST IM HANDWERK (est.1897)

Workshops producing designs for ceramics executed by *Swaine and other potteries. Designers include Max Rossbach (1871-1947), T.*Schmuz-Baudiss; workshops also produced *metalwork, jewellery, furniture. Printed mark.

VIERTHALER, Ludwig (1875-1967)

L·VIERTHALER

Sculptor, designer. Worked for *Karlsruhe, *Rosenthal, *Teichert. Moulded signature, printed monogram.

VILLEROY & BOCH (est.1748)

Manufacturers. Designers include P.*Behrens, Hans Eduard Berlepsch-Valendas (1849-1921), P.E.*Berthon (*see* French graphics), H.*Christiansen, Julius Diez (1870-1954), Hermann Gretsch (1895-1950), Adelbert Niemeyer (1867-1932), J.M.*Olbrich, Gustav Partz (fl.c.1930), R.*Riemerschmid (*see* German metalwork),

VILLEROY & BOCH (continued)

J.J.*Scharvogel, Gustav Spoerri (fl.c.1930). Also produced glass. Impressed/printed marks.

 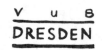

WÄCHTERSBACHER STEINGUTFABRIK (est.1832)

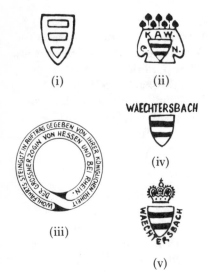

(i) (ii)

(iii) (iv)

(v)

Manufacturers. Designers include Ernst Aufseeser (fl.c.1930), Carl Bull (fl.c.1930) , H.*Christiansen, Heinrich Diehl (fl.c.1930), Ursula Fesca (1900-75), A.*Müller, C.*Neureuther, J.M.*Olbrich, E.*Riegel (see German metalwork), Eduard Schweitzer (1870-1939). Impressed (i), printed (ii-vi), printed/painted (vii) marks.

(vi) (vii)

WACKERLE, Josef (1880-1959)

WACKERLE.

(i)

(ii)

Sculptor, modeller, designer. Worked for *Berlin, *Karlsruhe, *Nymphenburg. Moulded (i) and incised (ii) signatures.

WEBER, Rolfe (b.1907)

Potter, designer, decorator. Impressed initial.

WEINGARTEN, Porzellanfabrik (est.1882)

Manufacturers. Designers include
C.*Kornhas.
Impressed mark.

WERNER, Edwin, & Co. (fl.c.1930)

Manufacturers.
Impressed (i), printed (ii) marks.

(i)   (ii)

WEWERKA, Hans (1888-1917)

H.WEWERKA.

Sculptor, modeller. Worked for
A.*Hanke, *Merkelbach.
Impressed signature.

WYNAND, Paul (1879-1956)

PAUL WYNAND

Sculptor, designer. Worked for
A.*Hanke, *Merkelbach.
Impressed mark.

ZEILLER, Paul (1880-1915)

Paul Zeiller .

Sculptor, modeller. Worked for
*Heubach, *Meissen, *Metzler &
Ortloff.
Moulded signature.

ZOELCH, Tono (1897-1955)

Sculptor, painter, modeller,
decorator. Worked for *Rosenthal.
Painted monogram.

AUSTRIAN CERAMICS

AUGARTEN (est.1922)

Manufacturers.
Designers/decorators include
F.*Barwig, Walter Bosse (b.1904),
H.*Bucher, M.*Flögl, J,*Hoffmann,
Mathilde Jaksch (b.1899), Dina
Kuhn (b.1891), Jakob Löw (1887-
1935), M.*Powolny, O.*Prutscher
(*see* Austrian metalwork, graphics),
Ena Rottenberg (1893-1950), Karl
Schwetz (b.1888), Ida Schwetz-
Lehmann (1883-1971),
V.*Wieselthier.
Impressed/printed marks.

'AUSTRIA' KUNSTGEWERBLICHE WERKSTÄTTE (fl.c.1920)

Pottery workshop.
Printed mark.

BARWIG, Franz (1868-1931)

Sculptor, modeller. Worked for
*Augarten, *Wienerberger and
independently.
Incised initials and signature.

BAUDISCH-WITTKE, Gudrun (1906-82)

Sculptor, potter, designer,
decorator. Worked for E.Fessler,
*Gmundner, Hallstatter Keramik,
*Wiener Werkstätte and ran her
own workshops; also designed
textiles.
Incised signature, painted initials.

BAUER, Leopold (1872-1938)

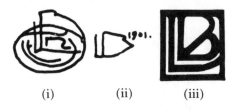

(i)　　　(ii)　　　(iii)

Architect, designer; also designed glass.
Incised (i, ii) and impressed (iii) monograms.

BIHL, G., & Co. (est.1882)

Bohemian/Czechoslovakian manufacturers.
Printed mark.

BÖCK, Josef, Wiener Porzellanmanufaktur (1879-1960)

Manufacturers. Designers include Remigius Geyling (1878-1974), Guido Heigl (1890-c.1926), J.*Hoffmann, Gustav Kalhammer (1886-1919), Hans Kalmsteiner (b.1886), Rosa Krenn (b.1894), M.*Likarz-Strauss (see Austrian metalwork), B.*Löffler, Fritzi Löw-Lazar (1891-1975), E.J.*Margold (see German ceramics), K.*Massanetz (see Austrian glass), K.*Moser, D.*Peche, M.*Powolny, O.*Prutscher (see Austrian metalwork, graphics), J.*Sika, T.*Trethan (see Austrian furniture), V.*Wieselthier, Karl Witzmann (b.1883), J.*Zimpel (see Austrian metalwork), Ugo Zovetti (b.1879). Impressed/printed marks.

BUCHER, Hertha (1898-1960)

Potter, designer, modeller, decorator. Worked for *Augarten, E.Fessler, M.*Goldscheider, *'Keramos', *Wienerberger, *Wiener Werkstätte and independently.
Incised monogram.

BUDAPEST KUNSTGEWERBESCHULE (O.M.K.I.I.)

Hungarian school of industrial art with a ceramics studio run by V.*Schleich from 1911 to 1914. Impressed mark.

BUSCH & LUDESCHER, Wiener Kunstkeramische Werkstätten (est.1908)

Workshop established when *Förster's ceramic studio was bought by two of the employees. Designers include Gertrude Dengg (b.1885), B.*Emmel, Lotte Frömmel-Fochler (b.1884), Elza Kövesházi-Kalmár (fl.c.1910), R.*Obsieger, Anton Puchegger (c.1890-1917). Printed/impressed marks.

CALM-WIERINK, Lotte (b.1897)

Designer, modeller. Worked for *Wiener Werkstätte; also worked as a fashion and jewellery designer. Incised initials.

CANDIA (1921-39)

Retail shop and pottery; also produced and sold a range of other decorative arts. Impressed mark.

CARLSBADER PORZELLANFABRIK CARL MOLL (est.1844)

Bohemian/Czechoslovakian manufacturers. Printed/impressed mark.

DACHSEL, Paul (est.1904)

Bohemian/Czechoslovakian
manufacturers.
Printed mark.

DRASCHE-FABRIK (est.1838)

Hungarian manufacturers.
Impressed mark.

DUXER PORZELLANMANUFAKTUR (est.1860)

(i)

(ii)

Bohemian/Czechoslovakian
manufacturers of 'Royal Dux'
porcelain. Designers include
E.*Strobach.
Raised pad (i) and printed
mark (ii).

EMMEL, Bruno (1877)

Potter, designer. Worked for *Busch
& Ludescher and independently.
Painted initials.

FISCHER, Emil (est.1890)

Hungarian manufacturers.
Succeeded Ignác *Fischer.
Printed mark.

FISCHER, Ignác (1864-90)

Hungarian manufacturers.
Succeeded by Emil *Fischer.
Printed marks.

FLÖGL, Mathilde (1893-1950)

Designer, modeller. Worked for
*Augarten, *Wiener Werkstätte
and ran her own workshop; also
designed glass, enamels, posters,
textiles, wallpapers and worked as
a fashion designer.
Painted initial, incised signature.

FÖRSTER, A., & Co. (1899-1908)

Design and decoration studios
established by sculptor Alexander
Förster (b.1861). Taken over by
*Busch & Ludescher; also
produced a range of other
decorative arts.
Printed mark.

GMUNDNER KERAMIK (1909-12)

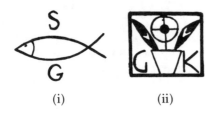

(i)   (ii)

(iii)

Pottery established by husband and
wife F.*Schleiss and E.*Simandl-
Schleiss. Other designers include
G.*Baudisch-Wittke, J.*Hoffmann,
M.*Likarz-Strauss (see Austrian
metalwork), Erna Pamberger
(fl.c.1910), Ida Schwetz-Lehmann
(1883-1971), V.*Wieselthier.
Merged with *Wiener Keramik to
become Vereinigte Wiener und
Gmundner Keramik.
Painted (i, ii) and impressed (iii)
marks.

GOLDSCHEIDER, Friedrich (1885-1954)

Manufacturers. Run by Walter and
Marcell Goldscheider (1920-26).
Designers include Ida Erdös
(b.1897) V.*Gemignani (see Italian

ceramics), J.*Lorenzl (*see* Austrian metalwork), Johanna Meier-Michel (b.1876), Ida Schwetz-Lehmann (1883-1971).
Printed/impressed marks.

GOLDSCHEIDER, Marcell, Vereinigte Atelier für Kunst und Keramik (1926-c.1938)

Manufacturers. Designers include H.*Bucher, Rudolf Knörlein (b.1902), Dina Kuhn (b.1891), Grete Neuwalder-Breuer (b.1898), Ena Rottenberg (1893-1950), S.*Singer-Schinnerl, V.*Wieselthier.
Printed mark.

HANAK, Anton (1875-1934)

Sculptor. Designed ceramic stoves manufactured by Rudolf Sommerhuber.
Painted monogram.

HEREND (est.1838)

(i)　　　(ii)　　　(iii)

Hungarian manufacturers. Designers/decorators include Jenö Farkasházi Fischer (1863-1926), who owned the firm from 1896 to 1926.
Painted (i, ii), relief-moulded (iii) and impressed (iv) marks.

HEREND (iv)

177

HOFFMANN, Josef (1870-1956)

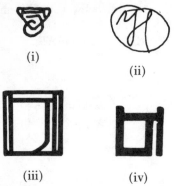

(i)

(ii)

(iii)

(iv)

Architect, designer. Worked for *Augarten, *Böck, *Gmundner, *Wiener Werkstätte; also designed *glass, *metalwork, jewellery, furniture, textiles, bookbinding (*see* Austrian graphics). Painted (i, ii) and impressed (iii, iv) monograms.

HOLLÓHÁZA (Istvanyi Co.) (est.1831)

HOLLÓHÁZA

Hungarian manufacturers. Printed mark.

HÜTTL (est.1854)

HÜTTL
BUDAPEST

HÜTTL
PORCZELLÁN
GYÁRA
BUDAPESTEN

Hungarian manufacturers. Designers include Pál Horti (1865-1907). Printed/impressed marks.

ISKRA, Franz Xaver (b.1897)

Potter, designer. Impressed mark.

KARAU, Werkstätte (1919-25)

Workshops which produced pottery as well as other decorative arts. Impressed mark.

KERAMISCHE WERKGENOSSENSCHAFT (1911-20)

Pottery established by Helena Johnova (1884-1962), Rosa Neuwirth (fl.c.1915) and Ida Schwetz-Lehmann (1883-1971). Designers include Julie Sitte (1881-1959).
Impressed mark.

'KERAMOS' WIENER KUNSTKERAMIK UND PORZELLANMANUFAKTUR (est.1920)

Pottery. Designers include H.*Bucher, E.*Klablena, O.*Prutscher (*see* Austrian graphics, metalwork), Ida Schwetz-Lehmann (1883-1971).
Printed mark.

KIRSCH, Hugo F. (1873-1961)

Potter, designer. Established his own pottery in 1906 where some of his vases were designed by Karl Krenek (1880-1948). Work sold through *Wiener Werkstätte.
Printed mark and painted/incised monograms.

KLABLENA, Eduard (1881-1933)

Potter, designer, modeller. Worked for *Berlin (*see* German ceramics), and *'Keramos' before establishing his own pottery, *Langenzersdorfer Keramik.
Painted monogram.

KOPRIVA, Erna (1894)

Designer, modeller. Worked for
*Wiener Werkstätte; also designed
textiles.
Painted initials.

KOSSUCH, János (est.c.1890)

Hungarian manufacturers.
Designers/decorators include
János Örley (fl.c.1895).
Impressed mark.

LANGENZERSDORFER KERAMIK (est.1911)

Pottery established by E.*Klablena.
Work sold through *Wiener
Werkstätte.
Painted mark.

LÖFFLER, Bertold (1874-1960)

Painter, designer, decorator. Co-
founder of *Wiener Keramik.
Worked for *Böck and Vereinigte
Wiener und Gmundner Keramik;
also designed glass, jewellery,
posters, books (see Austrian
graphics).
Painted initials.

MOSER, Koloman (1868-1918)

Painter, designer. Worked for
*Böck; also designed *glass,
*metalwork, jewellery, posters,
books (see Austrian graphics),
furniture, textiles, carpets.
Incised/painted monogram.

OBSIEGER, Robert (1884-1958)

R·OBSIEGER

Potter, designer, decorator.
Worked for *Wienerberger, *Busch
& Ludescher and independently.
Incised signature.

PECHE, Dagobert (1886-1923)

Designer, modeller. Worked for
*Böck, Vereinigte Wiener und
Gmundner Keramik, *Wiener
Werkstätte; also designed *glass,
*metalwork, jewellery, posters,
books (*see* Austrian graphics),
furniture, carpets, textiles,
wallpapers.
Incised/painted initials.

POWOLNY, Michael (1871-1954)

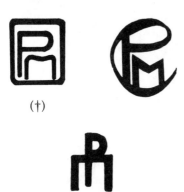

(†)

Sculptor, potter, designer,
modeller, decorator. Co-founder
of *Wiener Keramik. Worked for
*Augarten, *Bock, Brüder
Schwadron, Rudolf Sommerhuber,
*Wienerberger, *Wiener
Werkstätte; also designed *glass,
silver.
Impressed (†) and painted
monograms.

RIESSNER, STELLMACHER & KESSEL (est.1892)

Bohemian/Czechoslovakian
manufacturers of 'Amphora'
porcelain and other wares.
Impressed marks.

RIPPL RÓNAI, József (1861-1930)

Hungarian painter, designer.
Worked for *Zsolnay; also
designed tapestries.
Painted monogram.

RIX-UVENO, Felice (1893-1967)

F.R.

Designer, modeller, decorator.
Worked for *Wiener Werkstätte;
also designed glass, enamels,
textiles.
Painted initials.

SCHLEICH, Vilmos or Wilhelm (b.1881)

Hungarian sculptor, potter,
modeller. Ran ceramics studio at
*Budapest Kunstgewerbeschule
and worked for Vereinigte Wiener
und Gmundner Keramik.
Painted initials and monogram.

SCHLEISS, Franz (b.1884)

Potter, designer, decorator. With
wife E.*Simandl-Schleiss
established *Gmundner Keramik.
Also worked for Vereinigte Wiener
und Gmundner Keramik.
Painted monogram.

SIKA, Jutta (1877-1964)

Designer. Worked for *Böck,
*Wiener Werkstätte; also designed
glass, metalwork, and worked as a
fashion designer.
Painted monogram.

SIMANDL-SCHLEISS, Emilie (1880-1962)

Ɛ, S,

Potter, designer, decorator. With husband F.*Schleiss established *Gmundner Keramik. Also worked for Vereinigte Wiener und Gmundner Keramik.
Painted initials.

SINGER-SCHINNERL, Susi (1881-1965)

S.S.

Potter, designer, decorator. Worked for Marcell *Goldscheider, *Wiener Werkstätte before establishing her own pottery, Grünbacher Keramik; also designed textiles.
Painted initials.

STROBACH, Elly (fl.c.1930)

Elly Strobach

Designer, modeller. Worked for *Duxer Porzellanmanufaktur. Moulded signature.

TEPLITZ, Fachschule (est.1874)

Bohemian/Czechoslovakian pottery training school. Impressed mark.

VÁROSLÖD (est.c.1850)

VÁROSLÖD

Hungarian manufacturers. Printed mark.

VIKTORIA (est.1883)

Bohemian/Czechoslovakian manufacturers. Printed mark.

WAHLISS, Ernst (est.1897)

Retailers and manufacturers of 'Serapis-Fayence', among other wares. Designers include Karl Gallé (fl.c.1910), Karl Klaus (b.1889), E.J.*Margold (*see* German ceramics), O.*Prutscher (*see* Austrian graphics, metalwork), T.*Trethan (*see* Austrian furniture), Karl Witzmann (b.1883). Printed marks.

WIEN, Kunstgewerbeschule

School of industrial art offering instruction in pottery from c.1900. Impressed/printed marks.

WIENERBERGER WERKSTÄTTENSCHULE FÜR KERAMIK (est.1919)

Training workshops run by R.*Obsieger until 1932. Designers include F.*Barwig, H.*Bucher, Hugo Gorge (1883-1934), Ernst Lichtblau (1883-1963), Jakob Löw (1887-1935), Viktor Lurje (b.1883), Ella Max (b.1897), M.*Powolny, O.*Prutscher (*see* Austrian metalwork, graphics), Franz von Zülow (1883-1963). Impressed mark.

WIENER KERAMIK (1905-11)

Pottery established by B.*Löffler and M.*Powolny. Other designers include Fritz Dietl (b.1880), Anton Kling (1881-1963), Emil Meier

(b.1877), Ida Schwetz-Lehmann (1883-1971). Merged with *Gmundner Keramik to become Vereinigte Wiener und Gmundner Keramik.
Impressed marks.

WIENER KUNSTKERAMISCHE WERKSTÄTTEN BUSCH & LUDESCHER *see* BUSCH & LUDESCHER, Wiener Kunstkeramische Werkstätten

WIENER WERKSTÄTTE (est.1903)

(i)

(ii)

(iii)

Craft workshops and retail outlets. Pottery made from 1913. Designers/decorators include Adele Appoyer (b.1904), G.*Baudisch-Wittke, Leopold Blonder (b.1893), H.*Bucher, L.*Calm-Wierink, C.*Ehrlich (*see* Dutch metalwork), Otto Fenzl (1898-1945), M.*Flögl, Eva Frieberger (1892-1950), István Gádor (b.1891), J.*Hoffmann, Sofie Iszkowska (b.1897), Lilly Jacobsen (b.1895), H.F.*Kirsch, Rudolf Knörlein (b.1902), E.*Kopriva, Eva Kowarcz (b.1905), Dina Kuhn (b.1891), M.*Likarz-Strauss (*see* Austrian metalwork), B.*Löffler, Jakob Löw (1887-1935), Fritzi Löw-Lazar (1891-1975), Viktor Lurje (b.1883), Ella Max (b.1897), Antoni Mutter (b.1892), A.*Nechansky (*see* Austrian glass), Grete Neuwalder-Breuer (b.1898), Erna Pamberger (fl.c.1910), D.*Peche, M.*Powolny, Margarete Reinhold (b.1901), F.*Rix-Uveno, Kitty Rix-Tichacek (fl.c.1925), Ena Rottenberg (1893-1950), Reni Schaschl-Schuster (b.1895), Hans Scheibner (b.1897), Hedwig

WIENER WERKSTÄTTE (continued)

Schmidl (b.1889), Anny Schröder-Ehrenfest (1898-1972), Ida Schwetz-Lehmann (1883-1971), J.*Sika, S.*Singer-Schinnerl, Julie Sitte (1881-1959), Oskar Strnad (1879-1935), Alice Teichtner (b.1896), Trude Weinberger (b.1897), V.*Wieselthier, Gustav Zimpel (1904-57), J.*Zimpel (*see* Austrian metalwork). Workshops also produced *glass, *furniture, textiles, *metalwork, graphics. Impressed (i, ii) and incised (iii) marks.

WIESELTHIER, Vally (1895-1945)

Potter, designer, modeller, decorator. Settled in USA 1929. Worked for *Augarten, *Böck, *Gmundner Keramik, Marcell *Goldscheider, Sebring Pottery Co., *Wiener Werkstätte; also designed glass, posters, textiles, wallpapers.
Painted monogram.

WILHELMSBURGER STEINGUTFABRIK (est.1882)

Manufacturers.
Printed mark.

ZSOLNAY (est.1865)

(i)

Hungarian manufacturers. Designers/decorators include Sándor Apáti Abt (fl.1898-1908), László Beszédes (fl.c.1915), Henrik Darilek (fl.1898-1906), Lajos Mack

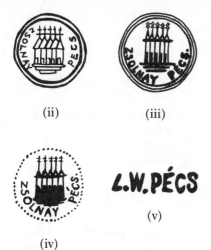

(ii)　　　　(iii)

L.W.PÉCS

(v)

(iv)

(fl.1899-1916), László
Mattayasovszky (fl.1910-35), Rezsö
Mihály (fl.c.1910), Mihály K. Nagy
(fl.c.1900), Adelbert Niemeyer
(1867-1932), Géza Nikelszky
(fl.1899-1949), Sándor Hidasi Pilló
(fl.c.1910), J.*Rippl Rónai, Táde
Sikorski (fl.1890-1910), Júlia
Sikorski-Zsolnay (fl.1880-1910),
Teréz Zsolnay (fl.c.1890), Vilmos
Zsolnay (fl.1865-1900).
Printed (i-iii), relief-moulded (iv)
and impressed (v) marks.

ITALIAN CERAMICS

ACQUAVIVA, Giovanni (1900-71)

Painter, designer. Worked for Ceramiche Artistiche Savonesi and *Mazzotti.
Painted signature.

ARTE DELLA CERAMICA FIRENZE, L' [A.D.C.F.] (1896-1907)

Pottery established in Florence by painter and potter Galileo Chini (1873-1956). Other designers/decorators include V.*Gemignani, Domenico Trentacoste (fl.c.1900). In 1904 the pottery was moved to Fontebuoni near Florence.
Painted marks.

BALLA, Giacomo (1871-1958)

Painter, designer. Worked for R.*Gatti.
Painted signature.

BUCCI, Anselmo (fl.c.1925)

Potter. Executed figures modelled by F.*Nonni.
Painted signature and mark.

CANTAGALLI, Figli di Giuseppe (est.1878)

Manufacturers.
Designers/decorators include Agostino Andrei (fl.c.1890), Luigi Cecconi (fl.c.1890), V.*Gemignani, L.*Paoletti, Adolfo Rapi (fl.c.1890).
Painted mark.

CHINI & Co. (1907-44)

Pottery established by painter and potter Galileo Chini (1873-1956). Other designers/decorators include V.*Gemignani.
Painted marks.

CIAURRO, Ilario (b.1889)

Designer, decorator. Worked for *Vascellari before establishing his own pottery and, later, *FOCAC.
Painted signature.

DAL MONTE, M.G. (b.1906)

DIS- DALMONTE

Painter, designer. Worked for R.*Gatti, M.*Ortolani.
Painted signature.

DIATO, Albert (1927-85)

Monegasque potter, designer, decorator working largely in Italy.
Incised monogram.

DOTTORI, Gerardo (1884-1977)

PIS. DOTTORI

Painter, designer. Worked for M.*Ortolani.
Painted signature.

DUSE, Mario (fl.1925-35)

MARIO
DVSE

Painter, designer. Worked for *Mazzotti.
Painted signature.

FAÏENCE, La (est.1919)

Pottery established by P.*Melandri and Paolo Zoli (fl.1920-33); made figures modelled by F.*Nonni. Painted marks.

'FARFA' (1881-1964)

Painter, designer. Real name Vittorio Osvaldo Tommasini. Worked for *Mazzotti and Maioliche Artistiche Savonesi. Painted signature.

'FILLIA' (1904-1936)

Painter, designer. Real name Luigi Colombo. Worked for *Mazzotti. Painted signature.

FOCAC [Fabbrica Orvietana delle Ceramiche Artistiche 'Ciaurro'] (1936-38)

Pottery established by I.*Ciaurro. Other designers/decorators include Angelina Suadoni (b.1905). Painted mark.

GATTI, Riccardo (1886-1972)

Potter, designer, modeller, decorator. Established his own pottery where he made ceramics designed by G.*Balla, M.G. *Dal Monte and others. Painted rebus and signature.

GAUDENZI, Alfredo (b.1908)

Painter, desginer. Worked for
*Mazzotti.
Painted signature.

GEMIGNANI, Valmore (b.1879)

Gemignani

Painter, sculptor, modeller.
Worked for L'*Arte della Ceramica
Firenze, *Cantagalli, *Chini,
*Goldscheider (*see* Austrian
ceramics).
Printed signature.

GIACOMINI, Ugo (b.1907)

Designer, decorator. Worked for
*Vascellari and independently.
Painted signature.

LENCI (est.1919)

Lenci

Craft workshops including a
ceramics studio.
Printed mark.

LUCERNI, Ugo (b.1900)

Sculptor, potter.
Incised signatures on raised
panels.

MAOLONI, Salvatore (fl.1920-30)

MAOLONI
SALVATORE

Designer, decorator. Worked for
*Vascellari.
Painted signature.

MAZZOTTI, Bottega di Giuseppe (est.1903)

Pottery established in Albisola by Giuseppe Mazzotti (b.1865) and after his death run by his sons Torido (b.1895) and Tullio, called *Tullio d'Albisola. Other designers/decorators include G.*Acquaviva, Giuseppe Mario Anselmo (b.1913), Romeo Bevilacqua (1908-58), F.*Depero (see Belgian furniture), Nicolaj Diulgheroff (b.1901), M.*Duse, *'Farfa', *'Fillia', Dino Gambetti (b.1907), A.*Gaudenzi, Bruno Munari (b.1907), U.*Pozzo, E.*Prampolini, *'Tullio d'Albisola'. Painted marks.

MELANDRI, Pietro (1885-1976)

Painter, potter, designer, modeller, decorator. Worked for La *Faïence and collaborated with F.*Nonni, Gio Ponti (b.1891) and others, and worked independently.
Painted signature and initial.

NONNI, Francesco (1885-1976)

Sculptor, modeller. Worked for A.*Bucci, La *Faïence, Società Cooperativa Ceramisti di Imola and other factories. Sometimes collaborated with P.*Melandri; also designed graphics.
Painted signature.

ORTOLANI, Mario (1901-55)

Potter, designer, decorator. Established his own pottery where he made ceramics designed by

M.G. *Dal Monte, G.*Dottori,
Remo Fabbri (1890-1977), Pippo
Rizzo (1897-1964) and others.
Painted mark.

PAOLETTI, Luigi (fl.c.1890)

Decorator. Worked for *Cantagalli.
Painted initials.

POZZO, Ugo (1900-81)

Painter, designer. Worked for
*Mazzotti.
Painted signature.

PRAMPOLINI, Enrico (1894-1956)

Painter, designer. Worked for
Mazzotti.
Painted initials.

RICHARD GINORI, Società Ceramica (est.1896)

Amalgamation of manufacturers
Giulio Richard and the Doccia
factory belonging to the Ginori
family. Designers include Giovanni
Garibaldi (b.1908), B.*Kaipiainen
(*see* Scandinavian ceramics), Gio
Ponti (b.1891).
Printed marks.

'TULLIO D'ALBISOLA' (1899-1971)

Potter, designer, modeller,
decorator. Real name Tullio
Mazzotti. Worked for family
pottery *Mazzotti.
Painted signatures.

VASCELLARI DI ORVIETO (est.1920)

(i)   (ii)

(iii)

Pottery established by Pericle Perali (1884-1949). Other designers/decorators include I.*Ciaurro, U.*Giacomini, S.*Maoloni, Leonello Solini (1905-72), Angelina Suadoni (b.1905). Painted (i, ii) and printed (iii) marks.

SCANDINAVIAN CERAMICS

ALUMINIA (est.1863)

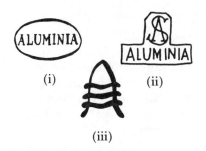

(i)

(ii)

(iii)

Danish manufacturers.
Amalgamated in 1882 with
*Copenhagen.
Designers/decorators include
J.P.*Dahl-Jensen, Christian Hans
Joachim (1870-1943), A.E.*Krog,
Harald Slott-Møller (1864-1937).
Printed (i,ii), painted (iii) marks.

ANDERSEN, Valdemar (1875-1928)

Danish painter, designer, modeller.
Worked for *Bing & Grøndahl; also
designed books and posters.
Painted monogram.

ANDERSSON & JOHANSSON (est.1910)

Swedish manufacturers. Designers
include John Andersson (fl.1924-
69), Hertha Bengtson (fl.from
1950).
Impressed mark.

ARABIA (est.1874)

Finnish manufacturers. Designers
include R.*Bryk, Kurt Ekholm
(1907-75), K.*Franck (*see*
Scandinavian glass), A.*Gallén
(*see* Scandinavian graphics), Greta-
Lisa Jäderholm-Snellman (1894-
1973), B.*Kaipiainen, Friedl
Kjellberg (b.1905), Toini Muona
(1904-87), Thure Öberg (1871-
1935), Eliel Saarinen (1873-1950),
Kyllikki Salmenhaara (1915-81).
Printed/impressed marks.

BING & GRØNDAHL (est.1853)

B&G

Danish manufacturers. Designers/decorators include V.*Andersen, Kay Bojesen (1886-1958), J.P.*Dahl-Jensen, E.*Drewes, F.*Garde, Jean Gauguin (d.1961), F.A.*Hallin, E.*Hegermann-Lindencrone, H.P.*Kofoed, Nathalie Krebs (1895-1978), Pietro Krohn (1840-1905), K.*Kyhn, Sven Lindhart (1898-c.1985), A.M.C.*Nielsen, Erik Nielsen (1857-1947), Kai Nielsen (1882-1924), Carl Petersen (1874-1923), Erik Reiff (b.1923), Ebbe Sadolin (b.1900), A.*Salto, Gertrud Vasegaard (b.1913), Myre Vasegaard (b.1936), Jens Ferdinand Willumsen (1863-1958). Printed mark.

BOBERG (est.1874)

(i)   (ii)

Swedish manufacturers. Designers include Gabriel Burmeister (fl.1920-50), Ewald Dahlskog (1894-1950), Allan Ebeling (fl.c.1925), Maud Fredin-Fredholm (fl.c.1950). Impressed (i), painted (ii) marks.

BØGELUND, Gerd (b.1923)

Danish potter, designer, decorator. Worked for *Copenhagen, and with Nathalie Krebs (1895-1978). Painted initials.

BRYK, Rut (b.1916)

BRYK

Swedish designer/decorator working in Finland. Worked for *Arabia, *Rosenthal (see German ceramics); also designed textiles. Painted signature.

COPENHAGEN, Royal, Porcelain Factory, (est.1775)

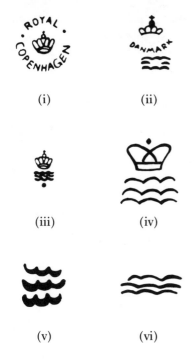

(i) (ii)

(iii) (iv)

(v) (vi)

Danish manufacturers.
Amalgamated in 1882 with
*Aluminia. Designers/decorators
include G.*Bøgelund, Elizabet
Castenschiold (1895-1986),
V.*Engelhardt, Vilhelm Theodor
Fischer (1857-1928), L.*Gaillard,
C.*Halier, F.A.*Hallin,
S.*Hammershøj, K.F.C.*Hansen-
Reistrup, G.*Heilmann, Gerhard
Henning (1880-1967), M.*Høst,
Oluf Jensen (1871-1934), Christian
Hans Joachim (1870-1943),
A.E.*Krog, K.*Kyhn, K.*Lange,
C.F.*Liisberg, F.*Ludvigsen,
Theodor Lundberg (1852-1926),
T.C.*Madsen, Arno Malinowski
(1899-1976), Olaf Mathiesen (1878-
1923), J.S.*Meyer, B.*Nathanielsen,
Erik Nielsen (1857-1947),
J.*Nielsen, P.*Nordström,
T.*Olsen, J.*Oppermann, Emil
Orth (1833-1919), G.A.A.*Rode,
A.*Salto, E.*Staehr-Nielsen,
C.*Thomsen, N.*Thorsson, Georg
Thylstrup (1884-1930), Nicolai
Tidemand (1888-1975), S.*Ussing.
Printed (i-iv), painted (v-vi) marks.

DAHL-JENSEN, Jens P. (b.1874)

Danish sculptor, modeller. Worked
for *Bing & Grøndahl and Norden
before setting up his own factory in
1925.
Printed mark.

DREWES, Elisabeth (b.1877)

Danish designer, decorator.
Worked for *Bing & Grøndahl.
Painted signature.

197

EKBERG, Josef (1877-1945)

Ekberg

Swedish painter, designer. Worked for *Gustavsberg.
Painted signature.

ENGELHARDT, Valdemar (1860-1915)

VE

Danish potter, designer. Worked for *Copenhagen.
Painted monogram.

ERIKSSON, Algot (1868-1930)

AE

Swedish designer, decorator. Worked for *Rörstrand.
Painted initials.

FINCH, A. *see* Belgian ceramics.

FORSETH, Einar (1892-1988)

FORSETH

Swedish designer. Worked for *Lidköping, *Rörstrand, *Upsala-Ekeby; also designed stained glass, mosaics.
Printed mark.

GABRIEL-VERKEN (est.1925)

Swedish pottery run by Gabriel Burmeister (fl.1920-50).
Painted mark.

GAILLARD, Lucien (b.1861)

French designer. Worked for *Copenhagen; also made *metalwork (*see* French metalwork), jewellery, enamels.
Printed initials.

GARDE, Fannie (1855-1928)

Danish designer, decorator.
Worked for *Bing & Grøndahl.
Painted signature.

GEFLE PORSLINSFABRIK (est.1913)

Swedish manufacturers. Designers
include A.*Percy.
Painted mark.

GÖTEBORGS PORSLINSFABRIK (est.1898)

GÖTEBORG   GÖTEBORG
   (i)   (ii)

Swedish manufacturers.
Impressed (i), printed (ii) marks.

GUSTAVSBERG (est.1825)

(i)

(ii)   (iii)

GUSTAVSBERG
(iv)

Swedish manufacturers. Designers
include Karin Björquist (b.1927),
Ferdinand Boberg (1860-1946),
Bibi Breger (b.1927), J.*Ekberg,
Berndt Friberg (1899-1981),
W.*Kåge, S.*Lindberg, August
Malmstrøm (1829-1901),
M.*Simmulson, Gunnar
Wennerberg (1863-1914).
Painted (i-iv), printed (v) marks.

(v)

HALD, Edward (1883-1980)

Hald

Swedish designer. Worked for
*Karlskrona, *Rörstrand; also
designed *glass.
Printed mark.

HALIER, Carl (1873-1948)

)€(.

German-born designer, modeller
(Danish citizen from 1915).
Worked for *Copenhagen.
Painted monogram.

HALLIN, F. August (1865-1947)

JAK

Swedish designer, decorator
working in Denmark for *Bing &
Grøndahl, *Copenhagen; also
designed books.
Painted initials.

HAMMERSHØJ, Sven (1873-1948)

S B

Danish painter, designer, decorator.
Worked for *Bing & Grøndahl,
*Copenhagen, *Kähler; also
designed silver and bookbindings.
Painted initials.

HANSEN-REISTRUP, Karl Frederik Christian (1863-1929)

KHR

Danish painter, sculptor, designer,
ceramic decorator. Worked for
*Copenhagen, *Kähler.
Painted initials.

HEGERMANN-LINDENCRONE, Effie (1860-1945)

E Hegermann-Lindencrone   44

Danish designer, decorator.
Worked for *Bing & Grøndahl.
Painted signature and monogram.

HEILMANN, Gerhard (1859-1946)

GHeilmann

Danish designer, decorator.
Worked for *Copenhagen; also
designed and illustrated books.
Painted signature.

HJORTH (est.1859)

Danish pottery run by successive generations of Hjorth family. Impressed mark.

HÖGANÄS-BILLESHOLMS (1903-26)

HÖGANAS
(i)

(ii)

Swedish manufacturers. Designers/decorators include Edgar Böckman (1890-1960), Berndt Friberg (1899-1981), M.*Kardell. Impressed (i) and printed (ii) marks.

HØST, Marianne (1865-1943)

MHost

Danish designer, decorator. Worked for *Copenhagen, *Meissen (see German ceramics). Painted signature.

IPSENS ENKE, P. (fl.20th century)

Danish manufacturer. Output includes figures modelled by Georg Thylstrup (1884-1930). Printed mark.

IRIS WORKSHOPS (1899-1902)

IRIS

Craft workshops in Finland including a pottery directed by A.*Finch (see Belgian ceramics). Incised mark.

KÅGE, Wilhelm (1889-1960)

KÀGE
(i)

(ii)

Swedish painter, designer, decorator. Worked for *Gustavsberg. Painted (i) and printed (ii) signatures.

KÄHLER KERAMIK (est.1839)

Danish pottery. Designers include Thorvald Bindesbøll (1846-1908), O.*Eckmann (*see* German graphics), S.*Hammershøj, K.F.C.*Hansen-Reistrup, Hermann August Kähler (1846-1917), Herman J. Kähler (b.1904), Nils A. Kähler (b.1906), Sten Lykke Madsen (b.1937), T.*Madsen, Erik Nielsen (1857-1947), Jens Thirslund (1897-1942). Incised mark.

KAIPIAINEN, Birger (1915-88)

Finnish designer, decorator. Worked for *Arabia, *Richard Ginori (*see* Italian ceramics), *Rörstrand. Painted signature.

KARDELL, Maria (fl.c.1915)

Swedish designer, decorator. Worked for *Höganäs. Painted signature.

KARLSKRONA PORSLINSFABRIK (est.1918)

Swedish manufacturers. Designers include Eva Bladh (fl.c.1955), Walter Garstecki (fl.1930-60), E.*Hald, V.*Lindstrand (*see* Scandinavian glass), A.C.*Percy, M.*Simmulson, Sven-Erik Skawonius (1908-81). Printed marks.

KOFOED, Hans Peter (1868-1908)

Danish painter, designer, decorator. Worked for *Bing & Grøndahl. Painted signature.

KROG, Arnold Emil (1856-1931)

Danish designer, decorator.
Worked for *Aluminia,
*Copenhagen.
Painted monogram.

KYHN, Knud (1880-1969)

Danish sculptor, modeller. Worked
for *Bing & Grøndahl,
*Copenhagen, *Kähler.
Painted monogram.

LANGE, Kaj (b.1905)

Danish designer, decorator.
Worked for *Copenhagen.
Painted monogram.

LIDKÖPINGS PORSLINSFABRIK (est.1911)

Swedish manufacturers. Designers
include E.*Forseth, Knut Hallgren
(fl.c.1925).
Printed mark.

LIISBERG, Carl Frederik (1860-1909)

Danish painter, sculptor, designer,
modeller, decorator. Worked for
*Copenhagen.
Painted signature.

LINDBERG, Stig (1919-82)

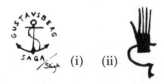 (i)   (ii)

Swedish designer. Worked for
*Gustavsberg and independently;
also designed textiles.
Printed (i) and painted (ii) marks.

LINDSTRÖM, Karl (1865-1936)

Swedish designer, modeller, decorator. Worked for *Rörstrand. Painted initials.

LINDSTRÖM, Waldemar (fl.1890-1940)

W. L.

Swedish designer, decorator. Worked for *Rörstrand. Incised initials.

LUDVIGSEN, Frederik (1883-1958)

I

Danish potter. Worked for *Copenhagen and independently. Painted monogram.

MADSEN, Theodor Christian (1880-1965)

M̄

Danish sculptor, modeller. Worked for *Copenhagen, *Kähler. Painted monogram.

MEYER, Jenny Sofie (1866-1927)

Danish designer, decorator. Worked for *Copenhagen. Painted signature.

NATHANIELSEN, Bertha (1869-1914)

BNathaniel

Danish designer, decorator. Worked for *Copenhagen. Painted signature.

NIELSEN, Anna Marie Carl (b.1863)

AMC- n

Danish sculptor, modeller. Worked for *Bing & Grøndahl. Painted initials.

NIELSEN, Jais (1885-1961)

Danish designer, modeller.
Worked for *Copenhagen and
independently.
Painted mark.

NITTSJÖ LERKÄRLSFABRIK (est.1847)

Swedish manufacturers. Designers
include Edgar Böckman (1890-
1960), Erik Mornils (fl.1925-67).
Impressed mark.

NORDSTRÖM, Patrick (1870-1929)

Swedish potter, designer working
in Denmark for *Copenhagen and
independently.
Painted monogram.

OLSEN, Thorkild (1890-1973)

Danish designer, decorator.
Worked for *Copenhagen.
Painted monogram.

OPPERMANN, Johannes (1860-1939)

Danish designer, decorator.
Worked for *Copenhagen.
Painted signature.

PERCY, Arthur Carlsson (1886-1976)

PERCY

Swedish designer. Worked for
*Gefle, *Karlskrona; also designed
glass, textiles.
Printed mark.

PORSGRUNDS PORSELAENSFABRIK (est. 1886)

Norwegian manufacturers. Designers include Henrik Bull (1864-1953), Tias Eckhoff (b.1926), Hans Flygenring (1881-1958), Konrad Galaaen (b.1923), Nora Gulbrandsen (1894-1978), Thorolf Holmboe (1866-1935), G.P.*Munthe (*see* Scandinavian graphics, textiles), Eystein Sandnes (b.1924). Printed mark.

RODE, Gotfred Andrew Andersen (1862-1937)

Danish designer, decorator. Worked for *Copenhagen. Painted monogram.

RÖRSTRANDS PORSLINSFABRIK (est. 1726)

Swedish manufacturers. Designers/decorators include Louise Adelborg (fl.1920-60), Hertha Bengtson (fl.from 1950), A.*Eriksson, E.*Hald, B.*Kaipiainen, K.*Lindström, W.*Lindström, Tyra Lundgren (fl.1930-50), Gunnar Nylund (b.1904), C.-H.*Stålhane, A.*Wallander (*see* Scandinavian furniture), Marianne Westman (b.1925). Printed/impressed mark.

SALTO, Axel (1889-1961)

Danish painter, potter, designer. Worked for *Bing & Grøndahl, *Copenhagen, and collaborated with Nathalie Krebs (1895-1978);

also designed textiles and
illustrated books.
Printed signature.

SIMMULSON, Mari (b.1911)

Estonian designer working in
Sweden. Worked for *Gustavsberg,
*Upsala-Ekeby; also designed
textiles.
Impressed monogram.

STAEHR-NIELSEN, Eva (1911-76)

Danish potter, designer.
Collaborated with Nathalie Krebs
(1895-1978) and worked for
*Copenhagen.
Painted initials.

STÅLHANE, Carl-Harry (b.1920)

Swedish potter, designer,
decorator. Worked for *Rörstrand
before establishing his own pottery.
Incised signature.

S:T ERIKS LERVARUFABRIK (est.1888)

Swedish manufacturers. Designers
include Gertrud Lönegren
(fl.c.1935), Edvin Ollers
(1888-1959), Anna-Lisa Thomson
(fl.c.1930).
Impressed mark.

THOMSEN, Christian (1860-1921)

Sculptor, modeller. Worked for
*Copenhagen.
Painted monogram.

THORSSON, Nils (1898-1982)

Danish designer, decorator.
Worked for *Copenhagen; also
designed silver.
Painted monogram.

TÖRNGRENS KRUKMAKERI (est.1789)

Törngren

Swedish pottery run by successive
generations of Törngren family.
Incised mark.

UPSALA-EKEBY (est.1886)

EKEBY

(i)

(ii)

Swedish manufacturers. Designers
include Ingrid Atterberg
(fl.c.1950), Kjell Blomberg
(fl.c.1955), Gabriel Burmeister
(fl.1920-50), Allan Ebeling
(fl.c.1925), E.*Forseth,
V.*Lindstrand (see Scandinavian
glass), Lillemor Mannerheim
(fl.c.1955), Edvin Ollers
(1888-1959), Harald Östergren
(fl.1925-45), M.*Simmulson,
Sven-Erik Skawonius (1908-81).
Impressed (i) and printed (ii)
marks.

USSING, Stefan (fl.1894-1930)

St. Ussing

Danish designer, decorator.
Worked for *Copenhagen.
Painted signature.

WALLÅKRA STENKÄRLSFABRIK (est.1864)

WALLÅKRA

Swedish manufacturers.
Impressed mark.

BRITISH GLASS

COTTIER & CO. (1870-1907)

Cottier & Co

Firm of interior decorators with branches in Britain, the USA (est.1873) and Australia (est.1873), which produced stained glass. Designers included Daniel Cottier (1838-91). Also produced ceramic tiles, furniture.
Painted mark.

COUPER, James, & Sons (fl.1860-1900)

Manufacturers of 'Clutha' glass designed by C.*Dresser, George Walton (1867-1933).
Etched mark incorporating C.*Dresser's initials and the lotus mark of *Liberty.

DRESSER, Christopher (1834-1904)

Designer. Designed 'Clutha' glass for *Couper; also designed *ceramics, *metalwork, furniture, textiles, carpets, wallpapers.
Etched initials incorporated in *Couper mark.

EDINBURGH & LEITH FLINT GLASS WORKS
(fl. 20th century)

Manufacturers. Designers include H.*Monro, A.E. Morris (fl.c.1935), V. Trainer (fl.c.1935).
Etched marks.

FARQUHARSON, W. Clyne (1906-72)

Designer. Worked for *Stevens &
Williams, *Walsh.
Etched signature.

HARBRIDGE CRYSTAL GLASS CO. (1928-57)

Manufacturers.
Etched marks.

LIBERTY & CO. (est.1875)

London retailers. Sold glass
manufactured by G.*Argy-
Rousseau (*see* French glass),
*Couper, *Loetz (*see* Austrian
glass), *Moncrieff, James Powell &
Sons, among others; also retailed
*ceramics, *metalwork, jewellery,
*furniture, carpets, textiles.
Etched lotus mark incorporated in
*Couper mark.

MONCRIEFF, John (est.1965)

Manufacturers of 'Monart' glass,
designed by Isabel Moncrieff (1874-
1961), Salvador Ysart (1878-1955).
Paper labels and etched mark.

MONRO, Helen (b.1901)

Designer, decorator. Worked for
*Edinburgh & Leith and founded
Juniper Workshop in 1956.
Engraved signature.

MURRAY, Keith (1892-1981)

Architect, designer. Worked for
*Stevens & Williams; also designed
ceramics.
Etched signature

NASH, Paul (1889-1946)

Painter, designer. Worked for
*Stuart; also designed *ceramics,
textiles, carpets, posters, books.
Etched signature.

REDGRAVE, Richard (1804-88)

Painter, designer. Worked for
*Summerly's Art Manufactures;
also designed ceramics.
Etched signature.

RICHARDSON & SONS (est.c.1830)

Manufacturers. Designers include
Henry Cole (1808-82), John
Northwood I (1836-1902),
R.*Redgrave.
Printed mark.

ROSENKRANTZ, Arild (b.1870)

Arild
Rosen krantz

Danish painter, designer working
in Britain from 1899. Designed
stained glass for Lowndes & Drury,
*Tiffany (*see* American glass).
Painted signature.

STEVENS & WILLIAMS (est.1847)

ROYAL
BRIERLEY
ENGLAND

Manufacturers. Designers include
C.*Boyton (*see* British metalwork),
F.*Carder (*see* American glass),
W.C.*Farquharson, James Hill
(1850-1928), Joshua Hodgetts
(1857-1933), Deanne Meanley
(fl.c.1950), K.*Murray, John
Northwood I (1836-1902), John
Northwood II (1857-1907),
G.*Russell (*see* British furniture),
John William Wadsworth
(1879-1955), R.S. Williams-Thomas
(fl.c.1935).
Etched marks.

STOURBRIDGE GLASS CO., The (est.1922)

Manufacturers of 'Tudor' glass. Designers include Jack Lloyd (1879-1975). Etched marks.

STUART & SONS (fl.20th century)

Stuart

Stuart
ENGLAND

Stuart
ENGLAND

Stuart

Manufaturers. Designers include G.*Forsyth (*see* British ceramics), L.*Knight (*see* British ceramics), Ludvig Kny (fl.1900-40), John Luxton (fl.c.1955), P.*Nash, D.*Procter (*see* British ceramics), E.*Procter (*see* British ceramics), E.W.*Ravilious (*see* British ceramics), G.V.*Sutherland (*see* British ceramics). Etched marks.

SUMMERLY'S ART MANUFACTURES (est.1847)

Group of designers including Henry Cole (1808-82), a.k.a. Felix Summerly, R.*Redgrave. Designs manufactured by I.F. Christy, *Richardson and other glass houses; also designed ceramics, metalwork, jewellery, furniture. Etched mark.

WALSH, John Walsh (1851-1951)

WALSH

WALSH
ENGLAND

Manufacturers. Designers included W.C.*Farquharson, Walter Gilbert (fl.c.1930). Etched marks.

WEBB, Thomas, & Sons (est.1837)

Manufacturers. Designers include Anna Fogelberg (fl.c.1935), Homery Folkes (b.1906), David Hammond (fl.c.1950), Samuel Johnson (fl.1900-30), Ludvig Kny (fl.1900-40), John Northwood I (1836-1902), Daniel Pearce (1817-1907), Thomas F. Pitchford (b.c.1912), G.*Woodall, Thomas Woodall (1849-1926).
Etched marks.

WEBB, Thomas, & Corbett (fl. from mid 19th century)

Manufacturers. Designers include Albert E. Oakden (fl.c.1935), Irene M. Stevens (fl.c.1950), Herbert Webb (fl.c.1930).
Stamped/etched marks.

WHISTLER, Laurence (b.1912)

LW 1960

Designer, decorator.
Engraved initials.

WOODALL, George (1850-1925)

G. Woodall

Designer, decorator. Worked for *Webb & Sons.
Engraved signature.

AMERICAN GLASS

CARDER, Frederick C. (1863-1963)

ℱ Carder

English glassmaker, designer, decorator. Worked for *Stevens & Williams in England before moving in 1903 to the USA where he co-founded *Steuben Glassworks.
Engraved signature.

DREHOBL BROS. ART GLASS CO. (est.1919)

DREHOBL Bros

Manufacturers of stained glass. Designers include M.*Guler, Peter Kugel (fl.c.1920), Herman Schulze (fl.c.1920).
Painted mark.

ECKHARDT, Edris (b.1907)

Edris Eckhardt

Sculptor, glassmaker, designer, modeller, decorator; also modelled ceramic figures.
Painted signature.

FOSTORIA GLASS SPECIALTY CO. (1899-1917)

.IRIS.
FOSTORIA,O

Manufacturers.
Paper label.

GULER, Max (fl.1900-35)

Stained glass designer, decorator. Worked for *Drehobl, The *Munich Studio (co-founder).
Painted initials.

HANDEL & CO. (1893-1941)

Decorators.
Painted/stencilled mark.

HAVILAND & CO. (fl.19th and 20th century)

Importers and retailers; also
imported and retailed ceramics.
Printed mark.

HEATON, Maurice (b.1900)

M.H.

Glassmaker, designer, decorator.
Worked for American Designers'
Gallery, Lightolier and
independently.
Etched initials.

IMPERIAL GLASS CO. (est.1901)

Manufacturers.
Impressed marks.

LABINO, Dominick (1910-87)

Labino

Glassmaker, designer, decorator.
Etched signature.

LINDEN GLASS CO. (c.1888-1909)
LINDEN CO., The (1910-34)

LINDEN C°

Manufacturers. Produced stained
glass after designs by Frank Lloyd
Wright (1867-1956), George
Washington Maher (1864-1926)
and others.
Painted mark.

LITTLETON, Harvey K. (b.1922)

Glassmaker, designer, decorator.
Engraved signature.

MUNICH STUDIO, The (1903-32)

Stained glass studio. Designers
included M.*Guler (co-founder),
Peter Kugel (fl.c.1920), Herman
Schulze (fl.c.1920).
Painted mark.

PITKIN & BROOKS (1871-c.1923)

Manufacturers.
Engraved mark.

QUEZAL ART GLASS AND DECORATING CO. (1901-25)

Manufacturers.
Etched/engraved mark.

SMITH BROTHERS (1877-99)

Decorators.
Painted mark.

STEUBEN GLASSWORKS (est.1903)

Manufacturers. Produced a wide
range of glassware including
'Aurene' and 'Calcite'. Designers
included Thomas Benton
(1889-1975), Christian Bérard
(1909-49), F.C.*Carder
(co-founder), J.*Cocteau (*see*
French ceramics), Salvador Dali
(1904-90), Jacob Epstein
(1880-1959), John Monteith Gates

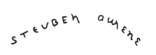

(fl.c.1935), Eric Gill (1882-1940), Marie Laurencin (1885-1956), Aristide Maillol (1861-1944), Paul Manship (b.1885), H.*Matisse (*see* French ceramics), Bruce Moore (b.1905), John Nash (1893-1977), Isamu Noguchi (b.1904), Georgia O'Keefe (b.1887), John Piper (b.1903), G.V.*Sutherland (*see* British ceramics), Walter Dorwin Teague (1883-1960), Sidney Biehler Waugh (1904-63). Printed (i, ii), etched (iii) and engraved (iv) marks.

TIFFANY, Louis Comfort (1848-1933)

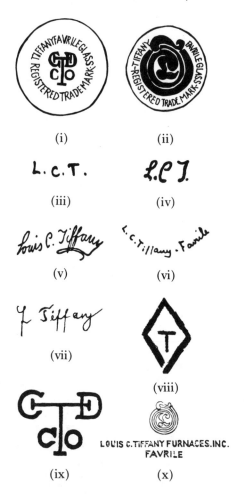

(i) (ii)

(iii) (iv)

(v) (vi)

(vii)

(viii)

(ix) (x)

Glassmaker, designer. Founded Tiffany Glass Co. (1886), Tiffany Glass & Decorating Co. (1892) and Stourbridge Glass Co. (1893), which became Tiffany Furnaces in 1902. Most glass made to designs by L.C.*Tiffany himself. Stained glass made to designs by Pierre Bonnard (1867-1942), F.*Brangwyn (*see* British graphics), E.S.*Grasset (*see* French graphics), H.*Ibels (*see* French graphics), Paul-Elie Ranson (1864-1909), A.*Rosenkrantz (*see* British glass), Ker-Xavier Roussel (1877-1944), Paul Sérusier (1863-1927), H. de *Toulouse-Lautrec (*see* French graphics), F.*Vallotton (see French graphics), Edouard Vuillard (1868-1940) among others. Lampshades made to designs by Clara Driscoll (fl.c.1900) and Tiffany himself; also designed ceramics, metalwork, jewellery, textiles, wallpapers. Paper labels/etched marks (i, ii), painted initials (iii, iv) and signatures (v-vii), engraved/painted initial (viii) and etched (ix, x) marks.

UNION GLASS CO. (1851-1924)

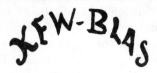

Manufacturers of art glass called 'Kew-Blas', an anagram of W.S. Blake (fl.c.1900), the factory superintendent.
Engraved mark.

WESTERN SAND BLAST MANUFACTURING CO. (est.1876)

WESTERN SAND BLAST CO. CHICAGO.

Manufacturers. Executed designs by Edgar Miller (b.1901), Louis Henry Sullivan (1856-1924) and others.
Sand-blasted mark.

FRENCH GLASS

ANDELYS, Verrerie d' (c.1933-55)

Verlys
France

Manufacturer. Made line of art glass called 'Verlys'.

ARGY-ROUSSEAU, Gabriel (1885-1953)

G. A-R.   G.ARGY-ROUSSEAU

Glassmaker, designer, decorator. Made figures modelled by Marcel Bouraine (fl.c.1925). Enamelled initials, moulded signature.

ARSALE (fl.1900-10)

drsale   *Arsale*

Probably a decorating studio. Relief-etched marks.

AVESN, Pierre d' (fl.1910-35)

P D'AVESN

FRANCE

Glassmaker, designer. Worked for Cristallerie de Choisi-le-Roi, *Daum, *Lorrain. Moulded signature.

BACCARAT (est.1764)

Manufacturers. Designers include H.P.*Berlage (*see* Dutch glass), Georges Chevalier (b.1894). Etched/impressed mark.

BADORD, Jacqueline (b.1917)

BADORD

Glassmaker, designer, decorator. Signature.

BERGÉ, Henri (1968-1936)

Designer, modeller, decorator.
Worked for *Daum, A.V.*Walter.
Moulded signature.

BRATEAU, Jules-Paul (1844-1923)

Glassmaker, designer, decorator;
also designed metalwork, jewellery,
enamels.
Gold-foil mark.

BROCARD, Philippe-Joseph (d.1896)

Glassmaker, designer, decorator.
From 1884, worked with his son
Émile.
Enamelled mark.

BURGUN, SCHVERER & CIE (est.1711)

Manufacturers.
Designers/decorators include
Armand Christian (1874-1953),
D.*Christian, François Christian
(fl.c.1900), Georg Frankenhausen
(fl.c.1900), Eugène Kremer (1867-
1941), Joseph Stenger (fl.c.1900).
Produced glassware for E.*Gallé.
Etched and printed marks.

CAMOT, Eugène (fl.1900-20)

Glassmaker, designer, decorator.
Relief-etched signature.

CARANZA, Amédée de (fl.1870-1906)

Glassmaker, designer, decorator.
Collaborated with Jeanne Duc
(fl.c.1900), worked independently
and for *Copillet; also designed
*ceramics.
Painted signatures.

CAYETTE, Jules (b.1882)

⊃ Cayette

Designer. Worked for A.V.*Walter; also designed ceramics, furniture. Moulded signature.

CHRISTIAN, Désirée (1846-1907)

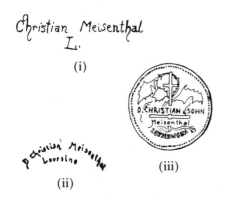

Christian Meisenthal
L.
(i)

(iii)

Christian Meisenthal
Lorraine
(ii)

Glassmaker, designer, decorator. Worked for *Burgun, Schverer, E.*Gallé, *Vallérysthal et Portieux. In 1903 set up his own workshop where he employed his brother François (fl.c.1900) and son Armand (1874-1953). Engraved signatures (i-ii) and mark (iii).

COLOTTE, Aristide (1885-1959)

Designer, decorator. Worked for Cristalleries de Nancy before establishing his own workshop. Engraved/etched signature.

COPILLET, H.A., & Cie (1903-06)

Manufacturers. Designers include A. de *Caranza, E. de* Neuville. Taken over by *Lhomme Lefèvre. Stencilled marks.

CROS, Henri (1840-1907)

H. CRoss

Sculptor, glassmaker, designer, modeller, decorator; also made ceramics. Moulded signature.

DAMMOUSE, Albert-Louis (1848-1926)

Glassmaker, designer, decorator. Made some pieces designed by brother E.A.*Dammouse (*see* French ceramics); also made *ceramics.
Moulded mark

DAMON, Louis (d.1947)

Designer, decorator; also decorated ceramics.
Engraved signatures.

DAUM FRÈRES (est.1879)

Manufacturers.
Designers/decorators include P. d'*Avesn, H.*Bergé, Eugène Dammann (fl.c.1900), Antonin Daum (1864-1931), Jean Daum (1885-1916), Michel Daum (b.1900), Paul Daum (1888-1944), J.*Gruber, V.*Prouvé (*see* French ceramics), Charles Schneider (1881-1953), Gustave Toussaint (fl.c.1900), A.V.*Walter, Sévère Winckler (fl.c.1900), Émile Wirtz (fl.c.1900).
Etched, relief-etched, gilt and engraved marks.

DÉCORCHEMONT, François-Émile (1880-1971)

Painter, glassmaker, designer, decorator; also made *ceramics.
Moulded signature.

DEGUÉ, Verrerie d'Art (est.1926)

Manufacturers founded by David Guéron (fl.1925-40). Designers include E.*Cazaux (*see* French ceramics).
Etched or relief-etched marks.

DELATTE, André (est.1921)

Manufacturers founded by designer, decorator André Delatte (b.1887). Etched/relief-etched marks.

DESCOMPS, Jean-Bernard (fl.c.1925)

Sculptor, modeller. Worked for A.V.*Walter.
Moulded signature.

DESPRET, Georges (1862-1952)

Despret

Belgian glassmaker and designer working in France. Made pieces modelled by A.*Charpentier (*see* French metalwork), Jean Goujon (fl.c.1910), P. *Le Faguays (*see* French ceramics), Georges Nicollet (fl.c.1910), Y.*Serruys, Charles Troché (fl.c.1910) and others. Engraved signature.

DIEUPART, Henri-German-Étienne (b.1888)

DIEUPART

Sculptor, designer. Worked for *Simonet Frères.
Moulded signature.

DUMOULIN, Georges (1882-1959)

y DUMOULIN

Glassmaker, designer; also made ceramics, enamels.
Engraved signature.

ETLING (fl.c.1925)

ETLING **FRANCE**

Retailers. Commissioned designs for glass from Georges Béal (b.1884), Geneviève Granger (b.1877, Jean-Théodore Delabassé (b.1902), Géza Hiez (fl.c.1925), Lucille Sévin (fl.c.1925); also commissioned *ceramics, *metalwork.
Moulded mark.

FEURE, Georges de (1868-1949)

(i)

(ii)

Painter, designer. Worked for Fauchon and other firms; also designed *ceramics, posters (*see* French graphics), furniture, carpets, textiles.
Moulded (i) and etched (ii) signatures.

FINOT, Alfred (1876-1947)

Sculptor, modeller. Worked for A.V.*Walter.
Moulded signature.

GALLÉ, Émile (1846-1904)

Manufacturer, designer, decorator. Designed much of his firm's output himself. Other designers/decorators include D.*Christian, A.*Herbst (*see* French furniture), Louis Hestaux (fl.c.1900), Paul Holderbach (fl.c.1900), V.*Prouvé (*see* French ceramics); also produced *ceramics, *furniture.
Etched, relief-etched, engraved and enamelled signatures.

GALLÉ, Émile (continued)

GOUPY, Marcel (1886-1954)

Glassmaker, designer, decorator. Many of his designs were executed by A.-C.*Heiligenstein; also designed *ceramics. Enamelled signature.

GRUBER, Jacques (1870-1936)

Designer, decorator. Worked for *Daum before establishing his own workshop making coloured glass panels; also designed *ceramics, bookbinding, furniture. Relief-etched signatures ('Géef = GF, for 'Gruber fecit'; 'Géer' = GR, first 2 letters of 'Gruber').

HEILIGENSTEIN, Auguste-Claude (1891-1976)

Designer, decorator. Worked for M.*Goupy, *Legras and independently; also designed ceramics, posters. Engraved signature.

HUNEBELLE, André (fl.1920-40)

Manufacturer, designer.
Moulded signature.

JEAN, Auguste (fl.c.1880)

Glassmaker, designer, decorator;
also made ceramics.
Moulded signature on applied pad.

LALIQUE, René (1860-1945)

Glassmaker, manufacturer,
designer, modeller, decorator.
Early pieces manufactured by
Saint-Gobain and *Legras.
Established his own glass house in
1908. After his death, firm run by
his son Marc (1900-77); also made
jewellery (*see* French metalwork)
and designed bookbindings.
Engraved, etched and moulded
marks.

LEGENDRE, Maurice (b.1928)

Glassmaker, designer, decorator.
Enamelled signature.

LEGRAS & CIE (est.1864)

(†)

Manufacturers.
Designers/decorators include
A.-C.*Heiligenstein.
Etched (†) and gilt marks.

LÉVEILLÉ, Ernest-Baptiste (fl.1870-1905)

E. Léveille

Designer, decorator. Worked for E.F.*Rousseau whose shop and studio he bought in 1885. Designers/decorators working for him included E.*Michel, A.-G.*Reyen.
Engraved signature.

LHOMME LEFÈVRE (est.1906)

LʰᵒᴹᴹE LE FEVRE

Manufacturers. Took over *Copillet.
Stencilled mark.

LORRAIN, Verreries d'Art (1927-32)

Lorrain

Manufacturers, subsidiary of *Daum. Designers include P. d'*Avesn.
Impressed mark.

LUCE, Jean (1895-1964)

Designer; also designed *ceramics.
Engraved/enamelled monogram.

MABUT, Jules (fl.1890-1909)

Paris retailers, decorators; glass workshop called Verrerie de la Paix. Designers/decorators include H.A.L.*Laurent-Desrousseaux (*see* French ceramics).
Etched mark.

MARINOT, Maurice (1882-1960)

m. marinot

Painter, glassmaker, designer, decorator.
Engraved signature.

MICHEL, Eugène (fl.1867-1910)

E Michel

Glassmaker, designer, decorator.
Worked for E.-B.*Léveillé,
E.F.*Rousseau before establishing
his own workshop.
Engraved signature.

MULLER FRÈRES (c.1895-c.1936)

(i)

(ii)

(iii)

(iv)

(v)

(vi)

(vii)

Manufacturers. From 1906 to 1907,
Désiré Muller (fl.1885-1925) and
Henri Muller (fl.1885-1925)
worked for *Val St Lambert (*see*
Belgian glass).
Engraved (i, ii, iii), etched (iv),
relief-etched (v) and enamelled
(vi) marks.

NAVARRE, Henri (1885-1971)

H.NAVARRE

Sculptor, glassmaker, designer,
modeller, decorator.
Engraved signature.

NEUVILLE, Edouard de (fl.c.1905)

E. de Neuville

Designer, decorator. Worked for
H.*Copillet.
Painted signature.

NICOLAS, Paul (1875-1952)

Glassmaker, designer, decorator.
Worked for E.*Gallé, *Saint-Louis
before establishing his own
workshop.
Engraved signature.

NOVERDY, Jean (fl.c.1925)

Glassmaker, designer, decorator.
Etched/relief-etched signature.

PANTIN, Cristallerie de (est.1855)

Glasshouse operated from c.1895
by manufacturers Stumpf, Touvier,
Viollot & Cie. Designers/decorators
include H.P.*Berlage (*see* Dutch
glass) C.T. de *Varreux.
Etched mark.

RASPILLER, G. (fl.c.1910)

Designer, decorator.
Relief-etched signature.

REYEN, Alphonse-Georges (fl.1875-1905)

Designer, decorator. Worked for
E.-B.*Léveillé, E.F.*Rousseau
before establishing his own
workshop.
Engraved signature.

RICHARD (fl.c.1905)

Probably a decorating studio.
Relief-etched mark.

ROUSSEAU, Eugène François (1827-91)

Retailer, designer, decorator.
Established a workshop where
E.-B.*Léveillé, E.*Michel,
A.*Reyen and others worked. Sold
business to Léveillé in 1885; also
designed, decorated and retailed
*ceramics.
Engraved signature.

SABINO, Marius Ernest (b.1878)

Sabino
France —.   **SABINO**
          PARIS

Italian manufacturer and designer working in France from c.1900. Moulded marks.

SAINT-LOUIS (est.1829)

d'Argental

Manufacturers. Designers/decorators include M.*Dufrène (*see* French ceramics), M.*Goupy, P.*Nicolas, J.*Sala. Relief-etched marks.

SALA, Jean (1895-1976)

J. Sala

Glassmaker, designer, decorator. Worked for *Saint-Louis and independently. Cast sculptures by Antoine Bourdelle (1861-1929) in glass, and made lamps in collaboration with E.-M.*Sandoz (*see* French ceramics). Engraved signature.

SANTINI, Paolo (b.1929)

Santini

Italian sculptor, glassmaker, working in France. Signature.

SCHNEIDER, Verrerie (1913-81)

Schneider   *Schneider*
(i)   (ii)
Le Verre Français
(iii)

Manufacturers. Output included a line called alternatively 'Le Verre Français' or 'Charder' (contraction of 'Charles Schneider'). Designers/decorators include Charles Schneider (1881-1953), Robert Henri Schneider (b.1917).

230

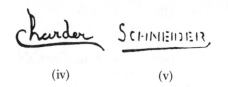

(iv)   (v)

Some items designed by
M.*Dufrène (*see* French ceramics)
for La Maîtrise (decorative art
department of Galeries Lafayette).
Engraved (i-iv) and etched (v)
marks.

SERRUYS, Yvonne (b.1874)

Sculptor, modeller. Worked for
G.*Despret.
Engraved monogram.

SÈVRES, Verrerie de (est.1870)

(i)

(ii)

Manufacturers.
Engraved (i) and etched (ii)
marks.

SIMONET FRERES (est. 19th century)

SIMONET FRS

Manufacturers of bronzework who
began making glass light fittings
and ornaments in 1919. Designers
include H.*Dieupart.
Moulded mark.

THIANCOURT (fl.c.1905)

Decorator or studio possibly
associated with *Pantin.
Engraved mark.

THURET, André (1898-1965)

andre
thuret

Glassmaker, designer, decorator.
Engraved signature.

VALLÉRYSTHAL ET PORTIEUX, Verreries Réunies de (est.1872)

Manufacturers. Designers include D.*Christian, F.A. Otto Krüger (b.1869), B.*Paul (*see* German graphics), Charles Spindler (1865-1938).
Engraved marks.

VARREUX, Camille Tutré de (fl.c.1910)

Designer. Worked for *Pantin. Etched signature (phonetic abbreviation: 'de V').

VESSIÈRE, Charles (fl.1900-10)

Designer, decorator. Worked for Vessière Frères.
Relief-etched signature.

WALTER, Almaric V. (1870-1959)

Glassmaker, designer, decorator. Worked in collaboration with Gabriel Lévy (fl.c.1900) and for *Daum before establishing his own glass works. Designers include J. and J.*Adnet (*see* French furniture), H.*Bergé, J.*Cayette, Jules *Chéret (*see* French graphics), E.-J.J.*Descomps (*see* French metalwork), J.-B.*Descomps, A.*Finot, V.*Prouvé (*see* French ceramics); also made *ceramics. Moulded signature.

BELGIAN GLASS

BERNARD, Paul (fl.1925-39)

P BERNARD

Designer, decorator. Worked for *Nationale, *Nouvelles; also decorated ceramics. Sandblasted/etched signature.

BOOM KRISTALFABRIEK (fl.c.1935)

ARTVER

Manufacturers of glassware including the 'Artver' line. Designers include Paul Heller (b.1914). Sandblasted mark.

CATTEAU, Charles (1880-1966)

French designer working in Belgium. Worked for *Scailmont; also designed *ceramics. Carved/moulded signature.

CENTRE, Verreries du (1924-38)

VERCENTRE

Manufacturers. Designers included L.*Mairesse. Engraved mark.

GRAFFART, Charles (1893-1967)

Designer, decorator. Worked for *Val St Lambert. Etched signature.

HEEMSKERK, Henri (1886-1953)

H. H.

Designer, decorator. Worked for *Scailmont; also decorated ceramics. Carved/moulded initials.

HOFMAN, Robert (1910-81)

R. HOFMAN

Designer, decorator. Worked for
*Nationale, *Scailmont and
independently.
Engraved signature.

MAIRESSE, Léon (1903-85)

L MAIRESSE

Designer, decorator. Worked for
*Centre, *Nouvelles and
independently.
Engraved signature.

NATIONALE, Gobeleterie (1927-38)

COBENA

Manufacturers.
Designer/decorators include
P.*Bernard, Désiré Dengis
(fl.c.1930), R.*Hofman.
Sandblasted/etched mark.

NOUVELLES, Verreries & Gobeleteries (est.1910)

Novelty

Manufacturers.
Designers/decorators include
P.*Bernard, Karl Heller
(1886-1932), Paul Heller (b.1914),
L.*Mairesse.
Enamelled/gilt mark.

SCAILMONT, Verreries de (1901-72)

Scailmont.

Manufacturers.
Designer/decorators include
C.*Catteau, H.*Heemskerk,
R.*Hofman.
Carved/moulded mark.

VAL ST LAMBERT, Cristalleries du (est.1826)

(i)

(ii)

(iii)

(iv)

(v)

(vi)

(vii)

VSL BELCIQUE

(viii)

Manufacturers.
Designers/decorators include René Delvenne (1902-72), Romain Gevaert (1875-1931), C.*Graffart, Léon Ledru (1855-1926), Désiré Muller (fl.1885-1925), Henri Muller (fl.1885-1925), Lucien Petignot (1874-1936), Joseph Simon (1874-1960), Jeanne Tisehon (1875-1955), H.C. van de *Velde (*see* German ceramics, metalwork, Belgian furniture), P.*Wolfers.
Etched (i), engraved (ii-vi), moulded (vii, viii) marks.

WOLFERS, Philippe (1858-1929)

Sculptor, designer. Worked for *Val St Lambert; also made jewellery and designed ceramics, *metalwork, furniture, textiles. Engraved signature.

DUTCH GLASS

AGTERBERG, Cris (1883-1948)

Designer, decorator; also designed
*ceramics, metalwork.
Enamelled initials.

ASCH VAN WIJCK, C.C. (1900-32)

Sculptor, designer. Worked for
*Leerdam.
Etched monogram.

BAZEL, Karel Petrus Cornelis de (1869-1923)

Architect, designer. Worked for
*Leerdam; also designed books,
furniture.
Etched monograms.

BERLAGE, Hendrik Petrus (1856-1934)

Architect, designer. Worked for
*Baccarat (*see* French glass),
*Leerdam, *Pantin (*see* French
glass); also designed *ceramics,
metalwork, furniture, carpets.
Etched monogram.

BLOCH, Lucienne (fl.c.1930)

Designer, modeller. Worked for
*Leerdam.
Etched monogram.

COPIER, Andries Dirk (b.1901)

Glassmaker, designer, decorator.
Worked for *Leerdam.
Etched monogram and mark, and
engraved initials and signatures.

EISENLOEFFEL, Jan (1876-1957)

Designer. Worked for *Kristalunie;
also designed *ceramics and made
*metalwork.
Etched mark.

FALKENBERG-LIEFRINCK, Ida (fl.c.1935)

Designer. Worked for *Leerdam.
Etched monogram.

GIDDING, Jaap (1887-1955)

Designer, decorator. Worked for
*Leerdam; also designed
*ceramics.
Etched monogram.

HEESEN, Willem (b.1925)

Glassmaker, designer, decorator.
Worked for *Leerdam.
Engraved signature.

KOOTEN, Anthonius Johannes van (1894-1951)

Glassmaker, designer, decorator.
Worked for *Leerdam before
establishing his own workshop.
Enamelled monogram.

KRISTALUNIE MAASTRICHT (1925-78)

Manufacturers.
Designers/decorators include
J.*Eisenloeffel, J. de *Meijer,
W.J.*Rozendaal, P.*Zwart.
Engraved marks.

LANOOIJ, Christiaan Johannes or Chris (1881-1948)

Painter, designer. Worked for
*Leerdam; also designed
*ceramics.
Etched mark and engraved
signature.

LEBEAU, Chris (1878-1945)

Designer. Worked for *Leerdam;
also designed ceramics, books,
posters, textiles.
Etched monogram and engraved
signature.

LEERDAM, Glasfabriek (est.1878)

Manufacturers.
Designers/decorators include
C.C.*Asch van Wijck, K.P.C. de
*Bazel, H.P.*Berlage, L.*Bloch,
A.D.*Copier, I.*Falkenberg-
Liefrinck, J.*Gidding, W.*Harzing
(see Dutch ceramics), W.*Heesen,
C.J.*Lanooij, C.*Lebeau, C. de
*Lorm, F.*Meydam, J.*Nicolas,
R.*Strebelle, W.*Stuurman,
S.*Uiterwaal, S.*Valkema,
J.*Vermeire, Frank Lloyd Wright
(1867-1956).
Engraved marks.

LORM, Cornelis de (1875-1942)

Designer. Worked for *Leerdam; also designed *ceramics. Etched monogram.

MEIJER, J. de (1878-1950)

Designer. Worked for *Kristalunie. Etched mark.

MEYDAM, Floris (b,1919)

Glassmaker, designer, decorator. Worked for *Leerdam. Engraved signature.

NICOLAS, Joep (1897-1972)

Glassmaker, designer, decorator. Worked for *Leerdam. Etched monogram.

ROZENDAAL, Willem Jacob (b.1899)

Painter, designer. Worked for *Kristalunie; also designed ceramics, illustrations. Engraved mark.

STREBELLE, Rodolphe (1880-1959)

Painter, designer. Worked for *Leerdam. Engraved signature.

STUURMAN, Willem (b.1908)

Designer, modeller. Worked for *Leerdam; also designed ceramics. Painted initials.

UITERWAAL, Stef (1889-1960)

G 回 L

Sculptor, designer, modeller.
Worked for *Leerdam.
Etched monogram.

VALKEMA, Sybren (b.1916)

Sybren Valkema

Glassmaker, designer, decorator.
Worked for *Leerdam; also
designed ceramics.
Engraved signature.

VERMEIRE, Jules (b.1885)

Belgian sculptor, designer,
modeller. Worked for *Leerdam.
Etched monogram.

ZWART, Piet (1885-1977)

Architect, designer. Worked for
*Kristalunie; also designed books,
furniture.
Engraved mark.

GERMAN GLASS

ALLESCH , Marianne von (b.1886)

Glassmaker, designer, decorator, modeller. Moved to USA c.1935. Painted monogram.

BAAR, Lotte (b.1901)

Decorator.
Engraved monogram.

BENNA, Edgar (b.1899)

Designer, decorator.
Engraved monogram.

BUCHENAU, Glashüttenwerke (est.1705/15)

Glass house run by successive generations of the Von Poschinger family. Designers include H.*Christiansen (*see* German ceramics, furniture), Julius Diez (1870-1957), R.*Riemerschid (*see* German metalwork), K.*Schmoll von Eisenwerth (*see* German graphics).
Gilt marks.

EIFF, Wilhelm von (1890-1943)

Glassmaker, designer, decorator.
Engraved initials and signature.

HESSISCHE EDELGLASMANUFAKTUR, Grossherzogliche (est.1901)

Manufacturers.
Designers/decorators include
J.E.*Schneckendorf (director).
Painted, gilt or stamped mark.

JOHN, Marie Elisabeth (b.1903)

Decorator.
Engraved monogram.

KLOSE, Arthur

Decorator.
Engraved mark.

KOEPPING, Carl (1848-1914)

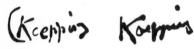

Designer. His designs were
executed first by F.*Zitzmann, and
then by a technical school in
Saxony; also illustrated books and
periodicals.
Painted signatures.

LÖWENTHAL, Arthur (b.1879)

Austrian decorator working in
Germany.
Engraved monogram.

MAUDER, Bruno (1877-1948)

Designer, decorator. In 1910
appointed director at *Zwiesel;
also designed ceramics.
Gilt mark.

PECHSTEIN, Max (1881-1955)

Painter, sculptor, designer of stained glass.
Painted monogram.

PETERSDORFER GLASHÜTTE (1866-1923)

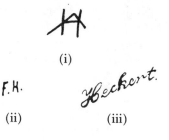

(i)

F.H.

(ii)   (iii)

Manufacturers owned by Fritz Heckert. Designers/decorators include Willy Meitzen (fl.c.1905), M.*Rade, Ludwig Sütterlin (1865-1917).
Enamelled (i, ii) and relief-cut (iii) marks.

RADE, Max (1840-1917)

Designer. Worked for *Petersdorfer, *Schappel (*see* Austrian glass).
Enamelled monogram.

RHEINISCHE GLASHÜTTE (1864-1931)

Manufacturers. Designers include P.*Behrens (*see* German graphics, metalwork, ceramics), K.*Moser (*see* Austrian ceramics).
Etched mark.

RIGOT, Edmond (b.1885)

Designer. Worked for *Villeroy & Boch.
Relief-cut signature.

SCHNECKENDORF, Josef Emil (1865-1949)

Glassmaker, designer, decorator. Worked independently and for *Hessische Edelglasmanufaktur; also designed and made jewellery.
Painted or gilt monogram.

SÜSSMUTH, Richard (b.1900)

Designer, decorator.
Engraved monogram.

VILLEROY & BOCH (est.1748)

Manufacturers. Designers include
E.*Rigot; also manufactured
*ceramics.
Relief-cut/etched mark.

VITTALI, Otto (b.1872)

Painter, designer, decorator; also
decorated ceramics.
Enamelled signature.

WENTZEL, Moritz (est. before 1870)

Manufacturers, decorators.
Engraved mark.

WIEGEL, Albert (1869-1943)

Designer, decorator.
Engraved signature.

ZITZMANN, Friedrich (1840-1906)

Glassmaker, designer, decorator.
Collaborated briefly with
C.*Koepping in 1895, otherwise
worked independently.
Signature in lustre.

ZWIESEL, Fachschule (est.c.1890)

Technical school. Instructors
include Stefan Erdös (fl.c.1950),
B.*Mauder (director), Rudolf
Rothemund (fl.c.1950).
Engraved mark.

AUSTRIAN GLASS

BECKERT, Adolf (1884-1929)

Glassmaker, designer, decorator. Worked for *Loetz-Witwe and taught at *Steinschönau where he became director. Relief-cut monogram.

CERNY, Jan (b.1907)

Czechoslovakian sculptor, glassmaker, designer, decorator. Engraved signature.

CONRATH & LIEBSCH (fl.c.1900)

Bohemian decorators. Engraved mark.

DRAHONOVSKY, Josef (1877)

Bohemian/Czechoslovakian designer, decorator. Engraved initials.

EISELT, Arnold (fl.1900-15)

Designer, decorator. Worked for *Haida, *Lobmeyr, *Steinschönau. Engraved monogram.

EISELT, Paul (fl.c.1910)

Decorator. Worked for *Steinschönau. Engraved initials.

FORSTNER, Leopold (1878-1936)

Mosaic and stained glass artist. Worked for Carl Geylings Erben, Tiroler Glasmalerei, *Wiener Werkstätte; co-founder of Wiener Kunst im Hause; founder of Wiener Mosaikwerkstätte. Painted monogram.

GOLDBERG, Carl (fl.1880-1910)

Glassmaker, designer, decorator. Established his own factory in 1881. Designers include J.*Hoffmann. Relief-cut signature.

HAIDA, Fachschule (est.1869)

(i)

(ii)

(iii)

Bohemian/Czechoslovakian technical school. Designers/decorators who instructed there include A.*Eiselt, R.*Muller. Engraved (i, ii) and etched (iii) marks.

HARRACH (est.1798)

Bohemian/Czechoslovakian manufacturers. Designers/decorators include Jaroslav Horejc (1886-1983), Pavel Janák (fl.c.1910), Julius Jelinek (1874-1918), Jan Kotéra (1871-1923). Relief-cut mark.

HLAVA, Pavel (b.1924)

Czechoslovakian glassmaker, designer, decorator. Engraved signature.

HOFFMANN, Josef (1870-1956)

Architect, designer. Worked for C.*Goldberg, *Lobmeyr, *Loetz-Witwe, *Moser, *Oertel, *Schappel, *Wiener Werkstätte; also designed *ceramics, *metalwork, jewellery, furniture, textiles, *graphics. Engraved signature.

JEZEK, Ladislav (b.1930)

Czechoslovakian designer, decorator. Engraved signature.

KIRSCHNER, Maria (1852-1931)

Painter, designer. Worked for *Loetz-Witwe; also designed and made embroidery. Engraved monogram.

KROMER, Emil (fl.c.1910)

E K

Decorator. Worked for *Steinschönau. Engraved initials.

KULKA, Wenzel (fl.20th century)

Bohemian/Czechoslovakian manufacturers. Etched mark.

LOBMEYR, J. & L. (est.1860)

Manufacturers with factories in Austria and Bohemia/Czechoslovakia. Designers/decorators include

LOBMEYR, J. & L. (continued)

J.*Divéky (*see* Austrian graphics),
A.*Eiselt, Lotte Fink (fl.c.1925),
Oswald Haerdtl (1899-1959),
J.*Hoffmann, Otto Hofner
(fl.c.1905), Jaroslav Horejc
(1886-1983), Urban Janke
(1887-1914), M.*Jung (*see* Austrian
graphics), Ludwig Jungnickel
(1881-1965), Antoinette Krasnik
(fl.c.1910), Rudolf von Larisch
(1856-1934), Ludwig Lobmeyr
(d.1917), Adolf Loos (1870-1933),
Viktor Lurje (b.1883),
R.F.*Marschall (*see* Austrian
metalwork), A.*Nechansky,
D.*Peche, M.*Powolny,
O.*Prutscher (*see* Austrian graphics,
metalwork), Marianne Rath
(b.1904), Stefan Rath (1876-1960),
Ena Rottenberg (1893-1950), Oskar
Strnad (1879-1935), Otto Tauschek
(fl.c.1905), V.*Wieselthier (*see*
Austrian ceramics), Karl Witzmann
(b.1883).
Etched mark.

LOETZ-WITWE, Johann (est.1848)

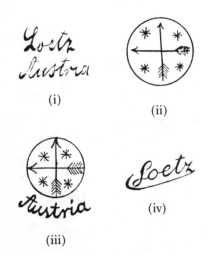

(i)

(ii)

(iii)

(iv)

Manufacturers.
Designers/decorators included
L.*Bauer (*see* Austrian ceramics),
A.*Beckert, Hans Bolek (fl.c.1905),
J.*Hoffmann, Franz Hofstätter
(fl.c.1905), Robert Holubetz
(fl.c.1905), M.*Kirschner,
K.*Moser, A.*Nechansky, D.*Peche,
M.*Powolny, O.*Prutscher (*see*
Austrian graphics, metalwork), M.
von *Spaun, M.*Weltmann, Marie
Wilfert-Waltl (fl.c.1905), Karl
Witzmann (b.1883).
Painted (i, ii, iii) and relief-etched
(iv) marks.

MASSANETZ, Karl (1890-1918)

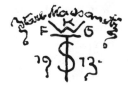

Bohemian designer, decorator. Worked for *Steinschönau before establishing his own workshop. Enamelled mark.

MAX, Hugo (fl.1896-1925)

Glassmaker, designer, decorator. Worked for *Steinschönau; also decorated ceramics. Enamelled initials.

MEYR'S NEFFE (1841-1922)

Bohemian/Czechoslovakian manufacturers. Designers included K.*Moser, J.M.*Olbrich (*see* German ceramics), O.*Prutscher (*see* Austrian metalwork, graphics), F.Schmoranz (1845-92). Taken over by L.*Moser. Engraved mark.

MOSER, Koloman (1868-1918)

Painter, designer. Commissioned by E. Bakalowits & Söhne to design glass manufactured by *Loetz-Witwe, *Meyr's Neffe; designed for *Rheinische Glashütte (*see* German glass); also designed *ceramics, metalwork, jewellery, posters, books, furniture, textiles, carpets. Engraved monogram.

MOSER, Ludwig, & Söhne (est.1857)

Bohemian/Czechoslovakian manufacturers.
Designers/decorators include Johann Hoffmann (1840-1922), J.*Hoffmann, Hilda Jesser-Schmidt (b.1894), Vera Lisková (b.1924), D.*Peche, Julius Urban (b.1855), E.*Wimmer (*see* Austrian metalwork).
Engraved marks.

MULLER, Rudolf (fl.c.1910)

Designer, decorator. Worked at *Haida, *Steinschönau.
Engraved initials.

NAGY, Sándor (1868-1950)

Hungarian painter, stained glass designer; also designed furniture, tapestries, posters.
Painted monogram.

NECHANSKY, Arnold (1888-1938)

Architect, designer. Worked for *Lobmeyr, *Loetz-Witwe; also designed ceramics, metalwork, jewellery, textiles, wallpaper.
Enamelled signature.

OERTEL, Johann, & Co. (est.1869)

Bohemian/Czechoslovakian manufacturers. Designers include J.*Hoffmann.
Printed marks.

PALLME-KÖNIG, Gebrüder (est.1786)

Bohemian/Czechoslovakian manufacturers. Designers include Alois Ritter (b.1870), Josef Velik (fl.1910-19).
Paper label.

PECHE, Dagobert (1886-1923)

ARCH.D.PECHE.
LOETZ.

Designer. Worked for *Lobmeyr, *Loetz-Witwe, *Moser, *Wiener Werkstätte; also designed *ceramics, *metalwork, jewellery, posters, books (*see* Austrian graphics), furniture, carpets, textiles, wallpapers.
Enamelled signature.

POWOLNY, Michael (1871-1954)

Prof, powolny
Loetz

Sculptor, designer. Worked for *Lobmeyr, *Loetz; also designed and made *ceramics and designed silver.
Enamelled signature.

REICH, S., & Co. (est.c.1840)

RKrasna

Bohemian manufacturers with several factories including one at Krasna.
Relief-cut mark.

SCHAPPEL, Carl (est.1857)

Bohemian/Czechoslovakian manufacturers. Designers include J.*Hoffmann, O.*Prutscher (*see* Austrian graphics, metalwork), M.*Rade (*see* German glass).
Printed mark.

SPAUN, Max von (d.1909)

Glassmaker, designer, decorator. Director of *Loetz-Witwe from 1879 to 1908. Painted signature.

STEINSCHÖNAU, Fachschule (est.1839)

KK$ST

Bohemian/Czechoslovakian technical school. Designers/decorators who instructed there include A.*Beckert, A.*Eiselt, P.*Eiselt, E.*Kromer, K.*Massanetz, H.*Max, R.*Muller. Engraved mark.

WELTMANN, Milla (fl.c.1905)

Designer. Worked for *Loetz-Witwe. Painted signature.

WIENER WERKSTÄTTE (est.1903)

WW

Craft workshops and retail outlets. Production of glass limited to simple pieces; designs executed by *Goldberg, *Loetz-Witwe, *Meyr's Neffe, *Moser, *Oertel. Designers/decorators include M.*Flögl (see Austrian ceramics), L.*Forstner, J.*Hoffmann, Hilda Jesser-Schmidt (b.1894), M.*Likarz-Strauss (see Austrian metalwork), Fritzi Löw-Lazar (1891-1975), D.*Peche, O.*Prutscher (see Austrian graphics, metalwork), F.*Rix-Uevno (see Austrian ceramics), Ena Rottenberg (1893-1950), Reni Schaschl-Schuster (b.1895), Anny Schröder-Ehrenfest (1898-1972), V.*Wieselthier (see Austrian ceramics), J.*Zimpel (see Austrian metalwork). Enamelled mark.

ITALIAN GLASS

BARBINI, Alfredo (b.1912)

$A\,B$

Glassmaker, designer, decorator.
Worked for Gino Cenedese & Co.
and Pauly & Co, and established
his own workshop.
Engraved initials.

BAROVIER & TOSO (est.1936)

barovier & toso
murano

Manufacturers.
Designers/decorators include
A.*Barovier, E.*Barovier.
Engraved mark.

BAROVIER, Angelo (b.1927)

Angelo
Barovier

Glassmaker, designer, decorator.
Worked for *Barovier & Toso.
Engraved signature.

BAROVIER, Ercole (1889-1974)

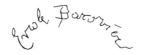

Glassmaker, designer, decorator.
Worked for *Barovier & Toso.
Engraved signature.

BIANCONI, Fulvio (b.1915)

FULVIO BIANCONI

Glassmaker, designer, decorator.
Worked for *Venini, *Vistosi.
Engraved signature.

SALVIATI & CO. (est.1856)

Manufacturers. Designers include Luciano Gaspari (fl.c.1950), Dino Martens (fl.1935-60).
Paper label.

SEGUSO, Archimede (b.1909)

Archimede Seguso

Glassmaker, designer, decorator. Worked for Seguso Vetri d'Arte before establishing his own workshop.
Engraved signature.

VENINI & CO. (est.1925)

venini murano

Venini Murano MADE IN ITALY

venini italia

venini. ITALY

venini murano ITALIA

venini murano aros

Manufacturers. Designers include Eugène Berman (1899-1972), F.*Bianconi, Tommaso Buzzi (1900-81), Ricardo Licata (fl.c.1955), Tyra Lundgren (1897-1979), Napoleone Martinuzzi (1892-1977), Gio Ponti (b.1891), Carlo Scarpa (1906-78), Tobia Scarpa (fl.c.1955), Thomas Stearns (b.1936), Paolo Venini (founder, 1895-1959), Massimo Vignelli (fl.c.1950), T.*Wirkkala (*see* Scandinavian ceramics), Vittorio Zecchin (1878-1947).
Etched marks.

VISTOSI, Vetreria (est.1945)

VISTOSI

Manufacturers. Designers include F.*Bianconi, Peter Pelzel (fl.c.1960), Alessandro Pianon (fl.c.1960), Gino Vistosi (fl.c.1950), Luciano Vistosi (fl.c.1950).
Engraved mark.

SCANDINAVIAN GLASS

BERGQVIST, Knut (fl.c.1920)

Swedish glassmaker. Worked for
*Orrefors.
Engraved initials.

BRØRBY, Severin (b.1932)

Norwegian glassmaker, designer,
decorator. Worked for Hadeland.
Engraved signature.

CYRÉN, Gunnar (b.1931)

Swedish designer. Worked for
*Orrefors; also made metalwork.
Engraved signature.

EDENFALK, Bengt (b.1924)

Swedish designer. Worked for
*Skrufs Glasbruk.
Engraved signature.

FLYGSFORS (fl.1930-1960)

Swedish manufacturers. Designers
include Viktor Berndt (b.1919),
P.*Kedelv, Edvin Ollers (1888-
1960).
Engraved mark.

FRANCK, Kaj (b.1911)

Finnish designer. Worked for
*Iittala, *Nuutajärvi, Riihimaki;
also designed ceramics, furniture,
textiles.
Engraved signature.

GATE, Simon (1883-1945)

Swedish designer, decorator.
Worked for *Orrefors; also
designed metalwork.
Engraved monogram and
signature.

HALD, Edward (1883-1980)

Swedish designer, decorator.
Worked for *Orrefors; also
designed ceramics.
Engraved marks.

HOLMEGAARDS GLASSVAERK (est.1825)

Danish manufacturers. Designers
include Jacob Bang (1899-1965),
P.*Lütken; also manufactured
ceramics.
Engraved mark.

HOPEA-UNTRACHT, Saara (1925-84)

Finnish designer. Worked for
*Nuutajärvi; also designed
ceramics, enamels, jewellery,
furniture, textiles.
Engraved signature.

IITTALA (est.1881)

Finish manufacturers. From 1915
to 1945 merged with Karhula and
known as Karhula-Iittala. Designers
include Aino Aalto (1894-1949),
Alvar Aalto (1898-1976), K.*Franck,
Greta-Lisa Jäderholm-Snellman
(1894-1973), Gunnel Gustafsson
Nyman (1909-48), T.*Sarpaneva,
T.*Wirkkala.
Engraved mark

KEDELV, Paul (b.1917)

Kedelv

Swedish designer. Worked for
*Flygsfors.
Engraved signature.

KOSTA (est.1742)

Kosta

Kosta

Swedish manufacturers. In 1946
merged with Åfors and Boda to
become Kosta Boda. Designers
include Elis Bergh (1881-1954),
Ferdinand Boberg (1860-1946),
Ewald Dahlskog (1894-1950),
K.*Lindeberg, Edvin Ollers
(1888-1960), Sven-Erik Skawonius
(1908-81), Edvard Strömberg
(1872-1946), A.*Wallander (*see*
Scandinavian furniture), Gunnar
Wennerberg (1863-1914).
Engraved marks.

LANDBERG, Nils (b.1907)

Nils Landberg

Swedish designer, decorator.
Worked for *Orrefors.
Engraved signature.

LINDEBERG, Karl (1877-1931)

KL   *K.Lindeberg*

Swedish designer, decorator.
Worked for *Kosta,
Engraved initials and signature.

LINDSTRAND, Vicke (1904-83)

Lindstrand

Swedish designer, decorator.
Worked for *Kosta, *Orrefors; also
designed ceramics, illustrations,
textiles.
Engraved signature.

LUNDIN, Ingeborg (b.1921)

J. Lundin

Swedish designer, decorator.
Worked for *Orrefors.
Engraved signature.

LÜTKEN, Per (b.1916)

Danish designer. Worked for
*Holmegaard.
Engraved monogram.

MOTZFELDT, Benny (b.1909)

BM

Norwegian designer. Worked for
Hadeland.
Engraved initials.

NUUTAJÄRVI (est.1793)

Nuutajärvi
Notsjö

Finnish manufacturers at first
known under Swedish name Notsjö.
Designers include K.*Franck,
S.*Hopea-Untracht, Gunnel
Gustafsson Nyman (1909-48).
Engraved mark.

ÖHRSTROM, Edvin (b.1906)

Edvin Öhrström

Swedish sculptor, designer.
Worked for *Orrefors.
Engraved signature.

ORREFORS GLASBRUK (est.1913)

orrefors

Orrefors

Swedish manufacturers.
Designers/decorators include
G.*Cyrén, S.*Gate, E.*Hald, Carl
Hermelin (1897-1979), Henning
Koppel (1918-81), N.*Landberg,
V.*Lindstrand, I.*Lundin,
E.*Öhrstrom, S.*Palmqvist.
Engraved marks.

PALMQVIST, Sven (1906-84)

[signature: Sven Palmqvist]

Swedish designer, decorator.
Worked for *Orrefors.
Engraved signature.

REIJMYRE GLASBRUK (est.1810)

[mark: Reijmyre Suède]

Swedish manufacturers. Designers
include Anna Katarina Boberg
(1864-1935), Ferdinand Boberg
(1860-1946), Monica Bratt
(1913-61), Edvin Ollers
(1888-1960), A.*Wallander (*see*
Scandinavian furniture).
Engraved mark.

SARPANEVA, Timo (b.1926)

[signature: TIMO SARPANEVA]

Finnish designer. Worked for
*Iittala; also designed ceramics,
metalwork, textiles.
Engraved signature.

SCHRADER, Åse Voss (fl.1936-60)

[mark: ÅVS ⊕ 1959]

Danish designer, decorator.
Engraved initials and mark.

SKRUFS GLASBRUK (est.1897)

[mark: Skruf]

Swedish manufacturers. Designers
include B.*Edenfalk.
Engraved mark.

WIRKKALA, Tapio (1915-85)

[signature: TAPIO WIRKKALA]

Finnish designer. Worked for
*Iittala, *Rosenthal (*see* German
ceramics), *Venini (*see* Italian glass);
also designed ceramics, metalwork.
Engraved signature.

BRITISH METALWORK & JEWELLERY

ADIE BROS. (est.1879)

Manufacturing silversmiths.
Designers include Fernand Piret
(fl.c.1930), H.*Stabler.
Stamped mark.

ARTIFICERS' GUILD (1901-42)

Manufacturers and retailers of
metalwork and jewellery. Designers
include N.*Dawson, E.*Spencer.
Stamped mark.

ASHBEE, Charles Robert (1863-1942)

Architect, designer of metalwork
and jewellery for the *Guild of
Handicraft (which he founded)
and cast iron for Coalbrookdale
Co.; also designed furniture,
wallpaper, books.
Stamped initials.

ASPREY & CO. (est.1781)

ASPREY
LONDON

Silversmiths and jewellers.
Stamped marks.

BARNARD, Edward, & Sons (est.1829)

Manufacturing silversmiths.
Designers include Jane Barnard
(b.1902), Charles Francis Annesley
Voysey (1857-1941).
Stamped mark.

BENHAM & FROUD (fl. late 19th century)

Manufacturers of copper and brass wares. Designers include C.*Dresser. Stamped mark.

BENSON, William Arthur Smith (1854-1924)

Architect, designer. Opened factory (1880) manufacturing silver, plate and other metalwork, designed cast iron for Coalbrookdale Co. and Falkirk Iron Co.; also designed furniture, wallpaper. Stamped marks.

BIRMINGHAM GUILD OF HANDICRAFT (est.1890)

BGH

Association of craftsmen and designers producing metalwork and jewellery. Designers include Arthur S. Dixon (1856-1929), Claude Napier-Clavering (fl.1895-1925) Stamped marks.

BLACKBAND, William Thomas (1885-1949)

Silversmith, jeweller. Stamped initials.

BOYTON, Charles, & Son (est.c.1900)

  charles Boyton

Manufacturing silversmiths. Designers include Charles Boyton (1885-1958). Stamped marks.

CENTURY GUILD (fl.1883-c.1892)

Group of architects, designers and craftsmen including A.H.*Mackmurdo, H.P.*Horne who designed metalwork; also designed *furniture, textiles, wallpapers. Chiselled mark.

COMYNS, William, & Sons (est.1848)

Manufacturing silversmiths. Stamped mark

CONNELL & CO. (fl. late 19th and early 20th century)

(i)

(ii)

Manufacturing silversmiths. Stamped mark until 1902 (i), from 1902 (ii).

COOPER, John Paul (1869-1933)

Silversmith, jeweller. Stamped marks.

COURTHOPE, Frederick (fl.1885-1915)

Silversmith. Made silver designed by John Dando Sedding (1838-91) and others. Stamped initials.

CUZNER, Bernard (1877-1956)

Silversmith, jeweller. Designed for *Goldsmiths & Silversmiths Co., *Liberty. Stamped initials.

DAISH, Florence Ada (fl.c.1930)

Silversmith, jeweller. Stamped initials.

DAWSON, Nelson (1859-1942)

(i)

(ii)

Painter, silversmith, jeweller, metalworker. Founded and designed for *Artificers' Guild. Work often decorated with enamels by Edith Dawson (whom he married in 1893). Stamped initials (i), enamelled initial (ii).

DEAKIN & FRANCIS (fl. 20th century)

Manufacturing silversmiths. Designers include A.E.*Harvey. Stamped mark.

DIXON, James, & Sons (est.1806)

Manufacturers of silver and plate. Designers include C.*Dresser. Stamped marks.

DRESSER, Christopher (1834-1904)

Architect, designer. Designed silver and plate for *Dixon & Sons, *Elkington, *Heath & Middleton, *Hukin & Heath, metalwork for *Benham & Froud, Chubb & Co., Deakin & Moore, Hardman & Co., *Liberty, *Perry, cast iron for Coalbrookdale Co.; also designed *ceramics, *glass, furniture, textiles, wallpapers. Stamped signatures.

DRYAD METAL WORKS (est.1912)

Firm of metalworkers. Designers include William Pick (fl.1905-25). Stamped mark.

DUNHILL, Alfred, & Co. (fl. 20th century)

Retailers who organised design and manufacture of gold and silver boxes, lighters, etc.
Stamped mark.

ELKINGTON & CO. (est.1836)

Manufacturers of silver, plate and other metalwork. Designers include C.*Dresser, Reginald Hill (fl.1920-40), Frank Neville (fl.1920-40), John Walker (fl.1920-40).
Stamped marks.

FISHER, Alexander (1864-1936)

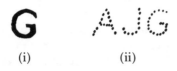

(i)   (ii)

Painter, sculptor, silversmith, jeweller, enamellist; also designed embroideries, decorated ceramics.
Stamped initials, enamelled monogram.

GASKIN, Arthur Joseph (1862-1928)

G   AJG

(i)   (ii)

Painter, silversmith, jeweller. Designed silver for *Liberty; also designed and illustrated books (*see* British graphics).
Engraved initial, hammered initials.

GOLDSMITHS & SILVERSMITHS CO. (1890-1952)

Manufacturing and retailing goldsmiths and silversmiths. Designers include B.*Cuzner, A.*Harvey, H.*Stabler.
Stamped mark.

GUILD OF HANDICRAFT (1888-1907)

Guild of artist-craftsmen founded by C.*Ashbee. Made metalwork and jewellery, most of it designed by Ashbee. Members included G.*Hart, F.*Partridge, J.*Pearson, J.*Williams.
Stamped mark.

HART, George (b.1882)

Silversmith and designer. Member of *Guild of Handicraft before establishing his own firm.
Stamped marks.

HARVEY, Arthur Edward (1893-1978)

Architect, designer. Designed silver and plate for *Deakin & Francis, *Goldsmiths & Silversmiths Co., *Hukin & Heath, *Mappin & Webb.
Stamped initials.

HASELER, W.H., & Co. (est.1850)

Manufacturers of silver, jewellery and other metalwork. From 1899 to 1927 manufactured silver for *Liberty.
Stamped mark.

HEATH & MIDDLETON (1887-1909)

Manufacturers of silver, plate and other metalwork. Designers include C.*Dresser.
Stamped mark.

HISLOP, D.W. (fl.c.1905)

Silversmith, jeweller. Made silver designed by C.R.*Mackintosh and others.
Stamped initials.

HODEL, Joseph (fl.1890-1915)

Designer of metalwork and jewellery. Worked with Bromsgrove Guild (est.c.1890).
Stamped signature.

HORNE, Herbert Percy (1864-1916)

Architect, designer. Designed metalwork made by *Century Guild; also designed furniture, textiles, wallpapers, books.
Chiselled monogram.

HORNER, Charles, & Sons (fl.1900-20)

Manufacturing silversmiths and jewellers.
Stamped mark.

HUKIN & HEATH (1855-1953)

Manufacturers of silver and plate. Designers include C.*Dresser, A.E.*Harvey.
Stamped marks.

HUNT, George (fl.1910-40)

Jeweller.
Stamped signature.

HUTTON, William, & Sons (1800-c.1925)

Manufacturers of silver, plate and other metalwork. Designers include Kate Harris (fl.c.1900). Stamped mark.

INSTONE, Bernard (b.1891)

Silversmith, jeweller, enamellist. Stamped initials.

JONES, Albert Edward (1879-1954)

Silversmith, jeweller. Stamped initials.

JONES & CROMPTON (fl.c.1900)

Manufacturing silversmiths. Stamped mark.

KESWICK SCHOOL OF INDUSTRIAL ART (est.1884)

$$S \quad \overset{K}{\underset{A}{}} \quad I$$

Produced silver and other metalwork. Designers include Herbert T. Maryon (fl.1890-1910), H.*Stabler. Stamped mark.

KRALL, Charles (est.1881)

CK

KRALL

Manufacturing silversmiths and jewellers; successors to Barkentin & Krall. Designers include John Dando Sedding (1838-91). Stamped marks.

LEGROS, Alphonse (1837-1911)

French painter, sculptor, medallist working in England. Cast signature.

LIBERTY & CO. (est.1875)

CYMRIC

ENGLISH PEWTER

O 2 2 1

MADE BY LIBERTY & CO

Retailers who organised the design and production of jewellery, silver and other metalwork, including 'Cymric' silver and 'Tudric' pewter. Silver manufactured by *Haseler from 1899 to 1927. Designers include Oliver Baker (1859-1938), B.*Cuzner, C.*Dresser, A.J.*Gaskin, A.E.*Jones, J.M.*King (*see* British graphics), Archibald Knox (1864-1933), Silver Studio (1880-1963); also retailed and supervised production of *ceramics, *glass, *furniture, textiles, carpets. Stamped marks.

MACKINTOSH, Margaret Macdonald (1865-1933)

Painter, designer, metalworker, jeweller; also designed graphics and made embroideries. Engraved signature.

MACKMURDO, Arthur Heygate (1851-1942)

Architect, designer. Designed metalwork made by *Century Guild; also designed furniture, textiles, wallpapers. Hammered initial.

McNAIR, J. Herbert (1868-1953)

Architect, designer. Designed metalwork and jewellery; also designed furniture, posters. Engraved signature.

MAPPIN & WEBB (Est.1863)

Manufacturing silversmiths. Designers include A.E.*Harvey, K.*Murray (*see* British ceramics, glass). Stamped mark.

MARKS, Gilbert Leigh (1861-1905)

Silversmith and metalworker. Engraved signature and stamped initials.

MURPHY, Henry George (1884-1939)

Silversmith and jeweller. Executed designs by Eric Gill (1882-1940). Stamped initials and mark.

MURRLE BENNETT & CO. (1884-c.1914)

Manufacturers and importers of jewellery. Sometimes collaborated with *Liberty and T.*Fahrner (*see* German metalwork). Stamped marks.

NAPPER & DAVENPORT (fl.1920-40)

Manufacturing silversmiths. Stamped mark.

NEWLYN INDUSTRIAL CLASS (1890-1939)

NEWLYN

Metalworkers, jewellers and enamellists. Designers include J.D.Mackenzie (fl.1880-1915), J.*Pearson. Stamped and engraved marks.

OGDEN & CO. (fl.1920-40)

OGDENS

Manufacturing silversmiths. Designers include H.*Stabler. Stamped mark.

PARTRIDGE, Frederick James (1877-1942)

PARTRIDGE

Jeweller. Worked briefly with *Guild of Handicraft. Stamped signature.

PEARSON, John (fl.1895-1925)

Silversmith, metalworker. Worked with *Guild of Handicraft, *Newlyn Industrial Class; also decorated *ceramics.
Stamped initials.

PERRY, Son & Co. (1876-83)

Manufacturers of metalwork. Designers include C.*Dresser.
Stamped mark.

POWELL, James, & Sons (est.1834)

Firm of glassmakers who arranged the manufacture of their own silver mounts, c.1900-10.
Stamped marks.

RAMSDEN, Omar (1873-1939)

Goldsmith, silversmith, jeweller.
Stamped initials and chiselled signature.

RAMSDEN & CARR (1898-1919)

Partnership between goldsmiths, silversmiths and jewellers O.*Ramsden and Alwyn C.E. Carr (1872-1940).
Stamped marks.

RATHBONE, Richard Llewellyn Benson (1864-1939)

 RATHBONE

Designer, metalworker, silversmith, jeweller.
Stamped signature and monogram.

REYNOLDS, William Bainbridge (1855-1935)

Architect, sculptor, silversmith.
Designed for *Starkie Gardner.
Stamped initials.

ROBERTS & BELK (est.1809)

Manufacturers of silver and plate.
Designers include Walter P. Belk
(fl.1925-40).
Stamped mark.

SHINER, Cyril James (b.1908)

Designer, silversmith. Designed for
*Wakeley & Wheeler.
Stamped initials.

SPENCER, Edward (1872-1938)

Designer, metalworker. Director of
*Artificers' Guild, for which he
designed; also designed ceramics.
Stamped signature.

STABLER, Harold (1872-1945)

Designer, metalworker. Director of
*Keswick School of Industrial Art
from 1898 to 1899. Designed for
*Adie Bros., Firth Vickers,
*Goldsmiths & Silversmiths,
*Ogden, *Wakeley & Wheeler; also
designed ceramics, glass, posters.
Stamped initials and signature.

STARKIE GARDNER & CO. (fl.1875-1940)

Manufacturers of metalwork.
Designers include W.B.*Reynolds.
Stamped initials.

THEW, Mary (fl.1900-30)

Silversmith, jeweller, enamellist.
Hammered initial.

WAKELEY & WHEELER (est.1909)

Manufacturing silversmiths.
Designers include R.M.Y.
Gleadowe (1888-1944),
C.J.*Shiner, H.*Stabler.
Stamped mark.

WALKER & HALL (est.1843)

Manufacturing silversmiths.
Stamped mark.

WALLIS, Hugh (fl.1895-1935)

Painter, metalworker.
Stamped initials.

WILLIAMS, John (fl.1890-1915)

Silversmith, metalworker. Member
of *Guild of Handicraft.
Stamped initials.

WILSON, Henry J. (1864-1934)

Architect, designer, metalworker,
jeweller. Designed metalwork for
Longden & Co. (fl.1885-1915); also
designed furniture, wallpaper.
Stamped initials.

AMERICAN METALWORK & JEWELLERY

ALVIN CORPORATION (est.1886)

Manufacturers of silver and plate.
Bought by *Gorham in 1928.
Stamped marks.

ART SILVER SHOP, The (1912-34)

Workshops founded by silversmiths
Edmund Boker (b.1886) and
Ernest Gould (1884-1954).
Stamped mark.

AVERBECK & AVERBECK (fl.c.1900)

A & A

Manufacturing jewellers.
Stamped mark.

BELLIS, John O. (d.1943)

JOHN O BELLIS.

Silversmith.
Stamped mark.

BLANCHARD, Porter George (1886-1973)

Silversmith.
Stamped mark.

CAMPBELL METCALF SILVER CO. (est.1892)

Manufacturing silversmiths.
Designers include Ernest W.
Campbell (b.1860).
Stamped mark.

CHICAGO SILVER CO. (est.1923)

Manufacturing silversmiths.
Designers include Knut L.
Gustafson (1885-1976).
Stamped mark.

COPELAND, Elizabeth (1866-1957)

Silversmith, jeweller, enamellist.
Chiselled initials.

CRAVER, Margaret (b.1907)

Silversmith.
Stamped mark.

DOOLITTLE, Harold Lukens (1883-1974)

Engineer and amateur craftsman.
Made brass plaques; also made
furniture, carved wood, and printed.
Signature.

FESSENDEN & CO. (1858-1922)

Manufacturing silversmiths.
Stamped mark.

FRIEDELL, Clemens (1872-1963)

FRIEDELL - PASADENA

CLEMENS FRIEDELL
PASADENA

Silversmith, metalworker.
Chased and stamped signatures.

GLESSNER, Frances M. (1848-1922)

Silversmith.
Stamped mark.

GORHAM MANUFACTURING CO. (est.1831)

Manufacturers of silver, other metalwork and jewellery. Designers include William Christmas Codman (1839-1923), Ernest W. Campbell (b.1860), E.*Magnussen. Stamped marks.

INTERNATIONAL SILVER CO. (est.1898)

Manufacturing silversmiths. Stamped mark.

JARVIE, Robert R. (1865-1940)

Silversmith and metaworker. Cast signature.

KALO SHOPS (1900-70)

HAND BEATEN AT KALO SHOPS PARKRIDGE STERLING

HAND WROUGHT AT THE KALO SHOPS CHICAGO AND NEW YORK

STERLING HAND WROUGHT AT THE KALO SHOP

Workshops producing silverware and jewellery. Designers include Clara Pauline Barck Welles (1868-1965); also produced textiles, leatherwork. Stamped marks.

KERR, William B., & Co. (1855-1906)

Manufacturing goldsmiths, silversmiths and jewellers. Bought by *Gorham in 1906. Stamped mark.

KIPP, Karl E. (1882-1954)

Silversmith, metalworker, designer. Worked at *Roycroft Copper Shop and ran his own firm, the Tookay Shop. Stamped initials.

LEBOLT & CO. (est.1912)

Manufacturing silversmiths.
Designers include Edmund Boker
(b.1886).
Stamped marks.

MARSHALL FIELD & CO.

Department store which started a
silver workshop in 1904.
Stamped mark.

MERIDEN SILVER PLATE CO. (est.1869)

Manufacturers of silver-plate.
Stamped marks.

OLD MISSION KOPPER KRAFT (1922-c.1925)

Metalworkers.
Stamped mark.

PETTERSON STUDIO, The (c.1912-19)

THE PETTERSON STUDIO
CHICAGO

HAND MADE

Workshops founded by silversmith
John Pontus Petterson (1884-
1949).
Stamped marks.

RANDAHL, Julius Olaf (1880-1972)

JOR
HAND WROUGHT
STERLING

Silversmith. Ran his own
workshops, The Randahl Shop
(1911-50).
Stamped mark.

REED & BARTON (est.1837)

Manufacturers of silver and of nickel-plated wares.
Stamped marks.

ROYCROFT COPPER SHOP

ROYCROFT
SHEFFIELD

Copper workshop of the Roycroft Community founded by Elbert Hubbard (1856-1915). Designers include Walter U. Jennings (fl.1909-27), K.E.*Kipp, D.*Hunter (*see* American graphics) Victor Toothaker (fl.1910-20); Community also produced ceramics, *furniture, printed books and periodicals.
Stamped marks.

SHREVE & CO. (est.1852)

Manufacturing silversmiths and jewellers.
Stamped mark.

SMED, Peer (1878-1943)

Silversmith. Designed for *Tiffany & Co.
Stamped mark.

SMITH, E.H.H., Silver Co. (c.1904-20)

◁ S ▷

Manufacturing silversmiths.
Stamped mark.

SPRATLING, William (fl.1925-45)

Architect, designer, silversmith.
Stamped mark.

STICKLEY, Gustav (1858-1942)

Designed and manufactured metalwork at his Craftsman Workshops (1899-1916); also produced *furniture.
Stamped marks.

STONE, Arthur J. (1901-37)

Workshops founded by silversmith and designer Arthur J. Stone (1847-1938).
Stamped mark.

THUMLER, Arthur (1886-1969)

THUMLER

STERLING

Silversmith.
Stamped mark and monogram.

TIFFANY & CO. (est.1837)

TIFFANY&COMPY   TIFFANY
&Cº
18 K

TIFFANY&CO
550 BROADWAY

Manufacturers and retailers in New York of silver, other metalwork and jewellery. Designers include Paulding Farnum (fl.c.1900), Edward Chandler Moore (1827-91), P.*Smed, James Horton Whitehouse (1833-1902).
Stamped marks.

TIFFANY STUDIOS (1879-1936)

**TIFFANY STVDIOS
NEW YORK**

(i)

TIFFANY STUDIOS

NEW YORK

(ii)

Workshops under the direction of Louis Comfort Tiffany (1848-1933) producing metalwork and jewellery. Designers include Julia Munson (1875-1971); also produced ceramics, mosaics, glass, stained glass, textiles.

(iii)

Stamped marks (i, ii), engraved
signature (iii).

UNGER BROS. (1878-1919)

Manufacturing silversmiths and
jewellers. Designers include
Philomen Dickson (fl.c.1900).
Stamped mark.

VAN ERP, Dirk, Copper Shop (1908-77)

Metalworkers. Designers include
Dirk van Erp (1860-1933), Eleanor
D'Arcy Gaw (1868-1944).
Stamped mark.

WALLACE, R., & Sons (1855-1959)

Manufacturing silversmiths.
Stamped mark.

WHITING, Frank M., & Co. (c.1875-1940)

Manufacturing silversmiths.
Stamped mark.

WHITING MANUFACTURING CO. (est.1866)

Manufacturing silversmiths and
jewellers. Bought by *Gorham in
1926.
Stamped marks.

FRENCH METALWORK & JEWELLERY

BAPST & FALIZE (est.1880)

Collaboration of jewellers Germain Bapst (fl.1875-95) and Lucien Falize (1838-97).
Stamped mark.

BARBEDIENNE (1838-1953)

Foundry and metalworkers; also made furniture.
Cast marks.

F BARBEDIENNE Fondeur
PARIS

BECKER, Edmond-Henri (b.1871)

L. BECKER

Sculptor, medallist, jeweller.
Designed for *Boucheron.
Cast signature.

BERNARD, Joseph (1866-1931)

Sculptor.
Cast signature.

BISEGLIA, Mario (fl.c.1900)

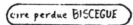

Foundry.
Cast mark.

BORREL, Alfred (b.1836)

A.BORREL

Sculptor, medallist.
Cast signature.

BOTTÉE, Louis Alexandre (1852-1941)

Sculptor, medallist.
Cast signature.

BOUCHERON, Maison (est.1858)

Jewellers. Designers include E.-H.*Becker, Jules-Paul Brateau (1844-1923), P. d'*Epinay de Briort, L.*Hirtz, Louis Rault (1847-1903).
Stamped marks.

BOULENGER, Maison (fl.1920-40)

Silversmiths.
Stamped mark.

BRACQUEMOND, Félix (1833-1914)

Designer of jewellery and enamels.
Designs executed by A.*Riquet; also designed furniture, ceramics, bookbindings.
Initial formed by cloisons.

BRANDT, Edgar (1880-1960)

E BRANDT

Metalworker and jeweller.
Stamped mark.

BRICTEUX, Antoine (fl.c.1900)

Manufacturing jewellers.
Stamped mark.

CALLOT, Jacques (fl.c.1900)

Sculptor, medallist.
Cast signature.

CARABIN, François Rupert (1862-1932)

Sculptor, medallist, designer of metalwork and jewellery; also designed ceramics, furniture. Cast signature.

CARDEILHAC, Maison (1802-1951)

Goldsmiths and silversmiths. Designers include Lucien Bonvallet (1861-1919). Firm merged with *Christofle in 1951. Stamped marks.

CARTIER (est.1869)

Jewellers. Designers include Louis Aucoc (b.1850), Georges Le Turcq (b.1859), P.*Wolfers (*see* Belgian metalwork). Stamped marks.

CAZIN, J.-M. Michel (1869-1917)

Sculptor, medallist; also made *ceramics. Cast monogram.

CHALON, Louis (b.1866)

Painter, sculptor. Designed for *Colin. Cast signature and monogram.

CHAPLAIN, Jules Clément (1839-1909)

J·C·C·

Sculptor, medallist. Cast initials.

CHAPU, Henri Michel Antoine (1833-91)

h. Chapuy

Sculptor, medallist.
Cast signature.

CHARPENTIER, Alexandre (1856-1909)

Alexandre Charpentier

Sculptor, medallist, designer.
Designed for Fontaine Frères
Vaillant; also designed ceramics,
glass, furniture.
Cast signature and monogram.

CHEURET, Albert (fl.1900-1930)

Albert Cheuret

Sculptor, designer of metalwork.
Cast signature.

CHRISTOFLE, Orfèvrerie (est.1830)

CHRISTOFLE

PROD.
CHRISTOFLE

Goldsmiths, silversmiths and
manufacturers of plate and other
metalwork. Designers include
Eugène Bourgouin (1880-1925),
M.*Dufrène, C.C.*Fjerdingstad,
P.*Follot, A.*Mare (*see* French
graphics), J.M.*Olbrich (*see*
German metalwork), Gio Ponti
(b.1981), O.*Roty, Lino Sabattini
(fl.c.1950), Louis Süe (1875-1968).
Stamped marks.

COLIN, E., & Cie (fl.c.1900)

E.COLIN&Cᴵᴱ
PARIS

Foundry and metalworkers.
Designers include L.*Chalon.
Cast mark.

COUDRAY, Marie Alexandre (b.1864)

Ḉoudray

Sculptor, medallist.
Cast signature.

DAMMANN, Paul-Marcel (1885-1939)

Sculptor, medallist.
Cast signature.

DEBAIN, A. (fl.c.1900)

Manufacturing silversmiths.
Output includes mounts designed
by H.C. van de*Velde (*see* German
ceramics, metalwork, Belgian
furniture) for ceramic vases sold at
La *Maison Moderne (*see* French
ceramics). Other designers include
Maurice Giot (fl.c.1900)
Stamped mark.

DELBET, Pierre (fl.c.1900)

Ð

Sculptor.
Cast monogram.

DÉRIOT (fl.1900-20)

Manufacturing silversmiths.
Stamped mark.

DESCOMPS, Emanuel-Jules Joë (1872-1948)

Sculptor, goldsmith, medallist,
enamellist; also modelled glass
figures.
Chiselled signature.

DESPRÈS, Jean (1889-1980)

Silversmith, metalworker, jeweller.
Stamped mark and engraved
signature.

DROPSY, Jean-Baptiste-Emile (1858-1923)

E.DROPSY

Medallist, jeweller.
Chiselled signature.

DUNAND, Jean (1877-1942)

Metalworker, designer of jewellery; also lacquer craftsman and *furniture designer.
Stamped initials.

DUPUIS, Jean-Baptiste Daniel (1849-99)

ᗪANIEL ᗪVPVIS

Painter, sculptor, medallist.
Cast signature.

EPINAY DE BRIORT, Prosper, Comte d' (b.1836)

ℬ

Sculptor, jeweller. Designed for Maison *Boucheron.
Stamped monogram.

ETLING (fl.1920-40)

ETLING . PARIS

Retailers who issued editions of objects and figures in metal. Designers include Dimitri Chiparus (fl 1915-35), Claire-Jeanne-Roberte Colinet (fl.1910-30), Maurice Guiraud-Rivière (fl.c.1920); also supervised design and production of *ceramics, *glass.
Cast mark.

FEUILLÂTRE, Eugène (1870-1916)

Sculptor, silversmith, jeweller, enamellist.
Engraved signature, stamped initials.

FJERDINGSTAD, Carl Christian (1891-1968)

Norwegian silversmith and designer who worked in Holland (1918-21) and France (1921-68). Designed for *Christofle.
Stamped mark.

FOLLOT, Paul (1877-1941)

Designer of jewellery, silver and other metalwork. Designed for La *Maison Moderne (*see* French ceramics), *Christofle, *Lapparra; also designed furniture, carpets, textiles.
Stamped monogram.

FONSÈQUE & OLIVE (est.1885)

Jewellers.
Stamped mark.

FOUQUET, Maison (est.c.1860)

Goldsmiths and jewellers. Designers include Eric Bagge (1890-1978), A.M.*Cassandre (*see* French graphics), Charles Desrosiers (fl.c.1900), Alphonse Fouquet (1828-1911), Georges Fouquet (1862-1957), Jean Fouquet (b.1899), Jean Lambert-Rucki (1888-1967), A.*Mucha (*see* French graphics).
Stamped marks.

FOUQUET-LAPAR (fl.1920-40)

Manufacturing silversmiths.
Stamped mark.

FROMENT-MEURICE, Emile (1837-1913)

FROMENT MEURICE

Goldsmith and jeweller.
Stamped signature.

GAILLARD, Lucien (b.1861)

Goldsmith, silversmith, jeweller, enamellist; also designed ceramics (*see* Scandinavian ceramics).
Stamped marks.

GARIOD, Léon (fl.1870-1910)

Jeweller, enamellist. Executed designs by L.*Gautrait.
Stamped mark.

GARNIER, Jean (fl.c.1900)

Sculptor.
Cast signature.

GAUTRAIT, Lucien (fl.c.1900)

Jeweller, enamellist, designer.
Designs executed by L*Gariod, Maison *Vever.
Stamped signature.

GOULDEN, Jean (1878-1947)

JEAN GOULDEN

Metalworker, enamellist.
Enamelled signature.

HARTZ & CIE (est.1904)

Jewellers. Successors to *Plisson & Hartz.
Stamped mark.

HÉNIN & CIE (fl.c.1930)

Manufacturing silversmiths.
Stamped mark.

HIRNÉ (fl.c.1900)

Jewellers and enamellists.
Executed designs by F.*Thesmar.
Chiselled mark.

HIRTZ, Lucien (b.1864)

LH

Jewellery and metalwork designer, enamellist. Designed for *Boucheron. Cast initials.

HUSSON, Henri (1852-1914)

Goldsmith, silversmith, jeweller, metalworker. Engraved signature.

JANVIER, Lucien Joseph René (b.1878)

L.JANVIER

Sculptor, medallist, jeweller. Cast signature.

KANN, Léon (fl.c.1900)

L Kann

Sculptor, designer; also designed ceramics. Cast signature.

KELLER, Gustave (est.1857)

Manufacturing silversmiths. Stamped marks.

LAFITTE, Gaston (fl.1900-10)

Jeweller, enamellist. Stamped mark.

LALIQUE, René (1860-1945)

 LALIQUE R.L.

R. LALIQUE

Designer, jeweller, enamellist, medallist, metalworker; also designed *glass, textiles. Stamped initials and signatures.

LAPPARRA (fl. early 20th century)

Manufacturing silversmiths.
Designers include P.*Follot.
Stamped mark.

LARCHE, François-Raoul (1860-1912)

Sculptor. Works cast by *Siot-Decauville.
Cast signature.

LEFÈBVRE, Eugène (est.1895)

Manufacturing jewellers and silversmiths.
Stamped mark.

LÉONARD, Agathon (b.1841)

Sculptor; some works cast in ceramic.
Cast signature.

MAISON DE L'ART NOUVEAU (1895-1905)

Retailers, founded by Samuel Bing (1838-1905). Supervised design and manufacture of jewellery, silver and other metalwork. Designers include Marcel Bing (1875-1920), Edward Colonna (1862-1948), Alfred Daguet (fl.c.1900), G. de *Feure (*see* French ceramics); also retailed and supervised design and production of *ceramics, glass, furniture, textiles, carpets, embroideries.
Stamped marks.

MAJORELLE, Louis (1859-1926)

L. Majorelle

Designer of metalwork; also designed ceramics, furniture.
Stamped signature.

OBIOLS, Gustave (fl.c.1900)

Spanish sculptor and jeweller working in France.
Engraved signature.

OLIER & CARON (fl.1910-40)

Manufacturing silversmiths.
Stamped mark.

PIEL FRÈRES (fl.c.1900)

Manufacturing jewellers.
Stamped mark.

PILLET, Charles (b.1869)

CH. PILLET.

Medallist.
Cast signature.

PLISSON & HARTZ (1898-1904)

Jewellers. Firm became *Hartz & Cie.
Stamped mark.

PONSCARME, Hubert (1827-1903)

H·Ponscarme.

Sculptor, medallist.
Cast signature.

PUIFORCAT, Jean Emile (1897-1945)

JEAN PUIFORCAT
PARIS

Sculptor, silversmith, designer.
Stamped mark.

RAVINET D'ENFERT (fl. 20th century)

Manufacturing silversmiths.
Stamped mark.

RIQUET, Alexandre (fl.c.1900)

Jeweller, enamellist. Executed designs by F.*Bracquemond. Monogram formed by cloisons.

RISLER & CARRÉ (fl.1920-60)

Manufacturing silversmiths. Stamped mark.

ROBIN, Maurice, & Cie (fl.1860-1900)

Goldsmiths, silversmiths, jewellers. Stamped mark.

ROCHE, Pierre (1855-1922)

Sculptor, medallist, metalworker; also designed ceramics, books. Cast initial.

ROTY, Oscar (1846-1911)

ROTY

Medallist, designer. Designed for *Christofle. Cast signature.

RUDIER, Alexis (fl.1880-1930)

ALEXIS . RUDIER.

FONDEUR . PARIS.

Foundry. Cast mark.

SAINT-YVES (fl.c.1900)

Designer. Designed jewellery for La *Maison Moderne (*see* French ceramics), Stamped mark.

SCHEIDECKER, Paul Frank (fl.1895-1915)

Jeweller, metalworker.
Chiselled monogram.

SIOT-DECAUVILLE

Foundry. Work cast for sculptors
including F.-R.*Larche.
Cast marks.

SIOT. FONDEUR. PARIS.

SOCIÉTÉ PARISIENNE D'ORFÈVRERIE (fl.c.1900)

Goldsmiths, silversmiths.
Stamped mark.

SPICER-SIMPSON, Théodore (1871-1959)

·T·S-S·

Sculptor, medallist; also printed
and illustrated books.
Cast initials.

SUSSE FRÈRES (est.1840)

Foundry.
Cast mark.

TEMPLIER, Raymond (1891-1968)

RAYMOND TEMPLIER

Designer of jewellery and enamels.
Stamped signature.

TÉTARD FRÈRES (est.1880)

Manufacturing goldsmiths and
silversmiths.
Stamped marks.

THESMAR, Fernand (1843-1912)

Designer, enamellist. Some designs executed by *Hirné; also decorated *ceramics. Monogram formed by cloisons.

THIEBAUT FRÈRES (fl. 19th and 20th century)

Foundry.
Cast mark.

TURIN, Pierre (1891-1968)

P.TURIN

Medallist.
Cast signature.

VALSUANI, C. (fl. 19th and 20th century)

Foundry.
Cast mark.

VERNIER, Séraphin Emile (1852-1927)

S. E. VERNIER

Medallist, jeweller.
Cast signature.

VEVER, Maison (est.1821)

VEVER PARIS

VEVER

Manufacturing jewellers. Designers include Edward Colonna (1862-1948), L.*Gautrait, E.S.*Grasset (*see* French graphics), Etienne Tourette (fl.1875-1915).
Stamped marks.

VOULOT, Félix (b.1865)

VouLot

Sculptor; also designed ceramics.
Cast signature.

YENCESSE, Ovide (1869-1947)

Ovide Yencesse   O YENCESSE

Sculptor, medallist.
Cast signatures.

BELGIAN METALWORK & JEWELLERY

ALTENLOH, E. (fl. 20th century)

Manufacturing silversmiths.
Designers include R.*Altenloh.
Stamped mark.

ALTENLOH, Robert (fl.1910-30)

ROBERT ALTENLOH

Silversmith, designer. Designed for
E.*Altenloh.
Stamped mark.

DELHEID (fl.c.1930)

Manufacturing silversmiths.
Stamped marks.

FEYS, Jacques (fl.c.1900)

FEYS, JACQUES
BRUXELLES

Jeweller.
Stamped mark.

VELDE, Henry Clemens van de *see* German metalwork

WISKEMANN (est.1872)

Manufacturers of silver, plate and
other metalwork.
Stamped mark.

WOLFERS FRÈRES (est.1812)

Goldsmiths, silversmiths, jewellers.
Designers include H.C. van de
*Velde (*see* German metalwork),
P.*Wolfers.
Stamped marks.

WOLFERS, Philippe (1858-1929)

Sculptor, jeweller, metalworker, designer. Designed for *Wolfers Frères; also designed *ceramics, *glass, furniture, carpets. Stamped mark.

DUTCH METALWORK & JEWELLERY

AMSTELHOEK (c.1900-1903)

Workshops making metalwork founded by Willem Hoeker (b.1862) of *Hoeker & Zoon. Designers include J.*Eisenloeffel, J.*Blinxma; workshops also made *ceramics, furniture. Stamped mark.

BEGEER, C.J. (1868-1919)

Manufacturing silversmiths. In 1919, merged with Van *Kempen & Zoon to become Van *Kempen, Begeer & Vos. Designers include C.J.A. *Begeer (see Dutch ceramics), J.*Eisenloeffel. Stamped marks.

BLINXMA, Johannes (1872-1941)

Silversmith, metalworker. Designed for *Amstelhoek. Stamped mark.

EERSTEN, Van den & HOFMEIJER (fl. 20th century)

Silversmiths and jewellers. Stamped mark.

EHRLICH, Christa (b.1903)

Real name: Christine Ehrlich.
Austrian designer working in
Holland from 1927. Designed for
*Voorschoten; also decorated
ceramics and designed textiles,
wallpapers.
Stamped monogram.

EISENLOEFFEL, Jan (1876-1957)

Silversmith, metalworker, designer.
Designed for *Amstelhoek,
C.J.*Begeer, *Hoeker & Zoon,
*Vereinigte Werkstätte für Kunst
im Handwerk (*see* German
metalwork); also designed
*ceramics, *glass.
Stamped initials and mark.

GERRITSEN & VAN KEMPEN, Koninklijke (1924-60)

Manufacturing silversmiths.
Designers include Gustav Beran
(b.1912).
Stamped mark.

HOEKER & ZOON (fl. 20th century)

Goldsmiths, silversmiths, jewellers.
Designers include J.*Eisenloeffel,
Willem Hoeker (b.1862),
B.*Nienhuis (*see* Dutch ceramics),
Elias Voet (1868-1940).
Stamped mark.

HOOGENDIJK, F.A. (1878-1934)

Silversmith, metalworker.
Stamped monogram.

JACOBS, J.A. (1885-1968)

Silversmith, jeweller.
Stamped initial.

KEMPEN, BEGEER & VOS, Van (1919-25)

Manufacturing silversmiths. In
1925, changed name to
Zilverfabriek *Voorschoten.
Designers include C.J.A. *Begeer
(*see* Dutch ceramics).
Stamped marks.

KEMPEN & ZOON, J.M. van (1789-1919)

Manufacturing silversmiths. In
1919 merged with C.J.*Begeer and
J. Vos to become Van *Kempen,
Begeer & Vos.
Stamped marks.

KOOTEN & ZOON, L.W. van (fl. 20th century)

Manufacturing silversmiths.
Stamped marks.

KRIEGE, Jan (1884-1944)

Sculptor, silversmith, jeweller.
Stamped mark.

SCHIJFSMA, J. (fl.c.1900)

Manufacturing silversmiths.
Stamped mark.

STICHTSCHE ZILVERFABRIEK (est.1904)

Manufacturing silversmiths started
by Cornelis L.J. Begeer (b.1868)
who had previously worked for
family firm C.J.*Begeer.
Stamped marks.

VOORSCHOTEN, Zilverfabriek (est.1925)

Manufacturing silversmiths.
Previously Van *Kempen, Begeer
& Vos. Designers include
C.*Ehrlich.
Stamped mark.

ZWOLLO, Frans (1872-1945)

Silversmith, metalworker, designer.
Designed for *Hagener
Silberschmiede (*see* German
metalwork).
Stamped initials and signature.

ZWOLLO, Frans (b.1896)

Silversmith, metalworker.
Stamped initial.

GERMAN METALWORK & JEWELLERY

BAHNER, Franz, Silberwaren-Fabrik (1895-c.1965)

Manufacturing silversmiths.
Designers include P.*Behrens.
Stamped mark.

BEHRENS, Peter (1868-1940)

Architect, painter, designer of silver, metalwork and jewellery. Designed for *Bahner, *Bruckmann & Söhne, *Hueck, *Mayer, *Mosgau, *Rückert, *Sächsische Metallwarenfabrik, K.M. Seifert & Co., *Wilkens & Söhne; also designed *ceramics, glass, posters, books (*see* German graphics), furniture, textiles, carpets. Stamped monogram.

BINDER, Wilhelm (est.1868)

Manufacturing silversmiths.
Stamped marks.

BING, Gebrüder (est.1895)

Manufacturers of metalwork, including pewter.
Stamped mark.

BOSSELT, Rudolf (1871-1938)

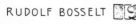 

Sculptor, medallist, designer of jewellery; also designed posters, books.
Cast signature, stamped monogram.

BRANDSTETTER, A. (fl.1890-1930)

GUSS VON A. BRANDSTETTER MÜNCHEN   Foundry.
Cast mark.

BREMER SILBERWARENFABRIK (BSF) (1905-81)

Manufacturing silversmiths.
Stamped mark.

BRUCKMANN, Peter, & Söhne (1805-1973)

Manufacturing silversmiths.
Designers include Adolf Amberg
(1874-1913), Friedrich Adler
(1878-c.1942), P.*Behrens,
H.*Christiansen (*see* German
ceramics, furniture), Friedrich
Felger (fl.c.1910-c.1920), Paul
Haustein (1880-1944), E.*Lettré,
E.J.*Margold (*see* German
ceramics), J.M.*Olbrich.
Stamped mark.

BUDER & WIBRECHT (fl.c.1900)

BUDER u. WIBRECHT   Foundry.
BLN   FRIEDENAU   Cast mark.

BÜRCK, Paul (1878-1947)

Painter, jewellery designer.
Designed for T.*Fahrner,
J.*Friedmann's Nachfolger; also
designed books (*see* German
graphics), *textiles.
Stamped signature.

CISSARZ, Johann Vincenz (1873-1942)

Painter, designer, medallist.
Designed silver for *Viëtor and
jewellery for Alfred Berger; also
designed posters, books,
bookbindings.
Cast signature.

CLARFELD & SPRINGMEYER (est.1858)

Manufacturers of silver and plate.
Designers include J.M.*Olbrich,
H.C. van de *Velde.
Stamped mark.

CRANACH, Wilhelm Lucas von (1861-1918)

Painter, designer of jewellery.
Designs executed by Louis Werner.
Stamped monogram.

DASIO, Ludwig (fl.c.1900)

Sculptor, medallist, metalworker;
also designed ceramics, graphics.
Cast signature.

DELL, Christian (1893-1974)

Silversmith, metalworker, designer.
Stamped monogram.

DEPPE, E. (est.1853)

Manufacturing silversmiths.
Stamped mark.

ELKAN, Benno (1877-1933)

Painter, sculptor, medallist.
Cast initials.

ENGELHARD, Roland (1868-1951)

Sculptor, medallist.
Cast signature.

ERBE, H.A. (fl.1885-1960)

Manufacturers of silver, plate and other metalwork.
Stamped mark.

FAHRNER, Theodor (1868-1929)

Son of founder of firm of manufacturing jewellers. Commissioned designs from Hans Eduard Berlepsch-Valendas (1849-1921), P.*Bürck, M.J.*Gradl, L.*Habich, P.*Huber, Georg Kleeman (1863-1932), Julius Müller-Salem (fl.1900-20), J.M.*Olbrich, H.C. van de *Velde among others.
Stamped monogram.

FEUCHT, Wilhelm (fl. late 19th and 20th century)

Manufacturing jewellers. Designers include Emil Riester (d.1925/26).
Stamped mark.

FRANCK, A.C. (fl.1900-40)

Manufacturing silversmiths.
Stamped mark.

FRIEDMANN'S NACHFOLGER, J. (D.& M. Löwenthal) (fl. 20th century)

JFN

Silversmiths, jewellers. Designers include P.*Bürck, H.*Christiansen (*see* German ceramics, furniture), J.M.*Olbrich.
Stamped mark.

GAUL, August (1869-1921)

A.GAUL

Sculptor, medallist; figures also cast in *ceramic.
Cast signature.

GEYGER, Ernest Moritz (b.1861)

E M. GEYGER

Painter, sculptor.
Cast signature.

GLADENBECK, H., & Sohn

Foundry, metalworkers.
Cast marks.

Akt-Ges.H.Gladenbeck&Sohn

GOSEN, Theodor von (1873-1943)

Designer of jewellery. Designed for
*Vereinigte Werkstätte für Kunst
im Handwerk.
Stamped monogram.

GRADL, Max Josef (b.1873)

Designer of jewellery. Designed for
T.*Fahrner; also designed books.

GROSS, Karl (1869-1934)

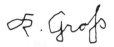

Jeweller, metalworker, designer.
Designed jewellery for Alfred
Berger, *Vereinigte Werkstätte für
Kunst im Handwerk, and
metalwork for L. Lichtinger; also
designed ceramics.
Engraved signature.

HABICH, Ludwig (1872-1949)

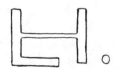

Sculptor, medallist, designer.
Designed for T.*Fahrner.
Cast monogram.

HAEGERMANN (c.1925-c.1950)

Manufacturing goldsmiths and silversmiths.
Stamped mark.

HAEGERMANN, Gustav (c.1900-c.1950)

Manufacturing silversmiths.
Stamped mark.

HAGENER SILBERSCHMIEDE (1910-1914)

Workshop. F.*Zwollo Sr (*see* Dutch metalwork) executed designs by F.H.*Ehmke, J.L.M. Lauweriks (1864-1932), F.H. Ernst Schneidler (1882-1956).
Stamped marks

HAHN, Hermann (1868-1942)

H.HAHN

Sculptor, medallist.
Cast signature.

HIRZEL, Hermann Robert Catumby (1864-1939)

HzL

Designer of jewellery. Designed for Louis Werner, *Vereinigte Werkstätte für Kunst im Handwerk; also designed graphics.
Stamped mark.

HOETGER, Bernhard (1874-1949)

Hoetger

Sculptor, painter, designer, architect. Designed for *Koch & Bergfeld; also made ceramic figures.
Cast signature.

HUBER, Patriz (1878-1902)

 Architect, designer. Designed jewellery for T.*Fahrner and silver for *Mayer, *Rückert; also designed furniture, textiles, carpets. Stamped monogram.

HUECK, Eduard (est.1864)

 Manufacturers of metalwork including pewter. Designers include P.*Behrens, A.*Müller, J.M.*Olbrich. Stamped mark.

HUTSCHENREUTHER, C.F., & Co. (est.c.1900)

 Manufacturers of silver and other metalwork; also made *ceramics. Stamped mark.

KALTENBACH, Karl, & Söhne (est.1870)

 Manufacturing silversmiths. Stamped mark.

KAYSER-SOHN, J.P. (est.1862)

Manufacturers of metalwork including 'Kayzerzinn' pewter. Designers include Hugo Leven (1874-1956). Stamped marks.

KIRCHGAESSNER & KRAFT (est.1904)

 Manufacturing silversmiths and jewellers. In 1909 R.*Kraft established his own company. Stamped mark.

KLINGER, Max (1857-1920)

Painter, sculptor; also designed books, posters.
Cast signature.

KÖBERLIN, Gebrüder (fl. 20th century)

Manufacturing silversmiths.
Stamped mark.

KÖBERLIN, Richard (fl. 20th century)

Manufacturing silversmiths.
Stamped mark.

KOCH & BERGFELD (est.1829)

Manufacturing silversmiths.
Designers include Gustav Elsass (fl.c.1930), B.*Hoetger, Hugo Leven (1874-1956), A.*Müller, H.C. van de *Velde.
Stamped mark.

KÖDDING, Johannes (b.1876)

Sculptor, medallist.
Cast signature.

KONEJUNG, Hermann (est.1873)

Manufacturers of gold, silver, plate and other metalwork.
Stamped marks.

KRAFT, Robert (est.1909)

Manufacturing silversmiths and jewellers. Previously part of *Kirchgaessner & Kraft. Stamped mark.

KÜNNE, Arnold (fl. late 19th century-c.1960)

Manufacturing silversmiths. Stamped mark.

LEMOR, Julius (fl.1900-50)

Manufacturing silversmiths. Stamped mark.

LETTRÉ, Emil (1876-1954)

Silversmith, designer. Designed for *Bruckmann & Söhne. Stamped initial.

LEVINGER, Heinrich (est.c.1875)

Manufacturing jewellers. Designers include O.*Prutscher (*see* Austrian metalwork). Stamped mark.

LEYRER, C. (fl. end 19th, early 20th. century)

GUSS C LEYRER. MUNCHEN

Foundry. Cast mark.

LUTZ & WEISS (est.c.1860)

Manufacturing silversmiths. Stamped marks.

MAGNUSSEN, Harro (1861-1908)

HARRO MAGNUSSEN

Sculptor, medallist.
Cast signature.

MAYER, Martin (est.1888)

Manufacturing silversmiths.
Designers include P.*Behrens,
H.*Christiansen (*see* German
ceramics, furniture), P.*Huber.
Stamped mark.

MAYRHOFER, Adolf von (1864-1929)

A von MAYRHOFER

Goldsmith, silversmith, jeweller.
Stamped signature.

MEYEN, H., & Co. (fl.1890-1920)

Manufacturing silversmiths.
Stamped mark.

MORY, Ludwig (est.1883)

Manufacturers of pewter.
Designers include Rudolf
Horrmann (fl.1880-1900), Fritz
Mory (fl.1905-20).
Engraved mark.

MOSGAU, Franz (1807-c.1960)

Manufacturing silversmiths.
Designers include P.*Behrens.
Stamped mark.

MÜLLER, Albin (1871-1941)

Architect, designer. Designed for Johann L. Brandner, J. Götz, *Hueck, *Koch & Bergfeld, *Wilkens & Söhne; also designed *ceramics, glass.
Stamped monogram.

MÜLLER, Theodor (fl. early 20th century)

Silversmith and jeweller. Executed designs by H.C. van de *Velde.
Stamped mark.

MÜLLER, Wilhelm (fl.1880-1940)

Manufacturing goldsmiths and silversmiths.
Stamped mark.

OLBRICH, Josef Maria (1867-1908)

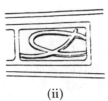

(i)

(ii)

Austrian architect and designer who settled in Germany in 1899. Designed for *Christofle (*see* French metalwork), *Clarfeld & Springmeyer, T.*Fahrner, *Friedmann's Nachfolger, *Hueck, Robert Koch (1852-1902), *Sächsische Metallwarenfabrik, *Schroeder, *Zerrenner; also designed *ceramics, furniture, posters.
Stamped (i) and cast (ii) monograms.

ORION (fl.c.1900)

Pewter manufacturers. Designers include Friedrich Adler (1878-c.1942).
Stamped mark.

PAUSER, Joseph (fl. 20th century)

J.P.

Silversmiths. Designers included
H.C. van de *Velde.
Stamped mark.

PFEIFER, Felix (1871-1945)

FELIX PFEIFER

Sculptor, medallist.
Cast signature.

PÖLLATH, Carl (fl.1890-1940)

C.PŒLLATH

Foundry.
Cast mark.

PREISS, Ferdinand (b.1882)

F.Preiss.

Sculptor, designer. Designed
bronze and ivory figures for PK.
Engraved signature.

RIEGEL, Ernst (1871-1939)

R.

Goldsmith, silversmith, jeweller;
also designed ceramics.
Engraved rebus (German for
hedgehog is Igel).

RIEMERSCHMID, Richard (1868-1957)

Painter, architect, designer.
Designed for *Bruckmann &
Söhne, Dresdner Werkstätten für
Handwerkskunst (est.1898),
Konrad König, *Vereinigte
Werkstätten für Kunst im
Handwerk, *Weishaupt; also
designed ceramics, glass, furniture,
textiles, wallpapers.
Stamped monogram.

ROMER, Georg (1868-1922)

G.R.   **CR**

Sculptor, medallist.
Cast initials and monogram.

RÜCKERT, M.J. (1901-c.1960)

RÜCKERT

R ⊛

Manufacturing goldsmiths and
silversmiths. Designers include
P.*Behrens, H.*Christiansen (*see*
German ceramics, furniture),
P.*Huber.
Stamped marks.

SÄCHSISCHE METALLWARENFABRIK AUGUST WELLNER SÖHNE (est.1854)

Manufacturers of silver, plate and
other metalwork. Designers
include P.*Behrens, J.M.*Olbrich.
Stamped marks.

SANDIG, Paul, & Co. (fl.c.1900-c.1940)

Manufacturing silversmiths.
Stamped mark.

SAUERLAND, Gebrüder (fl.1910-40)

Manufacturing silversmiths.
Stamped mark.

SCHERF, Walter, & Co. (est.1899)

O S I R I S

Manufacturers of metalwork
including 'Osiris' pewter.
Designers include Friedrich Adler
(1878-c.1942), Hermann Gradl
(1869-1934).
Stamped mark.

SCHMITZ, F.H. (1896-1906)

„ORIVIT"

Manufacturers of 'Orivit' pewter.
Taken over by *Württembergische
Metallwarenfabrik in 1906.
Stamped mark.

SCHROEDER, C.B. (fl.c.1900)

CBS 90

Manufacturing silversmiths.
Designers include J.M.*Olbrich.
Stamped mark.

SCHWECHTEN, W. (fl.1900-50)

S

Manufacturing silversmiths.
Stamped mark.

SEFFNER, Carl (1861-1932)

C· Seffner·

Sculptor, medallist.
Cast signature.

STUCK, Franz von (1863-1928)

FRANZ STVCK   FRANZ VON STVCK

Painter, sculptor, designer; also
designed furniture, posters, books.
Cast signatures.

STURM, Paul (b.1859)

PAVL STVRM

Sculptor, medallist.
Cast signature.

SY & WAGNER (est.c.1850)

SY & WAGNER.

Manufacturers of gold, silver and
plate.
Stamped mark.

VELDE, Henry Clemens van de (1863-1959)

Belgian architect and designer working largely in Germany. Designed silver made by *Clarfeld & Springmeyer, *Debain (see French metalwork), Albert Feinauer, *Koch & Bergfeld, T.*Müller, *Pauser, other metalwork by K.M. Seifert, jewellery by *Wolfers Frères (see Belgian metalwork); also designed *ceramics, glass, posters, books, *furniture (see Belgian furniture), textiles, embroideries, wallpaper. Stamped mark.

VEREINIGTE SILBERWAREN-FABRIKEN DÜSSELDORF (1810-c.1960)

Manufacturing silversmiths. Stamped mark.

VEREINIGTE WERKSTÄTTEN FÜR KUNST IM HANDWERK (est.1897)

Workshops for the production of jewellery, metalwork. Designers include T. von *Gosen, Paul Haustein (1880-1944), H.R.C.*Hirzel, B.*Paul (see German graphics), R.*Riemerschmid; also designed *ceramics and had workshops for the manufacture of furniture. Stamped mark.

VIËTOR, E.L. (fl.c.1900)

Manufacturing silversmiths. Designers include H.*Christiansen (see German ceramics, furniture), J.V.*Cissarz, Paul Haustein (1880-1944). Stamped mark.

VOGT, A. (fl.c.1900)

Manufacturing jeweller,
metalworkers, enamellists.
Designers include H.*Christiansen
(*see* German ceramics, furniture).
Stamped mark.

WEBER, Bernard (fl.1885-1915)

Manufacturing silversmiths and
jewellers.
Stamped mark.

WEISHAUPT, Carl (est.1802)

Manufacturing silversmiths.
Designers include
R.*Riemerschmid.
Stamped mark.

WENDE, Theodor (1883-1968)

TH·WENDE

Silversmith, jeweller.
Stamped signature.

WERNER, O. Max (fl.c.1900)

O.M.WERNER

Designer of jewellery. Designed for
family firm J.H. Werner.
Stamped signature

WILKENS, M.H., & Söhne (est.1810)

Manufacturing silversmiths.
Designers include P.*Behrens,
A.*Müller, H.*Vogeler (*see*
German graphics).
Stamped marks.

WINKELMANN, H.F. (fl.1910-50)

Manufacturers of silver, plate and other metalwork.
Stamped mark.

WOLLENWEBER, Eduard (fl. 20th century)

E.D.WOLLENWEBER

Manufacturing silversmiths and jewellers. Designers include Adelbert Niemeyer (1867-1932). Stamped mark.

WURM, H. (fl.1900-40)

Manufacturing silversmiths.
Stamped mark.

WÜRTTEMBERGISCHE METALLWARENFABRIK (WMF) (est.1880)

Manufacturers of silver, plate and other metalwork. Designers include F.A. Breuhaus (fl.c.1930), Paul Haustein (1880-1944), Wilhelm Wagenfeld (b.1900); also manufactured glass.
Stamped marks.

ZERRENNER, F. (fl.c.1900)

Ω

Manufacturing jeweller. Designers include J.M.*Olbrich.
Stamped mark.

ZIECH, Ludwig, & Co. (fl.c.1890-1928)

Z. & Co.

Manufacturers of silver, plate and other metalwork.
Stamped mark.

AUSTRIAN METALWORK & JEWELLERY

BECK, Vilmos Fémes (1885-1918)

Hungarian sculptor, medallist.
Cast monogram.

CZESCHKA, Carl Otto (1878-1960)

Designer of metalwork and
jewellery. Designed for *Wiener
Werkstätte; also designed ceramics,
*graphics, textiles.
Stamped monogram.

DIETRICH, Oscar (1853-1940)

Goldsmith, silversmith, jeweller.
Worked for family firm G.W.
Dietrich.
Stamped initials.

DUBB, Vincent Carl (1852-1922)

Silversmith.
Stamped initials.

FRIEDMANN, Eduard (1877-1920)

Manufacturing silversmiths and
jewellers. Designers include Hans
Bolek (b.1890), Philipp Häusler
(1887-1966), E.J.*Margold (*see*
German ceramics), O.*Prutscher.
Stamped marks.

GHEDINA, Agostino (fl.c.1900)

Jeweller.
Stamped initials.

HAGENAUER, Werkstätte (1898-1956)

Manufacturers of silver and other metalwork.
Stamped mark.

HOFFMANN, Josef (1870-1956)

Architect, designer of metalwork and jewellery. Designed for *Klinkosch, *Sturm, *Wiener Werkstätte, Würbel & Czokally; also designed *ceramics, *glass, furniture, textiles, *graphics. Stamped monogram.

HOSSFELD, Josef (fl.1900-25)

Silversmith. Worked for *Wiener Werkstätte.
Stamped monogram.

KALLERT, Carl (fl.c.1900)

Silversmith. Worked for *Wiener Werkstätte.
Stamped monogram.

KAUBA, Carl (fl.c.1900)

C. Kauba.

Sculptor.
Cast signature.

KAUTSCH, Heinrich (b.1889)

ნ KAUTSCH

Sculptor, medallist.
Cast signature.

KLINKOSCH, J.C. (est.1797)

Manufacturers of metalwork.
Designers included Oswald
Haerdtl (1899-1959), J.*Hoffmann,
M.*Powolny (*see* Austrian glass,
ceramics), O.*Prutscher, Richard
Teschner (1879-1948), Otto
Wagner (1841-1918), Karl
Witzmann (b.1883).
Stamped marks.

KOCH, Konrad (fl.1900-25)

Metalworker. Worked for *Wiener
Werkstätte.
Stamped monogram.

KOUNITSKY, Franz (b.1880)

Sculptor, medallist.
Cast signature.

KOWARZIK, Joseph (1860-1911)

Sculptor, medallist.
Cast signature.

KRUPP, Arthur (fl.1900-50)

Manufacturers of silver and other
metalwork. Designers include
Philippe Häusler (1887-1966),
Guido Heigl (1890-c.1926),
O.*Prutscher.
Stamped marks.

KURZER & WOLF (fl.1880-1925)

Manufacturing silversmiths and
jewellers.
Stamped mark.

LIKARZ-STRAUSS, Maria (b.1893)

L

Designer, enamellist. Worked for
*Wiener Werkstätte; also designed
ceramics, glass, graphics, textiles,
wallpapers.
Enamelled initial.

LORENZL, Joseph (fl.1920-40)

Sculptor. Modelled bronze and
ivory figures; also modelled
ceramic figures for
F.*Goldscheider.
Cast signatures.

MARSCHALL, Rudolf Ferdinand (b.1873)

Marschall fec.

Sculptor, medallist.
Cast signature.

MOSER, Koloman (1868-1918)

Designer of jewellery, silver and
other metalwork. Designed for
*Rozet & Fischmeister, *Scheid,
*Wiener Werkstätte; also designed
*ceramics, *glass, *graphics,
furniture, textiles, carpets.
Stamped monogram.

PECHE, Dagobert (1886-1923)

Designer of jewellery, silver and
other metalwork. Designed for
G.W. Dietrich, *Wiener Werkstätte;
also designed *ceramics, *glass,
furniture, textiles, carpets,
wallpapers, *graphics.
Stamped initial.

PFLAUMER, Eugen (fl.1900-25)

Goldsmith. Worked for *Wiener Werkstätte.
Stamped monogram.

POLLAK, Alfred (est.1878)

Manufacturing jewellers and silversmiths. Designers include Hans Bolek (b.1890), Rudolf Hammel (fl.c.1900), Ernst Lichtblau (1883-1963), A.*Nechansky (*see* Austrian glass). Stamped mark.

PRUTSCHER, Otto (1880-1949)

Architect, designer of jewellery, silver and other metalwork. Designed for *Friedmann, Anton Heldwein, Hutter & Schranz, *Klinkosch, *Krupp, *Levinger (*see* German metalwork), Rudolf Souval, *Wiener Werkstätte; also designed *ceramics, glass, furniture, textiles, carpets, posters (*see* Austrian graphics). Stamped monogram.

ROZET & FISCHMEISTER (fl.c.1900)

Manufacturing jewellers. Designers include K.*Moser, Hubert von Zwickle (1875-1950). Stamped mark.

SCHEID, Georg Adam (est.1862)

Manufacturing silversmiths, jewellers, enamellists. Designers included K.*Moser. Stamped marks.

SIESS, Joseph (fl.c.1900)

Manufacturing jeweller.
Stamped mark.

STURM, Alexander (est.1882)

Manufacturing silversmiths.
Designers included J.*Hoffmann,
Antoinette Krasnik (fl.c.1900).
Stamped marks.

SUCHARDA, Stanislas (1866-1916)

Bohemian sculptor and medallist.
Cast signature.

SUDFELT, Hermann, & Co. (est.1835)

(H·S)

Manufacturing silversmiths.
Stamped mark.

SZANDRIK (fl.c.1900)

Manufacturing silversmiths.
Stamped mark.

TERESZCZUK, P. (fl.c.1900)

P. Tereszczuk

Sculptor.
Cast signature.

TURRIET & BARDACH (fl.c.1900)

T. B.

Manufacturing jewellers.
Stamped mark.

WESTELL ALLGAYER & CO. (fl.c.1900)

Foundry.
Cast mark.

WIENER WERKSTÄTTE (1903-32)

Workshops producing jewellery, silver and other metalwork, enamels. Designers include Artur Berger (1892-1981), L.*Calm-Wierink (*see* Austrian ceramics), C.*Czeschka, Philipp Häusler (1887-1966), J.*Hoffmann, M.*Likarz-Strauss, B.*Löffler (*see* Austrian ceramics), K.*Moser, A.*Nechansky (*see* Austrian glass), D.*Peche, O.*Prutscher, Richard Teschner (1879-1948), E.J.*Wimmer, Karl Witzmann (b.1883), J.*Zimpel; workshops also produced *ceramics, *glass, *furniture, textiles, graphics. Stamped marks.

WIMMER, Eduard Josef (1882-1961)

Designer of jewellery, silver and other metalwork. Designed for *Wiener Werkstätte; also designed glass, furniture, carpets, graphics. Stamped monograms.

ZIMPEL, Julius (1896-1925)

Painter, designer of silver. Designed for *Wiener Werkstätte; also designed ceramics, glass, carpets, textiles. Stamped monogram.

SCANDINAVIAN METALWORK & JEWELLERY

ANDERSEN, Just (est.1915)

Danish manufacturing silversmiths. Designers include Just Andersen (1884-1943), Ellen Schlanbusch (fl.c.1950). Stamped mark.

BOJESENS, Kaj, Sølvsmedie (est.1913)

Danish manufacturing silversmiths. Designers include Kaj Bojesen (1886-1958), Magnus Stephensen (b.1903). Stamped mark.

BOLIN, W.A. (est.1845)

Firm of jewellers founded in Russia by Swedish family. Moved to Sweden in 1916. Stamped mark.

COHR, Carl M. (est. 1860)

Danish manufacturing silversmiths. Stamped mark.

DITZEL, Nanna (b.1923)

Danish designer of silver and other metalwork. Designed for *Jensen, *Michelsen; also designed ceramics, furniture, textiles. Stamped monogram.

FROM (fl. 20th century)

Danish silversmiths and jewellers.
Stamped mark.

GROTH, S.

Danish assay master 1863-1904.
Stamped monogram.

HAMMER, Marius (fl. late 19th and 20th century)

M

Norwegian manufacturing
silversmiths, enamellists. Designers
include Marius Hammer (1847-
1927), Emil Høye (1875-1958).
Stamped mark.

HANSEN, Hans (est.1906)

Danish manufacturing silversmiths.
Designers include Hans Hansen
(1884-1940), Karl Gustav Hansen
(b.1914).
Stamped mark.

HEISE, C.F.

Danish assay master 1904-32.
Stamped monogram.

HINGELBERG, Franz (est.1897)

Danish manufacturing silversmiths.
Designers include Svend
Weihrauch (b.1899).
Stamped mark.

JENSEN, Georg (est.1904)

Danish manufacturing silversmiths and jewellers. Designers include Gundorph Albertus (fl.1920-40), Sigvard Bernadotte (b.1907), N.*Ditzel, Georg Jensen (1866-1935), Henning Koppel (1818-81), E.*Nielsen, H.*Nielsen, J.*Rohde, Magnus Stephensen (b.1903). Stamped marks.

MAGNUSSEN, Erik (1884-1961)

Danish silversmith and designer. Designed for *Gorham (*see* American metalwork). Stamped monogram.

MICHELSEN, Anton (est.1841)

Danish manufacturing silversmiths and jewellers. Designers include Mogens Ballin (1871-1914), Thorvald Bindesbøll (1846-1908), N.*Ditzel, Jørgen Ditzel (fl.c.1950), Kaj Fisker (1893-1965), Harald Slott-Møller (1864-1937). Stamped marks.

NIELSEN, Evald Johannes (1879-1958)

Danish silversmith and designer. Designed for *Jensen. Stamped signature.

NIELSEN, Harald (1892-1977)

Danish silver designer. Designed for *Jensen. Stamped initials.

ROHDE, Johann (1856-1935)

Danish silversmith and designer.
Designed for *Jensen; also
designed furniture, textiles.
Stamped monogram.

SIGSGAARD, J.

Danish assay master 1933-60.
Stamped monogram.

SINDING, Stephan Abel (1846-1922)

Norwegian sculptor, modeller.
Cast signature.

SUOMEN KULTASEPPÄT (fl. late 19th and 20th century)

Finnish manufacturing
silversmiths.
Stamped mark.

RUSSIAN METALWORK AND JEWELLERY

FABERGÉ (1842-1918)

Goldsmiths, silversmiths, jewellers, enamellists. Craftsmen include A.W.*Holmström, M.E.*Perchin, H.*Wigström.
Stamped marks.

FABERGÉ, Peter Carl (1846-1920)

Goldsmith, jeweller, designer. Worked for family firm *Fabergé from 1870.
Stamped initials.

GRACHEV BROS (1866-c.1917)

Silversmiths, enamellists.
Stamped mark.

HOLMSTRÖM, August Wilhelm (1829-1903)

Finnish goldsmith and jeweller working in Russia for *Fabergé from 1857. Adopted son Albert (1876-1925) used same mark.
Stamped initials.

KLINGERT, Gustav G. (fl.1890-1915)

Manufacturing silversmiths.
Stamped mark.

OVCHINNIKOV, Pavel (1853-c.1917)

Manufacturing silversmiths.
Stamped mark.

PERCHIN, Michael Evlampievich (1860-1903)

Goldsmith. Worked for *Fabergé.
Stamped initials.

TILLANDER, A. (est.1860)

Manufacturing silversmiths. In
1917, moved to Finland.
Stamped marks.

WIGSTRÖM, Henrik (1862-c.1930)

Finnish goldsmith working in
Russia for *Fabergé.
Stamped initials.

BRITISH GRAPHICS

BEARDSLEY, Aubrey Vincent (1872-98)

 AVBREY BEARDSLEY

Graphic artist, illustrator, book designer, poster designer. Printed signature and mark.

BEGGARSTAFF BROTHERS

Name adopted by the brothers-in-law James Pryde (1869-1941) and William Nicholson (1872-1949), when they collaborated on the design of posters during the 1890s. Printed signature.

BELL, Robert Anning (1863-1933)

R·Aη·B

Painter, sculptor, graphic artist, illustrator, book designer; also designed stained glass and mosaics. Printed signature.

BRANGWYN, Frank (1867-1956)

FB

Painter, graphic artist, illustrator, poster designer; also designed *ceramics, *furniture, textiles. Printed initials.

BRICKDALE, Eleanor Fortescue (1871-1945)

EFB

Painter, graphic artist, illustrator, book designer. Printed initials.

CALDECOTT, Randolph (1846-86)

R C

Painter, graphic artist, illustrator.
Printed initials.

CHESWORTH, Frank (b.1868)

FRANK CHESWORTH

Painter, graphic artist, poster
designer, book designer.
Printed signature.

COOPER, Austin (b.1890)

AVSTIN
COOPER

Painter, graphic artist, poster
designer.
Printed signature.

CRAIG, Edward Gordon (1872-1966)

C

Poster designer, stage designer.
Printed initial.

CRANE, Walter (1845-1915)

Painter, graphic artist, illustrator,
book designer, poster designer.
Also designed wallpapers, textiles,
ceramics.
Printed monogram and rebus.

DAVIS, Louis (1861-1941)

Illustrator, book designer; also
designed stained glass.
Printed monogram.

DUNCAN, John (1866-1945)

Painter, graphic artist, illustrator.
Printed mark.

ECKERSLEY, Tom (b.1914)

ECKERSLEY

Painter, graphic artist, poster designer.
Printed signature.

GASKIN, Arthur Joseph (1862-1928)

A
J
G

Painter, graphic artist, poster designer.
Printed signature.

GEORGE, T. (fl.1905-30)

Painter, graphic artist, poster designer.
Printed signature.

GERE, Charles March (1869-1957)

Painter, graphic artist, illustrator.
Printed monogram.

GREENAWAY, Kate (1846-1901)

K.G.

Painter, graphic artist, illustrator.
Printed initials.

HARDY, Dudley (1866-1922)

Dudley Hardy

Painter, graphic artist, illustrator, poster designer.
Printed signature.

HASSALL, John (1868-1948)

Painter, graphic artist, illustrator, poster designer; also designed ceramic figures.
Printed signature and monograms.

HAVINDEN, Ashley (b.1903)

Painter, graphic artist, poster designer; also designed textiles.
Printed signature.

HOUSMAN, Laurence (1865-1959)

Graphic artist, illustrator, book designer, stage designer.
Printed initials.

IMAGE, Selwyn (1849-1930)

Graphic artist, illustrator, book designer; also designed furniture, needlework, stained glass.
Printed initials.

KING, Jessie Marion (1876-1949)

Graphic artist, illustrator, book designer; also designed jewellery, decorated *ceramics, made batik-printed textiles.
Printed signature.

KNOWLES, Reginald Lionel (1879-1950)

Illustrator, book designer, poster designer.
Printed intials.

MACKINTOSH, Charles Rennie (1868-1928)

Architect, painter, graphic artist, poster designer; also designed furniture, metalwork, textiles.
Printed initials.

MACKINTOSH, Margaret Macdonald (1865-1933)

Painter, graphic artist, poster designer; also made *metalwork, embroideries.
Printed initials.

McKNIGHT KAUFFER, Edward (1890-1954)

Painter, graphic artist, illustrator, poster designer; also designed carpets (*see* British furniture) and tapestries.
Printed initials.

MORRIS, Talwin (1865-1911)

Book designer; also designed metalwork.
Printed monogram.

MUCKLEY, Leonard Fairfax (fl.1890-1920)

≡L·F·M≡

Illustrator.
Printed initials.

PAINE, Charles (fl.1920-40)

CPAINE

Poster designer.
Printed signature.

PARTRIDGE, Bernard (1861-1945)

Painter, graphic artist, illustrator, poster designer.
Printed signature.

PISSARRO, Lucien (1863-1944)

Painter, graphic artist, illustrator, book designer.
Printed initials.

RANSOM, Sidney (fl.1890-1910)

Painter, graphic artist, poster designer.
Printed signature.

RAVEN-HILL, Leonard (1867-1942)

Painter, graphic artist, illustrator, poster designer.
Printed signatures.

RICKETTS, Charles de Sousy (1866-1931)

Painter, sculptor, graphic artist, illustrator, book designer, stage designer; also designed jewellery, needlework.
Printed monogram.

RITCHIE, Alick P.F. (fl.1890-1910)

Illustrator, poster designer.
Printed signature.

ROBERTSON, Walford Graham (1866-1948)

Painter, graphic artist, illustrator, poster designer.
Printed monogram.

ROGERS, William S. (fl.1890-1910)

W.J. Rogers

Poster designer.
Printed signature.

RYLAND, Henry (1856-1924)

HENRY RYLAND

Painter, graphic artist, illustrator, book designer, poster designer.
Printed signature.

SCOTSON-CLARK, George Frederick (fl.1890-1910)

SCOTSON-CLARK.

Painter, graphic artist, poster designer.
Printed mark and signature.

SUMNER, Heywood (1853-1940)

HS

Painter, graphic artist, illustrator; also designed *furniture, metalwork, stained glass, wallpapers, *textiles.
Printed initials.

TAYLOR, Frederick (1875-1963)

FRED
TAYLOR

Painter, graphic artist, poster designer.
Printed signature.

TURBAYNE, Albert Angus (1866-1940)

Graphic artist, book designer, poster designer.
Printed monograms.

WEBB, Archibald Bertram (b.1887)

Painter, graphic artist, poster designer.
Printed signature.

WELLS, Reginald Fairfax (1877-1951)

Sculptor, illustrator; poster designer; also made *ceramics.
Printed signature.

WHITE, Ethelbert (1891-1972)

ЄThεllεrГWhiℓε

Painter, graphic artist, poster designer.
Printed signature.

WOODROFFE, Paul Vincent (1875-1954)

P W

Painter, graphic artist, illustrator, book designer; also designed stained glass.
Printed initials.

AMERICAN GRAPHICS

ARMSTRONG, Margaret Neilson (1867-1944)

Painter, illustrator, book designer.
Printed monogram.

BATCHELDER, Ernest Allan (1875-1957)

Illustrator; also designed ceramics.
Printed initials.

BINDER, Joseph (1898-1972)

binder

Painter, graphic artist, poster
designer.
Printed signature.

BIRD, Elisha Brown (1867-1943)

⋅BIRD⋅

Graphic artist, illustrator, poster
designer.
Printed signature.

BOBRITSKY, Vladimir (b.1898)

BOBRITSKY

BOBRI

Russian painter, graphic artist,
poster designer, stage designer
working in USA from 1921; also
designed textiles.
Printed signatures.

BRADLEY, William H. (1868-1962)

Graphic artist, illustrator, book
designer, poster designer; also
designed furniture, interior
decoration.
Printed initial and signature.

BRAGDON, Claude Fayette (1866-1946)

Architect, graphic artist, illustrator, book designer, poster designer, stage designer.
Printed monogram and mark.

BRODOVITCH, Alexey (1900-71)

A.Brodovitch

Russian graphic artist, poster designer working in USA from 1934 (*see also* French graphics).
Printed signature and monogram.

CARQUEVILLE, Will (1871-1946)

Will Carqueville

Graphic artist, poster designer.
Printed signature and monogram.

COVARRUBIAS, Miguel (1904-57)

Graphic artist, illustrator, poster designer. Also designed textiles.
Printed signature.

DECORATIVE DESIGNERS, The (1895-1932)

Graphic design studio founded in New York City by architect Henry Thayer.
Printed monogram.

DOW, Arthur Wesley (1857-1922)

Painter, graphic artist, poster designer.
Printed signature.

ELLIS, Harvey (1852-1904)

HARVEY ELLIS

Painter, sculptor, architect, poster designer.
Printed signature.

GARNET, Porter (fl.1890-1910)

Painter, graphic artist, illustrator.
Printed monogram.

GIBSON, Charles Dana (1867-1944)

Painter, graphic artist, illustrator, poster designer.
Printed signature.

GLENNY, Alice Russell (1858-1924)

ARG

Painter, poster designer.
Printed initials.

GOODHUE, Bertram Grosvenor (1869-1924)

B·G·G·

Architect, graphic artist, book designer, poster designer.
Printed initials.

GOULD, Joseph J., Jr. (fl.1895-1920)

J J Gould

Graphic artist, illustrator, poster designer.
Printed signature.

HAPGOOD, Theodore Brown, Jr. (1871-1938)

T B HAPGOOD JR

T.B.H.

B
H
T

Sculptor, graphic artist, book designer, poster designer.
Printed signature and initials.

HAZENPLUG or (from 1911) HAZEN, Frank (1874-1931)

Graphic artist, illustrator, book designer, poster designer; also designed and decorated ceramics and designed metalwork, furniture.
Printed monogram.

HUNTER, Dard (1883-1966)

Graphic artist, illustrator, book designer. Also designed ceramics, stained glass and metalwork.
Printed monogram.

LOEWY, Raymond (b.1893)

L O E W Y

Product designer, graphic artist, illustrator, poster designer, stage designer.
Printed signature.

LUNDBORG, Florence (1871-1949)

Painter, graphic artist, illustrator, poster designer.
Printed initials.

McMANUS, Blanche (b.1870)

Painter, graphic artist, illustrator, book designer, poster designer.
Printed initials.

McVICKAR, Henry Whitney (b.1860)

Illustrator, poster designer.
Printed signature.

O'KANE, Helen Marguerite (b.1879)

Graphic artist, illustrator.
Printed monogram.

PARRISH, Maxfield (1870-1966)

M.P.

Painter, graphic artist, illustrator,
poster designer.
Printed initials and signature.

PENFIELD, Edward (1866-1925)

Graphic artist, illustrator, poster
designer.
Printed signature and monograms.

PLANK, George Wolf (fl.1910-1940)

Graphic artist, illustrator.
Printed initials.

PRENDERGAST, Maurice Brazil (1859-1924)

M.B.P.

Painter, graphic artist, illustrator,
poster designer.
Printed initials.

RAMSDELL, Frederick Winthrop (1865-1915)

Painter, graphic artist, poster
designer.
Printed signature.

REED, Ethel (b.1874)

Graphic artist, illustrator, book
designer, poster designer.
Printed signature.

RHEAD, Louis John (1857-1926)

English graphic artist, illustrator, book designer, poster designer working largely in USA.
Printed signature and initials.

RHYS, Dynevor (fl.1915-35)

Illustrator.
Printed initials.

SACKER, Amy M. (b.1876)

Illustrator, book designer.
Printed monogram.

SLOAN, John (1871-1952)

Painter, graphic artist, illustrator, book designer, poster designer.
Printed signature.

STOWELL, M. Louise (fl.1895-1930)

Painter, poster designer.
Printed monogram

VERTÈS, Marcel (1895-1962)

Painter, graphic artist, poster designer, stage and film designer.
Printed signature.

WOODBURY, Charles Herbert (1864-1940)

Painter, poster designer.
Printed signature.

FRENCH GRAPHICS

ALEXEIEFF, Alexander (1901-1982)

Alexeïeff

Graphic artist, poster designer,
stage designer.
Printed signature.

ATCHÉ, Jean (fl.1890-1915)

Atché

Poster designer.
Printed signature.

AURIOL, George (1863-1938)

G.A

Painter, graphic artist, illustrator,
book designer, poster designer.
Printed monogram.

AVELOT, Henri (d.c.1934)

H. Avelot

Painter, graphic artist, illustrator,
poster designer.
Printed signature.

BAC, Ferdinand (1859-1952)

Bac

Graphic artist, illustrator, poster
designer.
Printed signature.

BARBEY, Maurice (fl.1920-40)

mauricebarbey.

Graphic artist, poster designer.
Printed signature.

BARBIER, George (1882-1932)

C. BARBIER

Painter, graphic artist, illustrator, poster designer, stage designer; also designed textiles, wallpapers. Printed signature.

BASTARD, Marc Auguste (1863-1926)

Bastard

Painter, graphic artist, poster designer. Printed signature.

BELLENGER, Pierre (b.1909) and Jacques (fl.1930-50)

Bellenger

Brothers who designed posters in collaboration. Printed signature.

BENITO, Eduardo Garcia (b.1891)

B E N I T O

Spanish painter, graphic artist, illustrator working largely in France. Printed signature.

BERTHON, Paul Emile (1872-1909)

 Paul Berthon

Painter, graphic artist, poster designer; also designed ceramics. Printed signature.

BONNARD, Pierre (1867-1947)

Painter, graphic artist, illustrator, poster designer, stage designer. Printed initials.

BRODOVITCH, Atelier Alexey (fl.1925-30)

ATELIER AB

Graphic design studio founded in France by Russian artist A.*Brodovitch (*see* American graphics) before going to USA. Printed mark.

CAPPIELLO, Leonetto (1875-1942)

Italian painter, graphic artist, illustrator, poster designer working in France from 1898.
Printed signature.

CARLU, Jean (1900-83)

JEAN
CARLU

Graphic artist, illustrator, poster designer.
Printed signature.

CASSANDRE, Adolphe Mouron (1901-68)

A.M. CASSANDRE

Painter, poster designer. Also designed jewellery.
Printed signature.

CHÉRET, Jules (1836-1932)

Painter, poster designer; also designed glass.
Printed signature.

COLIN, Paul (b.1892)

PAUL
COLIN

Poster designer, stage designer.
Printed signature.

COULON, Eric de (b.1888)

Coulon

Graphic artist, poster designer.
Printed signature.

DOMERGUE, Jean Gabriel (1889-1962)

Painter, graphic artist, illustrator, poster designer.
Printed signature.

DUFAU, Clémentine Hélène (b.1869)

CH Dufau

Graphic artist, poster designer.
Printed signature.

DUPAS, Jean (1882-1964)

Jean - Dupas

Painter, graphic artist, illustrator, poster designer.
Printed signature.

ERTÉ (1892-1988)

Real name: Romain de Tirtoff.
Russian painter, sculptor, graphic artist, illustrator, poster designer, stage designer, fashion designer working largely in France; also designed textiles.
Printed signature.

FAY, Georges (fl.1890-1910)

Graphic artist, poster designer.
Printed signature.

FEURE, Georges de (1868-1928)

Painter, graphic artist, illustrator, poster designer. Also designed furniture, *ceramics, *glass, carpets, textiles.
Printed monograms.

GESMAR, Charles (1900-28)

Poster designer, stage designer.
Printed signature.

GIRBAL, Gaston (fl.1920-40)

Poster designer.
Printed signature.

GRASSET, Eugène Samuel (1841-1910)

Painter, graphic artist, illustrator,
book designer, poster designer;
also designed furniture, ceramics.
Printed monogram.

GRUN, Jules Alexandre (1868-1934)

Graphic artist, poster designer.
Printed signature.

HERBIN, Auguste (1882-1960)

Painter, graphic artist, poster
designer.
Printed signature.

HERMANN-PAUL, René Georges (1874-1940)

Graphic artist, illustrator, poster
designer.
Printed monogram.

IBELS, Henri Gabriel (1867-1936)

Painter, graphic artist, illustrator,
poster designer.
Printed signature.

JOSSOT, Henri Gustave (b.1866)

Painter, graphic artist, illustrator,
poster designer.
Printed signature.

KIFFER, Charles (b.1902)

Ch.Kiffer.

Poster designer.
Printed signature.

KOW, Alexis (1901-78)

A. KOW.

Painter, graphic artist, illustrator,
poster designer.
Printed signature.

LEPAPE, Georges (1887-1971)

Painter, graphic artist, illustrator,
poster designer, fashion designer.
Printed signature.

LOUPOT, Charles (1892-1962)

Loupot

Graphic artist, illustrator, poster
designer.
Printed signature.

MARE, André (1887-1932)

Painter, poster designer, book
designer. Also designed furniture,
textiles, interiors.
Printed initials.

MARTIN, Charles (1884-1934)

Painter, graphic artist, illustrator,
poster designer, stage designer;
also designed furniture, wallpapers,
textiles, scent bottles.
Printed signature.

MARTY, André Edouard (1882-1974)

Painter, graphic artist, illustrator, poster designer; also designed jewellery, enamels.
Printed signature.

MÉTIVET, Lucien (1863-1932)

Painter, graphic artist, illustrator, poster designer.
Printed initials.

MISTI (1865-1923)

Real name: Ferdinand Mifliez.
Graphic artist, poster designer.
Printed signature, monogram.

MOURGUE, Pierre (fl.1920-40)

Graphic artist, poster designer.
Printed signature.

MUCHA, Alphonse (1860-1939)

Bohemian painter, sculptor, graphic artist, poster designer working in France; also designed interiors, jewellery, ceramic decoration, carpets.
Printed signature and initial.

ORAZI, Manuel (1860-1934)

Graphic artist, illustrator, poster designer.
Printed signature.

PAL (1860-1942)

Real name: Jean de Paléologue.
Graphic artist, illustrator, poster
designer.
Printed signatures.

PONTY, Max (fl.1920-40)

M.PONTY

Graphic artist, poster designer.
Printed signature.

RAPIN, Henri (b.1873)

Painter, poster designer; also
designed furniture, ceramics.
Printed signature.

RIVIÈRE, Henri (1864-1951)

Painter, graphic artist, illustrator.
Printed initials.

SAUVAGE, Sylvain (1888-1948)

Graphic artist, illustrator.
Printed signature.

SAVIGNAC, Raymond (b.1886)

Savignac

Painter, graphic artist, poster
designer.
Printed signature.

STEINLEN, Théophile Alexandre (1859-1923)

Graphic artist, illustrator, poster
designer.
Printed signature.

TOULOUSE-LAUTREC, Henri de (1864-1901)

Painter, graphic artist, illustrator, poster designer; also designed ceramics, stained glass.
Printed monogram.

VALLOTTON, Félix (1865-1925)

Painter, graphic artist, illustrator, poster designer.
Printed initials.

VALTAT, Louis (1869-1952)

L.Valtat

Painter, graphic artist, poster designer, stage designer; also decorated ceramics.
Printed signature.

VERNEUIL, Maurice Pillard (1869-1942)

MRV.

Graphic artist, poster designer.
Printed initials.

VINCENT, René (1879-1936)

*RENE
UINCENT*

Graphic artist, illustrator, poster designer, stage designer.
Printed signature.

ZACK, Léon (1892-1980)

Léon Zack

Painter, graphic artist, poster designer.
Printed signature.

BELGIAN GRAPHICS

ACKER, Florimond van (1858-1940)

Painter, graphic artist, poster designer.
Printed signature.

BERCHMANS, Emile (1867-1947)

Painter, graphic artist, illustrator, poster designer, stage designer.
Printed signature and monogram.

CASSIERS, Hendrich (1858-1944)

Painter, graphic artist, illustrator, poster designer.
Printed signature.

COMBAZ, Gisbert (1869-1941)

Painter, graphic artist, illustrator, poster designer; also designed ceramics.
Printed monogram.

CRESPIN, Adolphe (1859-1944)

Painter, poster designer, stage designer.
Printed initials.

CRETEN, Victor C.J. (1878-1966)

Architect, painter, poster designer.
Printed signature.

DELVILLE, Jean (1867-1953)

Painter, graphic artist, illustrator, poster designer.
Printed monogram.

DONNAY, Auguste (1862-1921)

Painter, graphic artist, illustrator, poster designer.
Printed monogram.

EVENEPOEL, Henri (1872-99)

h.evenepoeL.

Painter, graphic artist, illustrator, poster designer.
Printed signature.

GAUDY, Georges (b.1872)

Painter, poster designer.
Printed signature.

JORIS, Léontine (1870-1962)

Painter, illustrator, poster designer.
Printed signature.

KHNOPFF, Fernand (1858-1921)

Painter, sculptor, graphic artist, illustrator.
Printed monogram.

LEMMEN, Georges (1865-1916)

Painter, graphic artist, poster designer.
Printed monogram.

LIVEMONT, Privat (1861-1936)

Graphic artist, poster designer.
Printed signature.

MAGRITTE, René (1898-1967)

MAGRiTTE

Painter, sculptor, graphic artist, poster designer.
Printed signature.

MARFURT, Leo (1894-1977)

marfurt

Graphic artist, poster designer.
Printed signature.

MEUNIER, Henri Georges Isidore (1873-1922)

Graphic artist, illustrator, poster designer.
Printed signature.

OTTEVAERE, Henri (1870-1944)

Painter, graphic artist, poster designer.
Printed monogram.

RASSENFOSSE, Armand A.L. (1862-1934)

Painter, graphic artist, illustrator, poster designer.
Printed monogram.

ROPS, Félicien (1833-98)

Painter, graphic artist, illustrator, poster designer.
Printed initials.

RYSSELBERGHE, Théodore van (1862-1926)

Painter, poster designer.
Printed monogram.

STEVENS, Gustave Max (1871-1946)

G.M. STEVENS

Painter, poster designer.
Printed signature.

DUTCH GRAPHICS

CASPEL, Johann van (b.1870)

v. Caspel

Poster designer. Also designed furniture.
Printed signature.

HOYTEMA, Theo van (1863-1917)

Moytema

Painter, graphic artist, illustrator, poster designer.
Printed signature.

HUSZAR, Vilmos (1884-1960)

V. HUSZAR

Architect, graphic artist, poster designer.
Printed signature.

KLIJN, Albertus (1895-1981)

ALB.KLIJN

Graphic artist.
Printed signature.

LAAN, Kees van der (b.1903)

Kees van der Laan

Painter, poster designer.
Printed signature.

LECK, Bart van der (1876-1958)

BvoL

Painter, graphic artist, poster designer; also designed rugs, *ceramics.
Printed initials.

NIEUWENHUIS, Theodor Willem (1866-1951)

TN

Graphic artist; also designed
*ceramics.
Printed initials.

RAEMAEKERS, Louis (1869-1956)

Louis Raemaekers

Painter, graphic artist, poster
designer.
Printed signature.

SLUITER, Willy (b.1873)

Willy Sluiter—

Painter, graphic artist, illustrator,
poster designer.
Printed signature.

SLUYTERS, Jan (1881-1957)

·S

Painter, graphic artist, illustrator,
book designer.
Printed monogram.

TEN BROEK, Willem Frederik (b.1905)

TenBroek

Poster designer.
Printed signature.

TOOROP, Jan (1858-1928)

J.T.

Painter, graphic artist, book
designer, poster designer; also
designed ceramics.
Printed initials.

WENCKEBACH, L.W.R. (1860-1937)

(i)

(ii)

Painter, graphic artist, illustrator,
book designer.
Printed initials: (i) c.1900, (ii)
c.1925.

WIJDEVELD, Hendrikus Theodorus (b.1885)

H.Th.W.

Architect, graphic artist.
Printed initials.

GERMAN GRAPHICS

ALASTAIR (1887-1968)

Alastair

Real name: Baron Hans Henning Voigt. Graphic artist, illustrator. Printed signature.

ARPKE, Otto (1886-1943)

ARPKE

Painter, graphic artist, poster designer.
Printed signature.

BALUSCHEK, Hans (1870-1935)

HB

Painter, graphic artist, illustrator, book designer.
Printed monogram.

BEHMER, Markus (1879-1958)

 B

Painter, graphic artist, illustrator, book designer.
Printed monogram and initial.

BEHRENS, Peter (1868-1940)

Architect, painter, graphic artist, book designer, poster designer; also designed *metalwork, *ceramics, glass, furniture, textiles.
Printed monogram.

BERNHARD, Lucian (1883-1972)

BERN HARD

Architect, graphic artist, poster designer; also designed furniture rugs, wallpaper, lighting fixtures.
Printed signature.

BERNHARD ROSEN (fl.1925-35)

Graphic design studio founded by L.*Bernhard and Herr Rosen in Berlin.
Printed mark.

BÜRCK, Paul (1878-1947)

Painter, graphic artist, illustrator, book designer. Also designed *textiles (see German furniture), *jewellery (see German metalwork).
Printed initial.

CHRISTIANSEN, Hans (1866-1945)

Painter, graphic artist, poster designer. Also designed *furniture, textiles, wallpaper, jewellery, glass, stained glass, *ceramics.
Printed monogram.

CISSARZ, Johann Vincenz (1873-1942)

Painter, graphic artist, illustrator, book designer, poster designer; also designed medals (see German metalwork).
Printed initials and monogram.

DEUTSCH, Ernst (b.1883)

Graphic artist, poster designer.
Printed signature.

ECKMANN, Otto (1865-1902)

Painter, graphic artist, illustrator, book designer, poster designer. Also designed metalwork, *furniture, textiles, ceramics, jewellery, stained glass.
Printed monogram.

EDEL, Edmund (1863-1923)

Painter, graphic artist, poster designer.
Printed initials.

EHMKE, Fritz Hellmut (b.1878)

Graphic artist, illustrator, book designer.
Printed initials.

ENGELHARD, Julius Ussy (1883-1964)

Painter, graphic artist, illustrator, poster designer.
Printed signature.

ERDT, Hans Rudi (b.1883)

Graphic artist, poster designer.
Printed signature.

FENNECKER, Josef (1895-1956)

Painter, graphic artist, poster designer, stage designer.
Printed signature.

FUSS, Albert (b.1889)

Poster designer.
Printed signature.

GRIMM, Richard (1873-1952)

Painter, graphic artist, illustrator.
Printed monogram.

GULBRANSSON, Olaf (1873-1958)

OLAF. G.

Painter, graphic artist, illustrator.
Printed signature.

GUSSMANN, Otto (b.1869)

Painter, graphic artist, poster
designer.
Printed initial.

HEINE, Thomas Theodor (1867-1948)

Painter, graphic artist, illustrator,
book designer, poster designer.
Printed monogram.

HOFMANN, Ludwig von (1861-1945)

Painter, graphic artist, illustrator,
poster designer.
Printed monogram.

HOHLWEIN, Ludwig (1874-1949)

Graphic artist, poster designer.
Printed signature.

JUNGHANS, Julius Paul (fl.1900-15)

Painter, graphic artist, illustrator, poster designer.
Printed monogram.

KAMPMANN, Walter (b.1887)

Painter, graphic artist, book designer, poster designer.
Printed signature.

KANDINSKY, Wassily (1869-1944)

Russian painter, graphic artist, poster designer, working largely in Germany.
Printed initial.

KEIMEL, Hermann (b.1889)

KEIMEL

Painter, graphic artist, poster designer.
Printed signature.

KLEUKENS, Friedrich Wilhelm (b.1878)

Painter, graphic artist, illustrator, book designer, poster designer.
Printed monogram.

KLINGER, Julius (1876-1950)

J. KLINGER

Painter, graphic artist, illustrator, poster designer.
Printed signature.

KNAB-KOCH (fl.1920-30)

Graphic design studio founded by
Hans Heinrich Koch (1896-1977)
and Kaufmann Richard Knab.
Printed mark.

LECHTER, Melchior (1865-1937)

Painter, graphic artist, illustrator,
book designer; also designed
stained glass, furniture and textiles.
Printed monogram.

LOOSCHEN, Hans (1859-1923)

Painter, graphic artist, illustrator.
Printed monogram.

LUDWIG, Alois (fl.1895-1915)

Painter, graphic artist, illustrator.
Printed monogram.

MOOS, Carl (b.1878)

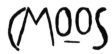

Painter, graphic artist, poster
designer.
Printed signature.

NEUMANN, Ernst (1871-1918)

Painter, graphic artist, illustrator,
poster designer.
Printed mark and initials.

NIGG, F. (fl.1890-1910)

Painter, graphic artist, illustrator.
Printed monogram.

PANKOK, Bernhard (1872-1943)

Painter, architect, graphic artist,
illustrator, book designer, stage
designer; also designed furniture.
Printed monogram.

PAUL, Bruno (1874-1968)

Architect, graphic artist, illustrator,
poster designer; also designed
ceramics, glass, furniture,
metalwork.
Printed monograms.

PREETORIUS, Emil (b.1883)

P

Illustrator, book designer, poster
designer, stage designer.
Printed initial.

SATTLER, Josef (1867-1931)

Painter, graphic artist, poster
designer.
Printed initials.

SCHEURICH, Paul (1883-1945)

Scheurich

Painter, graphic artist, poster
designer; also modelled ceramic
figures and designed tableware.
Printed signature.

SCHMOLL VON EISENWERTH, Karl (1879-1947)

KS·E

Painter, graphic artist, illustrator, poster designer; also designed glass.
Printed initials.

SCHNACKENBERG, Walter (1880-1961)

Painter, graphic artist, illustrator, poster designer, stage designer.
Printed signature.

VOGELER, Heinrich (1872-1942)

H ▨ V.

Painter, graphic artist, illustrator, book designer, poster designer; also designed ceramics, metalwork, carpets, furniture.
Printed mark and initials.

VOLKERT, Hans (b.1878)

HV.

Painter, graphic artist, illustrator; also designed medals.
Printed initials.

VOLZ, Wilhelm (1855-1901)

Painter, graphic artist, book designer.
Printed monogram.

WEISGERBER, Albert (1878-1915)

Painter, graphic artist, illustrator.
Printed monogram.

WEISS, Emil Rudolf (1875-1942)

.CÉ.X.M.

E.R.W.

Painter, graphic artist, illustrator, book designer.
Printed initials.

WITZEL, Josef Rudolf (b.1867)

I.R.W

Painter, poster designer.
Printed initials.

AUSTRIAN GRAPHICS

AUCHENTALLER, Josef M. (1865-1949)

ᔆᢲᢇ.

Painter, graphic artist, illustrator.
Printed monogram.

BEITEL, Carl (fl.1900-20)

Ⓑ

Book designer.
Printed monogram.

BÍLEK, Frantisek (1872-1941)

Ƀ·Ƒ

Bohemian/Czechoslovakian
sculptor, graphic artist, illustrator.
Printed initials.

BILKO, Franz (b.1894)

FBILKO

Painter, poster designer.
Printed signature.

BÖHM, Adolf (1861-1907)

Painter, graphic artist, illustrator;
also designed needlework.
Printed monogram.

CZESCHKA, Carl Otto (1878-1960)

Graphic artist, illustrator, book
designer, poster designer, stage
designer; also designed ceramics,
glass, furniture, textiles,
*metalwork, jewellery, wallpapers.
Printed monogram.

DIVÉKY, Josef (1887-1951)

D I

Hungarian graphic artist, illustrator, book designer, poster designer; also designed glass. Printed initials.

HOFFMANN, Josef (1870-1956)

Architect, illustrator, book designer, poster designer; also designed furniture, *glass, *ceramics, textiles, wallpaper, *metalwork, jewellery. Printed monogram.

JUNG, Moritz (1885-1915)

Graphic artist, illustrator, poster designer, book designer; also designed glass. Printed monogram.

KALVACH, Rudolf (1883-1932)

R· K·

Painter, graphic artist, illustrator, poster designer. Printed initials.

KLIMT, Gustav (1863-1918)

GVSTAV.
KLI MT.

GK·

Painter, graphic artist, illustrator, poster designer; also designed interior decoration (*see* Austrian furniture). Printed initials and signature.

KOKOSCHKA, Oskar (1886-1980)

Painter, graphic artist, illustrator, poster designer. Printed initials and monogram.

KÖNIG, Friedrich (1857-1941)

Painter, graphic artist, illustrator.
Printed monogram.

LÖFFLER, Bertold (1874-1960)

Painter, graphic artist, illustrator,
book designer, poster designer,
stage designer; also designed
furniture, textiles, *ceramics, glass,
metalwork, jewellery.
Printed monogram.

MOSER, Koloman (1868-1918)

Painter, graphic artist, illustrator,
book designer, poster designer,
stage designer; also designed
furniture, textiles, *ceramics,
*glass, *metalwork, jewellery.
Printed monogram.

ORLIK, Emil (1870-1932)

Painter, graphic artist, illustrator,
poster designer; also designed
interior decoration (*see* Austrian
furniture).
Printed monogram.

PECHE, Dagobert (1886-1923)

Graphic artist, book designer,
poster designer; also designed
furniture, carpets, wallpaper,
textiles, *metalwork, jewellery,
*ceramics, *glass.
Printed signature.

PRUTSCHER, Otto (1880-1949)

Architect, poster designer; also designed furniture, glass, stained glass, *metalwork, jewellery, ceramics, textiles.
Printed monogram.

ROLLER, Alfred (1864-1935)

Painter, graphic artist, illustrator, book designer, poster designer, stage designer.
Printed monogram.

SCHUFINSKY, Victor (b.1876)

Graphic artist, poster designer.
Printed monogram.

SCHWETZ, Karl (1888-1965)

SCHWETZ

Graphic artist, illustrator, book designer, poster designer; also designed ceramics.
Printed signature.

ITALIAN GRAPHICS

BISTOLFI, Leonardo (1859-1933)

$\mathcal{B}istolfi$

Sculptor, graphic artist, poster designer.
Printed signature.

BOMPARD, Luigi (b.1879)

ℓℬ

Painter, graphic artist, illustrator.
Printed monogram.

CALZAVARA, A. (fl.1920-40)

A. CALZAVARA

Poster designer.
Printed signature.

DUDOVICH, Marcello (1865-1927)

D

Graphic artist, illustrator, poster designer.
Printed initial.

GARRETTO, Paolo (b.1903)

Painter, graphic artist, illustrator, poster designer.
Printed signature.

HOHENSTEIN, Adolf (b.1854)

Hohenstein

Painter, graphic artist, poster designer.
Printed signature.

METLICOVITZ, Leopoldo (1868-1944)

Graphic artist, book designer,
poster designer.
Printed monogram.

RIZZI, Antonio (1861-1941)

Painter, graphic artist, illustrator.
Printed signature.

RUBINO, Antonio (1880-1964)

A RUBINO

Painter, graphic artist, illustrator,
poster designer.
Printed signature.

TERZI, Aleardo (b.1870)

Painter, graphic artist, illustrator,
poster designer.
Printed mark.

TOFANO, Sergio (b.1886)

sTo

Painter, graphic artist, illustrator.
Printed signature.

SCANDINAVIAN GRAPHICS

ANDERSEN, Valdemar (1875-1928)

Danish painter, graphic artist,
illustrator, book designer, poster
designer; also modelled ceramic
figures.
Printed monogram.

FISCHER, Paul (b.1860)

Danish painter, sculptor, poster
designer.
Printed signature

GALLÉN, Axel (1865-1931)

Changed name to Akseli Gallen-
Kallela in 1905. Finnish painter,
graphic artist, illustrator; also
designed furniture, textiles.
Printed monogram.

HEILMANN, Gerhard (1859-1946)

Danish painter, graphic artist,
illustrator, book designer; also
decorated ceramics.
Printed monogram.

KITTELSEN, Theodor (1857-1914)

Norwegian painter, graphic artist,
illustrator; also designed ceramic
decoration.
Printed initials.

LARSSON, Carl O. (1853-1919)

Swedish painter, graphic artist, illustrator.
Printed initials.

MUNTHE, Gerhard Peter (1847-1929)

Norwegian painter, graphic artist, illustrator; also designed ceramics, rugs and tapestries (*see* Scandinavian furniture).
Printed signature.

RUSSIAN GRAPHICS

AKIMOV, Nikolai Pavlovich (1901-68)

Painter, graphic artist, poster designer, stage designer.
Printed initial.

BAKST (1866-1924)

Real name: Leon Nikolayevich Rosenberg. Painter, illustrator, poster designer, stage designer.
Printed signature.

BILIBIN, Ivan Yakovlevich (1876-1942)

Painter, graphic artist, illustrator.
Printed signature and initials.

BORISOV, Grigori Ilych, and PRUSAKOV (b.1899)

Graphic artists who collaborated on poster designs.
Printed combined signature.

EL LISSITZKY (1890-1941)

Real name: Eleazar Lissitzky. Architect, painter, graphic artist, illustrator, poster designer, stage designer.
Printed monogram and initials.

FAVORSKY, Vladimir (1886-1964)

Graphic artist, illustrator, poster designer.
Printed monogram.

KUSTODIEV, Boris Mikhailovich (1878-1927)

Б. К.

Painter, graphic artist, illustrator, poster designer, stage designer.
Printed initials.

LANCERAY, Yevgeny Yevgenevich (1875-1964)

Painter, graphic artist, illustrator, stage designer.
Printed monogram.

LAVINSKY, Anton Mikhailovich (1893-1968)

ЛАВИНСКИИ

Poster designer, stage designer.
Printed signature.

MOOR, D. (1883-1946)

D.МООР

Real name: Dimitri Stakheyevich Orlov. Illustrator, poster designer.
Printed signature.

PAKHOMOV, Alexei Fyodorovich (b.1900)

Painter, graphic artist, illustrator, poster designer.
Printed initials.

RODCHENKO, Alexander Mikhailovich (1891-1956)

Painter, architect, poster designer; also designed furniture, textiles, ceramics.
Printed monogram.

SOMOV, Constantin Andreyevich (1869-1939)

CS   *K. Comob*   Painter, graphic artist, illustrator, poster designer.
Printed initials and signature.

STENBERG, Vladimir Augustovich (b.1899) and Georgi Augustovich (1900-33)

2 СТЕНБЕРГ 2   Brothers who collaborated on poster and stage design.
Printed joint signature.

SWISS GRAPHICS

BAUMBERGER, Otto (1889-1962)

B

Painter, graphic artist, poster designer.
Printed initial.

CARDINAUX, Emile (1877-1936)

€C

Painter, graphic artist, illustrator, poster designer.
Printed initials.

KREIDOLF, Ernst (1863-1956)

EK.

Painter, graphic artist, illustrator.
Printed initials.

MATTER, Herbert (1907-84)

matter

Graphic artist, poster designer.
Printed signature.

STEINER, Joseph (b.1882)

JO/TEINER

Architect, poster designer.
Printed signature.

SPANISH GRAPHICS

CLAVÉ, Antoni (b.1913)

Painter, illustrator, poster
designer.
Printed signature.

GALÍ I FABRA, Francesc d'Assis (1880-1965)

Painter, graphic artist, poster
designer.
Printed signature.

MORELL, José (1899-1949)

Poster designer.
Printed signature.

RIQUER I INGLADA, Alexandre de (1856-1920)

Painter, graphic artist, illustrator,
book designer, poster designer;
also designed furniture, lamps,
tiles, jewellery.
Printed signature.

BRITISH FURNITURE & TEXTILES

BRANGWYN, Frank (1867-1956)

Painter. Designed furniture made by E. Pollard & Co., Paul Turpin, *Rowley Gallery, carpets woven by James Templeton & Co. and tapestries woven by *Dovecot Studios; also designed *ceramics, posters (*see* British graphics). Woven monogram.

CENTURY GUILD (active 1883-c.1892)

Group of architects, artists, designers and craftsmen, including A.H.*Mackmurdo (*see* British metalwork), H.*Horne (*see* British metalwork), S.*Image (*see* British graphics), H.*Sumner, who designed furniture, textiles and wallpapers; the Guild also designed metalwork.
Monogram incoporated in design printed on textile.

DORN, Marion (1899-1964)

Textile and rug designer. Worked for Wilton Royal Carpet Co., Edinburgh Weavers.
Woven signature.

DOVECOT STUDIOS (founded 1912)

Tapestry workshops. Designers include John Armstrong (1893-1973), F.*Brangwyn, Henry Moore (1898-1990), S.R.*Shaw, S.*Spencer, G.V.*Sutherland (*see* British ceramics), Edward Wadsworth (1889-1949). Woven mark.

DUN EMER GUILD (1902-c.1950)

Guild of weavers and embroiderers founded by Evelyn Gleeson (1855-1944), Lily Yeats (1866-1949) and Elizabeth Yeats (1868-1940); the Guild also printed books.
Woven label on carpet.

GILLOW & CO. (1695-c.1900)

GILLOW

Furniture manufacturers. Designers include Thomas Collcutt (1840-1924), Bruce Talbert (1838-81). Became *Waring & Gillow after amalgamation with S.J. Waring & Sons c.1900.
Stamped mark.

GRIERSON, Ronald (b.1901)

Textile and rug designer. Worked for Wilton Royal Carpet Co.; also designed posters.
Woven initial.

HEAL & SON (est.1834)

Furniture manufacturers. Designers include Ambrose Heal (1872-1959), Arthur Greenwood (fl.1930-50).
Printed labels.

HEAL
& SON L?.

ISOKON FURNITURE CO. (1935-c.1941)

Furniture manufacturers. Designers include Walter Gropius (1883-1969), Marcel Breuer (1902-81) and R.D. Russell (b.1903).
Printed label.

JOEL, Betty (b.1896)

Designed furniture and rugs for Betty Joel Ltd, run by her and her husband.
Woven monogram.

KENTON & CO. (1890-92)

KENTON & C⁰ Lᵀᴰ

Group of furniture designers and makers. Designers include Sydney Barnsley (1865-1926), Reginald Blomfield (1856-1942), Ernest Gimson (1864-1919), William Lethaby (1857-1931).
Stamped mark.

LIBERTY & CO. (est 1874)

'Liberty' Art Fabrics.
No. CW 160
1/6
per yard.
Width 32 inches

(i)

LIBERTY
LONDON

(ii)

(iii)

Retailers who organised the design and production of furniture, textiles and carpets. Much of the furniture was designed by Leonard Wyburd (fl.1880-1910); also retailed and supervised production of *metalwork, jewellery, *ceramics, *glass.
Printed label on textiles (i), printed acetate (ii) and paper (iii) labels on furniture.

McKNIGHT KAUFFER, Edward (1890-1954)

EMCKK

Carpet and tapestry designer. Worked for Wilton Royal Carpet Co.; also designed posters (*see* British graphics).
Woven initials and monogram.

MORRIS & CO. (1861-1940)

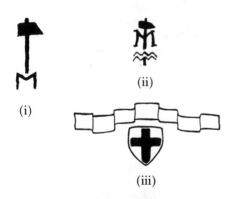

(i)

(ii)

(iii)

MORRIS & COMPANY 26 QUEEN Sᵠᴿ BLOOMSBURY

(iv)

MORRIS & COMPANY 449 OXFORD STREET LONDON W

(v)

MORRIS & C°
449 OXFORD Sᵀ W

(vi)

Firm run by William Morris (1834-96) that produced and retailed furniture, carpets, tapestries and wallpapers. Designers include Morris, W.A.S.*Benson (see British metalwork), Edward Burne-Jones (1833-99), Ford Madox Brown (1821-93), Henry Dearle (1860-1932), Kate Faulkner (fl.1860-90), Lucy Faulkner (fl.1860-90), George Jack (1855-1932), May Morris (1862-1938), Dante Gabriel Rossetti (1828-82), John Byam Shaw (1872-1919), Marian Stokes (1855-1927), H.*Sumner, Philip Webb (1831-1915); firm also produced tiles, stained glass. Woven marks on carpets (i, ii), on tapestries (iii), printed selvedge marks on textiles (iv, v), stamped mark on furniture (vi).

OMEGA WORKSHOPS (1913-19)

Workshops started by Roger Fry (1866-1934) for designing, making and decorating furniture, textiles, carpets. Designers/decorators include Fry, Vanessa Bell (1879-1961), Frederick Etchells (1886-1973), Duncan Grant (1885-1978), Percy Wyndham Lewis (1882-1956); workshops also produced ceramics.
Woven mark.

PEPLER, Marian (b.1904)

Carpet and rug designer. Some designs executed by Wilton Royal Carpet Co., Alexander Morton, & Co., Tomkinson Carpets Ltd, Gordon Russell Ltd (see Russell, G). Woven initial, monogram and signature.

ROWLEY GALLERY (est.1898)

ROWLEY
140 CHURCH ST KENSINGTON

ROWLEY

Furniture manufacturers.
Designers include F.*Brangwyn,
R.A.*Bell (*see* British graphics),
Henry Butler (fl.c.1900-c.1930),
William A. Chase (fl.c.1905).
Printed label and stamped mark.

RUSSELL, Gordon (1892-1980)

 **RUSSELL**
OF BROADWAY

Furniture designer. Founded
Russell Workshops Ltd (1927) and
Gordon Russell Ltd (1929); also
designed metalwork and glassware.
Printed label.

SEDDON, Thomas (fl.1820-60)

T.SEDDON.

Furniture manufacturers.
Designers include Augustus Welby
Northmore Pugin (1812-52), John
Pollard Seddon (1827-1906).
Stamped mark.

SHAPLAND & PETTER

S & P
B

Furniture manufacturers.
Designers include Maurice Adams
(1849-1933).
Stamped mark.

SHAW, Sax R. (fl.1945-60)

SAX R SHAW

Tapestry designer. Worked for
*Dovecot Studios.
Woven signature.

SPENCER, Stanley (1891-1959)

SS

Painter. Designed tapestries for
*Dovecot Studios.
Woven initials.

SUMNER, Heywood (1853-1940)

Painter and archaeologist. Designed wallpapers for Jeffrey & Co., textiles for Alexander Morton & Co, a tapestry for *Morris & Co., furniture for the *Century Guild; also illustrated books (*see* British graphics) and designed metalwork. Woven initials.

TRAQUAIR, Phoebe Anna (1852-1936)

Painter and embroiderer; also made enamels and illustrated books.
Stitched monogram.

WALDEN, J. (fl.1860-80)

Furniture maker. Made pieces designed by William Burges (1827-81).
Stamped initials.

WARING & GILLOW (est.c.1900)

WARING&GILLOW LTD
LANCASTER

Furniture maker. Previously *Gillow & Co. Designers include Serge Chermayeff (b.1900) and P.*Follot (*see* French metalwork).
Stamped mark.

WATT, William (fl.1860-90)

Furniture maker. Designers include Edward Godwin (1833-86).
Printed label.

AMERICAN FURNITURE & TEXTILES

ASSOCIATED ARTISTS (1879-1907)

Interior decorating firm founded by L.C.*Tiffany (*see* American glass), Candace Wheeler (1827-1923), Samuel Colman (1832-1920), Lockwood de Forest (1850-1932); partnership dissolved in 1883 after which the firm was run by C. Wheeler alone, producing textiles. Designers included D.*Wheeler. Embroidered initials.

DESKEY, Donald (b.1894)

Designed furniture made by Ypsilanti Reed Furniture Co., S. Karpen & Bros, Deskey-Vollmer, Royal Metal Co., and rugs woven by New England Guild; also designed products and packaging. Woven initial.

EAMES, Charles (1907-78)

Architect. Designed furniture for Herman *Miller Furniture Co. Signature on printed label.

FURNITURE SHOP (1906-20)

Store supplying furnishings including furniture designed by proprietors husband and wife Arthur (1860-1945) and Lucia (1870-1955) Mathews. Branded mark.

HUNZINGER, George (1835-98)

Furniture designer and manufacturer.
Stamped mark and printed label.

KIMBEL & CABUS (c.1863-82)

Furniture manufacturers.
Printed label.

LIMBERT, Charles P., Co., (1902-44)

Furniture manufacturers.
Branded mark.

MILLER, Herman, Furniture Co. (fl.1920-60)

Furniture manufacturers.
Designers include C.*Eames, George Nelson (b.1907), Gilbert Rohde (1894-1944).
Printed label and transfer monogram.

PABST, Daniel (1826-1910)

Designer and cabinetmaker. Made pieces designed by architect Frank Furness (1839-1912).
Carved signature.

PERI, Eve (fl.1935-50)

Embroiderer.
Stitched signature.

ROHLFS, Charles (1853-1936)

Designer and cabinetmaker.
Branded marks.

ROYCROFT FURNITURE SHOP (1895-1938)

Furniture workshop of the Roycroft Community founded by Elbert Hubbard (1856-1915) in East Aurora, New York; Community also produced *metalwork and printed books and periodicals.
Carved mark.

SHOP OF THE CRAFTERS (1904-20)

Furniture manufacturers.
Designers include Hungarian artist Paul Horti (1865-1907).
Printed label.

STICKLEY BROTHERS COMPANY (1891-1954)

Furniture manufacturers founded by brothers Albert (1863-1928) and John George Stickley (1871-1921). John George subsequently left to start L.& J.G.*Stickley.
Printed label.

STICKLEY, Gustav (1858-1942)

Designed and manufactured furniture at his Craftsman Workshops (1899-1916); also produced *metalwork.
Printed decals.

STICKLEY, L. & J.G. (est.1902)

Furniture manufacturers run by brothers Leopold (1869-1957) and John George Stickley (1871-1921).
Printed decals.

TOBEY FURNITURE COMPANY (1856-1954)

Furniture manufacturers. Designers include George Clingman (1857-1933), Joseph Twyman (b.1842).
Stamped copper label.

WHEELER, Dora (fl.1880-1900)

Ɗ.W.

Designed embroideries for
*Associated Artists.
Stitched initials.

FRENCH FURNITURE & TEXTILES

ADNET, Jacques and Jean (b.1901)

ADNET

Twins who jointly designed furniture and carpets for La Maîtrise and *Primavera (*see* French ceramics). From 1928 Jacques was director of *Compagnie des Arts Français; also designed ceramics, glass. Stamped signature.

BRAQUENIÉ, Atelier

Tapestry weaving workshop. Designers include J.*Lurçat. Woven mark.

BRUHNS, Bruno da Silva (fl.1920-40)

da Silva Bruhns

Carpet designer. Woven signature and monogram.

CHANAUX, Albert (fl.1910-1940)

CHANAUX&Cº

Cabinetmaker. Worked for J.E.*Ruhlmann, André Groult (1884-1967), Jean-Michel Frank (1895-1941). Stamped mark.

CHAREAU, Pierre (1883-1950)

Cabinetmaker, interior decorator. Branded monogram.

COMPAGNIE DES ARTS FRANÇAIS (est.1919)

Design studio and workshops founded by Louis Süe (1875-1968) and A.*Mare (*see* French graphics). Undertook the design and manufacture of furniture, tapestries, textiles, wallpapers. From 1928, Jacques *Adnet was director. Designers include Mathurin Meheut (1882-1958), Lucien Coutaud (b.1901), Gustave Jaulmes (1873-1959); also produced metalwork.
Woven monogram.

DELAUNAY, Sonia (1885-1979)

SD

Painter, embroiderer, designer of furniture, textiles, carpets and tapestries; also designed bookbindings, posters, stained glass, ceramics.
Woven initials.

DUNAND, Jean (1877-1942)

JEAN DUNAND

Lacquer craftsman, designer of furniture; also designed *metalwork and jewellery.
Signature in lacquer.

GALLÉ, Émile (1846-1904)

Manufacturer, designer. Designers/decorators include A.*Herbst; also designed and manufactured *ceramics, *glass.
Signatures in marquetry.

GOBELINS, Manfacture Nationale de (est.1662)

Tapestry and carpet weavers.
Designers include R.*Dufy (see French ceramics), J.*Lurçat.
Woven mark.

GOUBELY, Atelier

Tapestry weaving workshop.
Designers include M.*Gromaire, J.*Lurçat.
Woven marks.

GROMAIRE, Marcel (b.1892)

Painter, tapestry designer.
Tapestries woven at *Goubely, *Pinton.
Woven signature.

HERBST, August (fl.1885-1905)

Cabinetmaker worked for E.*Gallé.
Initial in marquetry.

JALLOT, Léon (b.1874)

Designed furniture and textiles.
Worked for *Maison de l'Art Nouveau (see French ceramics) before setting up on his own in 1904.
Monogram in lacquer.

LANSKOY, André (fl.1940-60)

LANSKOY

Painter. Designed tapestries.
Woven signature.

LE CORBUSIER (1887-1965)

L - C

Real name: Charles Jeanneret.
Swiss architect, painter, designer of
furniture and tapestries, working
in France. Furniture manufactured
by *Thonet (*see* Austrian
furniture); tapestries woven by
Atelier *Tabard.
Woven initials.

LELEU, Jules (1883-1961)

LELEU

Cabinetmaker, carpet designer.
Woven signature.

LURÇAT, Jean (1892-1966)

JLURÇAT.   LURÇAT

Painter and tapestry designer.
Tapestries woven at *Braquenié,
*Gobelins, *Goubely, *Pinton,
*Tabard. Also designed *ceramics.
Woven signatures and monograms.

MARTINE, Atelier (1911-c.1930)

Martine

Design studio set up by couturier
Paul Poiret (1879-1944). Designed
furniture, textiles, carpets,
wallpapers. Designers include
R.*Dufy, Guy Pierre Fauconnet
(fl.1900-20); also designed ceramics.
Woven mark.

PICART LE DOUX, Jean

JEAN PICART LE DOUX

Painter, tapestry designer.
Tapestries woven by Atelier
Berthaud.
Woven signature.

PINTON, Atelier

Tapestry weaving workshop at Felletin. Designers include M.*Gromaire, J.*Lurçat. Woven mark.

PRINTZ, Eugène (fl.1920-40)

Designed furniture, and carpets manufactured by the firm of Cogolin. Woven monogram.

RUHLMANN, Jacques Emile (1879-1933)

Designer of furniture, carpets, textiles; also designed ceramics. Stamped signature.

TABARD, Atelier

Tapestry weaving workshop. Designers include *Le Corbusier, J.*Lurçat. Woven mark.

BELGIAN FURNITURE & TEXTILES

HAESARTS, Paul (fl.1920-40)

Ⱶ

Painter, designed tapestries woven
by de *Saedeleer Soeurs.
Woven monogram.

LEPLAE, Charles (b.1903)

⌐C

Painter, sculptor, tapestry and
carpet designer. Designed for de
*Saedeleer Soeurs.
Woven initials.

SAEDELEER, De, Soeurs (fl.1920-40)

DSS

d
S
S

Weaving workshop. Designers
include Pierre Louis Flouquet
(fl.1920-40), P.*Haesarts,
C.*Leplae.
Woven initials.

VELDE, Henry Clemens van de (1863-1957)

Architect, painter. Designed
furniture for *Maison de l'Art
Nouveau (*see* French ceramics,
metalwork), *Maison Moderne (*see*
French ceramics), Löffler and his
own manufacturing company,
tapestries for *Scherrebek (*see*
German furniture), embroidery,
textiles and wallpapers; also
designed jewellery, metalwork (*see*
German metalwork), ceramics (*see*
German ceramics), glass, posters
and books.
Branded mark.

WOEDSTAD, Gaston (fl.1920-40)

Painter, weaver.
Woven monogram.

GERMAN FURNITURE & TEXTILES

BRAUCHITSCH, Margarethe von (1865-1957)

Painter. Designed textiles and wallpapers, and ran her own embroidery workshop; also designed ceramics, stained glass. Embroidered monogram.

BÜRCK, Paul (1878-1947)

Painter, textiles and carpet designer; also *graphic artist, illustrator, book and *jewellery designer.
Woven initial.

CHRISTIANSEN, Hans (1866-1945)

Painter. Designed furniture for Ludwig Schäfer, textiles for Marx & Kleinberger, tapestries for *Scherrebek, carpets for *Ginzkey (*see* Austrian furniture), wallpapers; also designed jewellery, glass, stained glass, *ceramics, posters (*see* German graphics). Woven monogram.

ECKMANN, Otto (1865-1902)

Painter. Designed tapestries for *Scherrebek, carpets for *Vereinigte Smyrna-Teppich-Fabrike, and furniture; also designed jewellery, metalwork, ceramics, stained glass, posters and books (*see* German graphics). Woven monogram.

GELDERN-EGMONT, Marie, Countess von (fl.c.1900)

Embroiderer.
Stitched initials.

GEYER, Marianne (fl.1905-30)

Tapestry designer and weaver.
Woven initials.

LECHTER, Melchior (1865-1937)

Painter. Designed furniture and
tapestries; also designed *graphics
and stained glass.
Woven monogram.

SCHERREBEK, Kunstwebschule (est.1896)

Weaving school. Designers include
H.*Christiansen, O.*Eckmann,
Walter Leistikow (1865-1908), H.C.
van de *Velde (see Belgian
furniture), H.*Vogeler (see
German graphics).
Woven mark (from top to bottom:
blue, white and red stripes).

VEREINIGTE SMYRNA-TEPPICH-FABRIKE

Carpet manufacturers. Designers
include O.*Eckmann, P.*Huber
(see German metalwork), Hans
Schmithals (1878-1964).
Woven initials.

AUSTRIAN FURNITURE & TEXTILES

BELMONTE, Leo (1870-1956)

Hungarian weaver. Wove tapestries designed by A.*Kriesch, S.*Nagy and others.
Woven monogram.

FREI, Rózsa (1887-1975)

Hungarian weaver. Wove tapestries designed by A.*Kriesch, S.*Nagy and others.
Woven monogram.

GINZKEY, Ignaz (fl. 19th and 20th centuries)

GINZKEY

Carpet manufacturers. Designers include H.*Christiansen (*see* German furniture, ceramics), J.*Hoffman (*see* Austrian ceramics, glass, graphics, metalwork), A.*Mucha (*see* French graphics), Charles Francis Annesley Voysey (1857-1941).
Woven mark.

GÜTERSLOH, Albert Paris von (1887-1973)

GÜTERSLOH FECIT

Real name: Albert Konrad Kiehtreiber. Painter and writer. Designed tapestries woven by *Wiener Gobelin Manufaktur.
Woven signature.

HEIDER, Ferdinand (fl.1900-20)

Leatherworker with *Wiener Werkstätte.
Stamped monogram.

KLIMT, Gustav (1862-1918)

Painter. Designed mixed media wall decoration for *Wiener Werkstätte; also designed posters (*see* Austrian graphics).
Monogram.

KOHN, Jakob & Joseph (fl. 19th and 20th centuries)

**J.&J.KOHN
Teschen Austria**

(i)

Manufacturers of bentwood furniture. Designers include J.*Hoffmann, (*see* Austrian ceramics, glass, graphics, metalwork), K.*Moser (*see* Austrian ceramics, glass, metalwork, graphics), Gustav Siegel (fl.1890-1915).
Branded mark (i) and printed label (ii).

(ii)

KRIESCH, Aladár Körösfói (1863-1920)

Hungarian painter, designer of tapestries and furniture. Tapestries woven by L.*Belmonte, R.*Frei; also designed stained glass, glass mosaics.
Woven monogram.

ORLIK, Emil (1870-1932)

Painter. Designed intarsia panels for *Wiener Werkstätte; also designed posters and books (*see* Austrian graphics).
Monogram.

RODER, Adolf (fl.1900-20)

Lacquer craftsman. Decorated furniture for *Wiener Werkstätte.
Monogram painted in lacquer.

THONET, Gebrüder (est.1849)

THONET
2

Manufacturers of bentwood and metal furniture. Designers include J.*Hoffmann (*see* Austrian ceramics, glass, graphics, metalwork), O.*Prutscher (*see* Austrian metalwork, graphics), *Le Corbusier (*see* French furniture), Otto Wagner (1841-1918).
Branded mark.

TRETHAN, Therese (b.1859)

Painter. Decorated furniture for *Wiener Werkstätte; also decorated ceramics.
Painted monogram.

WIENER GOBELIN MANUFAKTUR (fl. 19th and 20th centuries)

W·G·M·

Tapestry weaving workshops. Designers include A.P. von *Gutersloh.
Woven initials.

WIENER WERKSTÄTTE (1903-32)

(i)

(ii)

(iii)

(iv)

Workshops in Vienna producing furniture, textiles, leatherwork, embroidery, lace. Designers include G.*Baudisch-Wittke (*see* Austrian ceramics), Artur Berger (1892-1981), Leopold Blonder (b.1893), L.*Calm-Wierink (*see* Austrian ceramics), C.O.*Czeschka (*see* Austrian metalwork, graphics), C.*Ehrlich (*see* Dutch metalwork), M.*Flögl (*see* Austrian ceramics), Mitzi Friedmann-Otten (1884-1955), Lotte Frömmel-Fochler (b.1884), Philipp Häusler (1887-1966), F.*Heider, J.*Hoffmann (*see* Austrian ceramics, glass, graphics, metalwork), Hilda Jesser-Schmidt (b.1894), E.*Kopriva (*see* Austrian ceramics), M.*Likarz-Strauss (*see* Austrian metalwork), Fritzi Löw-Lazar (1891-1975), K.*Moser (*see* Austrian ceramics, glass, graphics, metalwork), A.*Nechansky (*see* Austrian glass), E.*Orlik, D.*Peche (*see* Austrian ceramics, glass, metalwork), Clara Posnanski (fl.1925-35), O.*Prutscher (*see* Austrian metalwork, graphics), F.*Rix-Uveno (*see* Austrian ceramics), Reni Schaschl-Schuster (1895-1979), Anny Schröder-Ehrenfest (1898-1972), S.*Singer-Schinnerl (*see* Austrian ceramics), Max Snischek (1891-1968), V.*Wieselthier (*see* Austrian ceramics), E.J.*Wimmer (*see* Austrian metalwork), J.*Zimpel (*see* Austrian metalwork), Ugo Zovetti (b.1879), Franz von Zülow (1883-1963); also produced *ceramics, *glass, jewellery, *metalwork, posters, books (*see* Austrian graphics).

Selvedge mark (i), costume label (ii), and textile labels (iii, iv).

ITALIAN FURNITURE & TEXTILES

BUGATTI, Carlo (1856-1940)

Furniture designer; also designed
metalwork.
Signature on vellum-covered chair.

DEPERO, Fortunato (1892-1960)

Painter. Designed tapestries and
interiors; also designed ceramics,
posters.
Woven signature.

SCANDINAVIAN FURNITURE & TEXTILES

ANTTILA, Eva (fl.c.1950)

Finnish tapestry weaver.
Woven monogram.

CHRISTENSEN, Augusta (fl.c.1900)

Norwegian weaver working for
*Nordenfjeldske
Kunstindustrimuseum.
Woven initials.

HANDARBETETS VÄNNAR (est.1874)

Swedish weaving workshops.
Woven monogram and mark.

HANSEN, Frida (1855-1931)

Frida Hansen

Norwegian weaver. Founded Det
*Norske Billedvaeveri.
Woven signature.

HANSEN, Johannes

JOHANNES HANSEN
COPENHAGEN
DENMARK

Danish furniture manufacturers.
Designers include Hans Wegner
(b.1914).
Branded mark and monogram.

KROGH, Henrik (1886-1927)

Henrik Krogh

Swedish tapestry designer. Some tapestries woven by M.*Määs-Fjetterström; also designed ceramics, metalwork. Woven signature.

LÖNNGREN, Frida (fl.c.1905)

Frida Lonngren

Swedish weaver working for *Svensk Konstslöjdställning Selma Giöbel. Woven signature.

MÅÅS-FJETTERSTRÖM, Marta (1873-1941)

MMF
(i)

AB MMF
(ii)

Swedish rug and tapestry weaver and designer. Founded workshops in 1919.
Woven initials (i), and workshop mark (ii).

MUNTHE, Gerhard Peter (1849-1929)

Norwegian painter. Designed tapestries for *Nordenfjeldske Kunstindustrimuseum, Det *Norske Billedvaeveri; also designed ceramics, *graphics. Woven signature and monograms.

NILLSSON, Barbro (b.1899)

B N

Swedish weaver. Founded workshops in 1927, and was art director at workshops of M.*Määs-Fjetterström from 1942. Woven initials.

NORDENFJELDSKE KUNSTINDUSTRIMUSEUM

Museum at Trondheim, Norway, which ran its own weaving workshop c.1900. Weavers included A.*Christensen and designers include G.*Munthe. Woven monogram.

NORSKE BILLEDVAEVERI, Det (est.1899)

Norwegian tapestry weaving school founded by F.*Hansen. Designers include G.*Munthe. Woven initials.

RYGGEN, Hannah (1894-1970)

HR

Swedish weaver who founded workshop in Norway. Woven monogram.

SVENSK KONSTSLÖJDSUTSTÄLLNING SELMA GIÖBEL

Swedish tapestry and textile manufacturers. Designers/weavers include F.*Lönngren, A.*Wallander. Woven mark.

WALLANDER, Alf (1862-1914)

ALF WALLANDER

Swedish designer of tapestries for *Svensk Konstslöjdsutställning Selma Giöbel, and furniture; also designed ceramics, glass, furniture. Woven signature.

ACKNOWLEDGEMENTS

Cameron Books is grateful to the London auction houses of Christie's and Phillips for permission to photograph marks on pieces in their sales, from which many of the illustrations in this book have been drawn. The source for a number of the Dutch ceramics and glass marks that did not appear in the first edition is *Nederlandse keramiek- en glasmerken* by M. Singelenberg-van der Meer, published by De Tijdstroom, Lochem.

Among the British, American and Austrian marks in this book that appeared in its first edition are some drawn from secondary sources. Cameron Books wishes to acknowledge: *The Encyclopaedia of British Pottery and Porcelain Marks* by Geoffrey Godden, published by Barrie & Jenkins, London; *Art Pottery of the United States* by Paul Evans, published by Charles Scribner's Sons, New York; *Wiener Keramik* by Waltraud Neuwirth, published by Klinkhardt & Biermann, Braunschweig; *Das Glas des Jugendstils* by Waltraud Neuwirth, published by Prestel Verlag, Munich.

INDEX

Page numbers in bold type refer to entry headings, Roman type to mentions in entries, and italic to trade names, etc., that appear in marks illustrated.